The Third Dimension

Jon Mathieu

THE THIRD DIMENSION

A COMPARATIVE HISTORY OF MOUNTAINS IN THE MODERN ERA

translated by Katherine Brun

Copyright © Jon Mathieu

Originally published in German as *Die dritte Dimension. Eine vergleichende Geschichte der Berge in der Neuzeit* (Basel: Schwabe Verlag 2011)

English translation published 2011 by
The White Horse Press, 10 High Street, Knapwell, Cambridge, CB23 4NR, UK

Set in 11 point Adobe Garamond Pro
Printed by Lightning Source

All rights reserved. Except for the quotation of short passages for the purpose of criticism or review, no part of this book may be reprinted or reproduced or utilised in any form or by any electronic, mechanical or other means, including photocopying or recording, or in any information storage or retrieval system.

British Library Cataloguing in Publication Data
A catalogue record for this book is available from the British Library

ISBN   978-1-874267-78-2

CONTENTS

List of Plates, Figures and Tables viii
Notes on the Author and Translator x
FOREWORD 1

1. THE GLOBALISATION OF PERCEPTION
1.1 1992: A Constitution for the Mountains 5
    Agenda 21 and the Mountain Chapter 6
    Global History – Many Voices 10
1.2 1492: Expansion and Change in Perception 12
    The Columbus Connection 13
    The Spanish and English Questionnaires 16
    World Map Plus Mountain System 20
1.3 Alexander von Humboldt 23
    'Humboldtian Science' 24
    Wanted: The Highest Mountain 27
    Profiles and World Mountains 30
1.4 Scientific Departure 33
    Specialisation and Globalisation 34
    Jules Blache (1893–1970) 37
    Carl Troll (1899–1975) 40
1.5 The Politicisation of the Environment 42
    Transitions to Organisation 43
    'A Global Priority' 47
    The Regions Under Study 49

PLATES . . . . between pages 50 and 51

2. POPULATION AND URBANISATION
2.1 Upland Demography 51
Population Distribution 52
Population Growth 55
2.2 Asynchrony of Settlement 59
Old-Settled Lands: South America, Mediterranean 59
Conquest of the 'Wilderness': China and North America 62
Highlands and Lowlands............................. 66
2.3 Urbanisation 70
Towards Town...................................... 70
Growth Factors 74
Aloft: Lhasa 77
Big and Bigger: Mexico City 78
2.4 Two Theories 80
Increasing Disparities 81
Interpretations Over the Course of Time 82
Two Theories...................................... 86

3. AGRICULTURE, FAMILY, MOBILITY
3.1 Agriculture 88
Verticality and Seasonality............................ 88
New Plants and Animals.............................. 92
Land Use Systems 94
Obstacles to Development 98
3.2 Animal Husbandry................................ 101
Mountain Nomadism, Transhumance 103
Transition to Stall-feeding 106
3.3 Family and Mobility 108
Spatial Organisation of Families 109
Variability and Change of Families 111

    Migration 114
    Relative Poverty 117

4. CULTURAL DIVERSITY AND MODERNITY
4.1 WESTERN MODERNISATION 120
    The Enlightenment and Romanticism in Europe 121
    The 'Wilderness' Movement in North America 124
    Mountain Sacredness – the Emergence of an Idea 127
4.2 THE SPIRITUAL EMPOWERMENT OF THE LANDSCAPE 129
    East Asia 129
    High Asia 132
    'To the Most Holy Mountain in the World' 135
    Cultural Diversity 137
4.3 NORTH–SOUTH CONFLICT COMMUNITY 140
    Colonialism 140
    Alpinism 143
    Tourism 147
    2002: The International Year of the Mountains 150

5. RESULTS AND OUTLOOK
    A Three-Dimensional World 155
    Major Ecosystems 157
    Towards Kamchatka 158

BIBLIOGRAPHY 161

INDEX 187

LIST OF FIGURES, TABLES AND PLATES

Figures

1. Single and Multiple Cropping Zones by Altitude in Karakoram (Gilgit), 1983 100

Tables

1. Major Scientific Works Pertaining to Mountains, 19th/20th Centuries... 35
2. Continental and Global Initiatives for the Mountains, 20th/21st Centuries 45
3. Population Density By Altitude and Continent, 1958 (persons per km^2) 53
4. Major Cities By Altitude and Continent, 2000 54
5. Estimated World Population By Continent, 1500–2000 (in millions) . 57
6. Urbanisation of Mountain Regions and Surrounding Areas on Three Continents, 1500–2000 57
7. Population of Cities in Early Modern Europe and China by Altitude (Based on Different Criteria in Each Region) 75
8. Development of the Olympic Winter Games, 1924–2006 149

Plates (between pages 50 and 51)

1. Regions Under Study: Mountain areas specifically examined in this book
2. Countries of the World with Mountain Percentages: Map from 2002
3. Altitude-Specific Vegetation in Three Climate Zones: Illustration from 1817

4. 'Heights of the Old and New World, An Illustrated Comparison': Drawing from 1813

5. Summits of the World as a Mountain Island: Illustration from 1875

6. Miao Warriors in Guizhou, South China: Illustration from the nineteenth century

7. Cherokee Indians on the Qualla Reservation in Appalachia, 1888

8. The Potala Palace in Lhasa: Illustration from 1667

9. Tenochtitlán, Later Mexico City: View from 1617

10. Potato Cultivation in the Andes: Illustration from 1615

11. Field Cultivation in the Highlands of Ethiopia, 1852

12. 'Wild Haymaking' in the Alps: Dramatised engraving from 1862

13. The Rocky Mountains with Lander's Peak: Oil painting by Albert Bierstadt, 1863

14. 'Image of the True Form of the Five Peaks': Chinese inscription, circa 1614

15. 'To the Most Holy Mountain in the World' by Herbert Tichy: Cover illustration from the 1953 reprint

16. International Year of the Mountains 2002: 'Celebrating Mountain Women'

NOTES ON THE AUTHOR AND THE TRANSLATOR

JON MATHIEU is Professor of history at the University of Lucerne and at the Swiss Federal Institute of Technology in Zurich. He was the founding director of the Instituto di Storia delle Alpi at the Università della Svizzera italiana and has organized several international conferences about the history of mountains. In 2008 he received the King Albert I Mountain Award for his research. Among his publications are *History of the Alps 1500–1900. Environment, Development, and Society* (Morgantown: West Virginia University Press 2009, with previous editions in German and Italian); *Religion and Sacredness in Mountains: A Historical Perspective*, Special Issue of *Mountain Research and Development*, 2006 (co-editor); and *Mountain Pastoralism and Modernity: Historical Approaches*, Special Issue of *Nomadic Peoples*, 2009 (co-editor). He is the proud owner of an Alpine hut in the Swiss mountains, built by his grandfather, where he plans to retire after having seen more of the world's mountains.

KATHERINE BRUN holds a Ph.D. in early modern European history from the University of California at Berkeley (2008). She is currently writing her first book, entitled *The Abbot and His Peasants: Building the Territorial State in Salem, 1473–1637*. While living at less than 100 metres above sea level, she is also a mountain enthusiast who has backpacked over 5,000 miles, including long distance hikes on the Appalachian and Pacific Crest Trails.

The Third Dimension

FOREWORD

The goal of this *Comparative History of Mountains in the Modern Era* is to encourage the investigation of human and social history in the third dimension. Other disciplines, such as botany, climatology and geography, have established an early interest in the three-dimensionality of the earth. If we choose to approach the subject from a historical perspective, however, we must move the central axis of history into the foreground – humans and their diachronic existence. Marc Bloch spoke of history as a science of people over time, *'une science des hommes dans le temps'*. Many issues appear in a different light with this shift from a primarily spatial to a primarily temporal perspective, affording us a reasonable hope of obtaining new insights. Examining the three-dimensionality from this angle makes no difference for the physical world and the summit's altitude, yet it allows the investigation of how various actors have perceived the mountains and how they have or have not used them at different points in time.

In recent decades there has been a remarkable increase in scientific mountain research and international mountain politics. Pivotal moments for public awareness were the passing of the 'Mountain Chapter' at the great environmental conference of Rio de Janeiro in 1992 and the designation of 2002 as the 'International Year of the Mountains', which sparked activities around the globe. If we want to understand how the world's mountains could become such a topic of political engagement at the turn of the twenty-first century, we must look further back in time. In fact, the roots of this globalised perception of mountains are to be found in the early modern period and in the nineteenth century, when science and mountaineering took off in Europe and moved well beyond traditional boundaries. The present study begins with the investigation of these long-term developments in science, culture and politics that have changed our attitudes toward mountains. It then takes up a series of historical problems that have been debated in recent scholarship, placing them in a comparative framework. We will consider various samples from mountainous regions around the world and in select periods since 1500. The themes of the investigation are: 1. Globalisation of Perception; 2. Population and Urbanisation; 3. Agriculture, Family, Mobility; and 4. Cultural Diversity and Modernity.

Foreword

Every historical study is in a certain sense 'comparative' but in this case the word certainly deserves a place in the title – for, in our discipline, the chosen spatial framework is unusual. It is composed, in principle, of countless regions scattered across the continents, with points of emphasis in a number of key areas. The Andes of South America span more than 7,000 kilometres, and when we link them with the adjoining mountain chains of Central and North America, this mountain system extends over an area reaching from 55 degrees South to 70 degrees North in latitude. In the Himalayas and in the Karakoram we encounter an impressive series of peaks, reaching more than 8,000 metres above sea level, which have been recognised since the nineteenth century as the world's highest mountains; these peaks form the heart of an immense mountain system, stretching from Siberia and China all the way to the Mediterranean. However, there are also many isolated and relatively inconspicuous mountains and hills. In Estonia – that flat, low-lying Baltic state – the highest point is 320 metres above sea level. The lookout tower built upon it, therefore, makes a considerable impression on the land's vertical profile.

This dispersed and starkly differentiated mountain world will not be treated here in a comprehensive manner. Our objective, as already mentioned, involves the examination of various sample regions, chosen from case to case depending on the subject of inquiry and the state of research. This study seeks to acquire new insights of a potentially global nature, using a comparative-historical approach that could be extended to include other major ecosystems such as deserts and oceans. In addition, one may hope that, by illuminating the subject from a general point of view, this project may benefit regional research. It will naturally require theoretical models, ideas and debates. These appear not at any special position within the text but, rather, wherever they seem essential to the point of investigation.

This book has a long history but there is one episode I remember most vividly. On 24 July 2002 I sat with a friendly Indian colleague and Himalayan expert in a restaurant on the Avenida de Mayo in Buenos Aires. Our Institute for Alpine History at the University of Italian Switzerland had organised a session there for an economic history congress and on the occasion of the International Year of the Mountains, historians of Latin American, Asian, and European mountain regions joined together in discussion for the first time. The title of the session was 'The Mountains in Urban Development'. Since I had been asked to write an introductory article for the proceedings, I had with me in Buenos Aires a series of historical population statistics for Indian cities. As a novice to this field I found the old Indian city names confusing, so

Foreword

I wanted to consult a specialist in order to determine which places belonged to the mountain regions and which did not.

In that restaurant on the busy avenue, my interlocutor answered every question I had with admirable clarity. Beyond that, his stories aroused in me the kind of excitement and longing for faraway landscapes that can stimulate research much more than dry, sober statistics. From the discussions and from the session there soon developed a small intercontinental network of historians of mountain regions, which led in turn to a series of conferences and university teaching invitations. Without the background of these experiences I would neither have thought to write this book, nor been able to do so to academic standards.

For valuable advice, scholarly inspiration and patient companionship at various stages, I would like to thank Jean-François Bergier, Michael Blatter, Heraclio Bonilla, Axel Borsdorf, Simona Boscani Leoni, Olivier Chave, Viviana Conti, Bernard Debarbieux, Mark Elvin, René Favier, Laurence Fontaine, Reto Furter, Raquel Gil Montero, Jean-François Giovannini, Toni Huber, Hermann Kreutzmann, Luigi Lorenzetti, Cla and Luisa Mathieu, Franz Mathis, Bruno Messerli, Claude Reichler, Thomas Scheurer, Chetan Singh, Delphine Spicq, Felicitas Sprecher Mathieu, Matthew Vester and Anne Zimmermann. I am also indebted to my students at the University of Lucerne, who have helped me refine parts of the book in various seminars. In addition I thank Katherine Brun, who translated the bulk of the text, and Benjamin Marschke for translating Chapters 4.1 and 4.2. Sarah Johnson from The White Horse Press in Cambridge has been a kind and very professional publisher. The Swiss National Science Foundation and the Research Commission of the University of Lucerne have supported the project with generous contributions. Switzerland's excellent multilingual library system has facilitated access to the vast field of publications on mountain regions, which serve as the most important foundation of this endeavour. Still, they cannot provide the exalted feeling of survey one might well experience up on top of the world. This is only the beginning.

~ 1 ~

THE GLOBALISATION OF PERCEPTION

1.1 1992: A Constitution for the Mountains

The Conference on Environment and Development, held in Rio de Janeiro during the first two weeks of June 1992, entered the history of the United Nations and of international relations as an unprecedented event. The conference broke all records and expanded unexpectedly into a cultural happening of global magnitude. Official representatives came from 172 countries, including over a hundred presidents and other heads of state. Also in attendance were several thousand non-governmental organisations, some integrated within the official conference channels, with others joining together in a colourful and exceedingly well-attended alternative summit, the so-called 'Global Forum'. A cultural programme with many celebrities provided entertainment and variety. Seven or eight thousand journalists covered the event, more according to some sources. In fact, no one knows exactly how many people were in Rio for the 'United Nations Conference on Environment and Development'. One frequently cited estimate spoke of 30,000. In addition there were the local people, who not only mingled among the participants but also made their voices heard in great demonstrations.[1]

Under the title 'Rio de Janeiro in Summit Fever', the climate at the meeting on 6 June 1992 was described by an internationally-oriented daily newspaper as follows: 'These days in the UNCED-city of Rio, a state of emergency prevails in nearly every sense – the military presence increases security but also the traffic chaos, tens of thousands flock to the Dalai Lama of Tibet, and the nightly alternative happenings and feminist events as well as street

---

1. Historians have not yet sufficiently examined the Rio conference; the following passages are based on commentary published after the conference, including newspaper reports, as well as interviews I conducted with the participants in the spring of 2006; for useful document collections from Rio, see United Nations 1993, Global Partnership; United Nations 1993, Agenda 21; Johnson 1993; Grubb 1993; Engelhardt/Weinzierl 1993. See also the recent study of Debarbieux/Rudaz 2010, pp. 220–6.

shows are only a few of the bewildering variety of cultural activities. The flood of attractions overwhelms everyone.' The official summit was designated an 'Earth Summit' and the alternative Global Forum soon came to be known as 'Eco-Woodstock'. Everything pointed to the meeting's lasting influence in future discussions and, indeed, by the next year it was already being hailed as legend.[2]

This should not obscure the fact that many in this multitude of conference participants were involved in diplomatic efforts and thereby became engaged in lengthy and arduous negotiations. Although the cold war had officially ended with the dissolution of the Eastern Bloc, the atmosphere was tense: the wealthy nations of the North demanded 'protection of the environment' from the less developed South, whereas the South called for a 'technology transfer' and financial compensation from the North. To make matters worse, the United States was very selective in its support for environmental protection, while at the same time claiming for itself more of a global leadership role than ever before.

Agenda 21 and the Mountain Chapter

A central document that was deliberated at Rio in the various committees and eventually adopted, was Agenda 21, a sort of world programme for environmental and developmental politics in the twenty-first century. The thirteenth of the Agenda's forty chapters was devoted to the mountains, and bore the title 'Managing fragile ecosystems: Sustainable mountain development'. It began by establishing that mountainous regions were not only important sources of water, energy and biological diversity but had other key resources to offer as well, such as minerals, forest and agricultural products and recreational opportunities: 'As a major ecosystem representing the complex and interrelated ecology of our planet, mountain regions contribute vitally to the survival of our global ecosystem.' Yet these regions were seen to be undergoing rapid change, accompanied by accelerated ground erosion, landslides and massive losses to habitat and genetic diversity. On the human side, the chapter identified widespread poverty among mountain people and the loss of indigenous knowledge. 'As a result, most global mountain areas are experiencing environmental degradation. Hence, the proper management of mountain resources and socio-economic development of the people deserves immediate action.'[3]

Following these introductory words, the chapter went on to list a comprehensive catalogue of problems and political directives. It stated that

---

2. *Neue Zürcher Zeitung*, 6/7 June 1992, p. 13; 3 June 1992, p. 2 (original German).
3. United Nations 1993, Agenda 21, p. 109.

1992: A Constitution for the Mountains

approximately ten per cent of the world population lived at higher elevations and in steep mountain areas, while another forty per cent inhabited the adjacent watershed areas below. Roughly half the world's people were therefore affected by these issues. At the same time mountain regions were described as being highly vulnerable and sensitive to human and ecological imbalances as well as climate change. The Mountain Chapter deemed it necessary on the one hand to expand our knowledge of mountains on a global scale through surveys, databases and information systems. On the other hand, it urged governments to promote these regions with comprehensive programmes in various sectors. The Agenda recommended more than three dozen fields of action for political measures. Mentioned by name were a few globally active research institutes and scientific disciplines (meteorology, hydrology, forestry and soil sciences, botany) but above all, the mountain regions and organisations of the South (such as the International Center for Integrated Mountain Development in Nepal, the African Mountain Association and the Andean Mountain Association). The total estimated cost necessary to implement these measures was thirteen billion US dollars per year.[4]

The comprehensive content and the dramatic tone of the Mountain Chapter might appear peculiar; yet it did not differ in this sense from the rest of Agenda 21. The Agenda stood as an official document, built upon chapters adopted one by one but for the individual governments it held no legal obligation. Commentators pointed out that, with its many general statements and wish lists, it exuded 'a different flavor' from the usual international agreements. This was due in part to the broad participatory process of its preparation. For the first time, non-governmental organisations and wider circles were deliberately included in the negotiations. The scope of the preparatory documentation drawn up for the conference was eventually estimated at 24 million pages and even the final synthesis adopted in Rio came to more than 500 pages.[5]

On the other hand, the Mountain Chapter truly was a special case. Many of the Agenda's other parts already belonged among the themes of international relations and to the historic traditions of the United Nations. For the oceans, a world environmental policy was already emerging shortly after 1900 and, when in 1972 the UN held its first environmental conference in Stockholm, desertification and the destruction of rain forests were the topics of passionate debate.[6] The mountains as a major ecosystem, however, were not

---

4. United Nations 1993, Agenda 21, pp. 109–113.
5. Grubb 1993, p. 97; *Neue Zürcher Zeitung* 4 June 1992, p. 2.
6. Biermann 1996, p. 197; Grubb 1993, pp. 4–6.

The Globalisation of Perception

yet an issue; it was at Rio that they were brought expressly, and for the first time, to the forefront of the global debate. Two sets of actors were primarily responsible for this: the first was known as the 'Mountain Agenda', a loosely-organised group of concerned scientists including the Swiss geography professor Bruno Messerli, the geography professor Jack D. Ives who worked in the United States, the Indian engineer Jayanta Bandyopadhyay who was then in Geneva, among others. The group formed in the fall of 1990, with an eye on the upcoming events at Rio and it met several times thereafter in the Bernese Oberland. From the beginning the Mountain Agenda also maintained personal ties to Swiss developmental policy, which contributed the second set of actors, though this one did not really become active until the eve of a conference held in preparation for Rio, at Geneva in March 1991. Apparently it required only a telephone call and immediately the director for developmental cooperation and humanitarian aid commissioned a young assistant, Olivier Chave, to ensure from the political and diplomatic side that the concerned scientists' ideas would gain entry to the negotiation process and that Agenda 21 would contain a chapter on the mountains.[7]

At first Chave felt, as he later reported, as if he were a parachute commando dropped behind enemy lines. He had only a little time left in Geneva and he began, after seeking advice from some knowledgeable UN insiders and with the help of a provisional catalogue of articles, to build conviction and forge alliances among state representatives. He recruited helpers from a core group of countries and, through their efforts, the project snowballed. The first line of action was to convince the numerous delegations that the mountains were an environmental and developmental issue of global importance and not merely a local or national affair. That Switzerland was so strongly committed at this point had to do not only with a long tradition of 'Alpine' foreign- and self-description but also with the fact that it allowed the country, in this moment, to take an offensive position behind a new theme uniting North and South. This became all the more obvious to the Swiss diplomats at the Rio conference as they found themselves in a delicate situation with respect to some of its central problems.[8]

---

7. Bandyopadhyay/Perveen 2004, pp. 16–7; interviews with Bruno Messerli and Oliver Chave on 18/26 April 2006; the details of the original proposals and contacts are difficult to reconstruct; the first publication of the Mountain Agenda (1992, flyleaf) hints at the roles played by the former Vice Director of Swiss Developmental Cooperation, Rudolf Högger, and the freelance environmental activist Peter Stone.

8. Interviews with Oliver Chave (see n. 7) and Jean-François Giovannini, head of the Swiss delegation in Rio, on 9 May 2006.

1992: A Constitution for the Mountains

The core group of states persuaded by the Mountain Chapter was composed of relatively small and poor mountainous countries, many of whom received developmental aid from the Swiss, such as Nepal, Bhutan, Bolivia and Peru. Some of the larger countries, however, reacted with initial scepticism. China and India seem to have feared, among other things, that it would divert attention from the central disparity between North and South. The United States did not view mountain regions as a problem, certainly not a global problem; its resistance, however, was merely passive.[9] The project was promoted at the Rio conference by the decisive support of the secretary general, who was an old friend of the mountains, and certainly also by the fact that the category of major ecosystems already belonged among the fundamental ideas of the conference. When defined ecologically, the mountain regions could join in as just one more constituent.

In any case, things now began to move very quickly: the chapter was accepted in principle, then the Mountain Agenda drafted a text, the secretary refined it and in New York the final preparatory conference approved it in March 1992. The chances were good that, at the upcoming Earth Summit in Rio, the world community would officially recognise the Mountain Chapter. In fact, it then passed so easily that the public barely took notice. Not even the Swiss press really drew attention to the issue. The newspaper *Neue Zürcher Zeitung*, which reported diligently and in great detail about the general event, devoted just one short section to the subject at the end of a long article.[10] Bruno Messerli, the informal spokesperson for the Mountain Agenda, reported moreover that one could hear the opinion expressed in conference corridors that the mountain regions were really a national, not a global, problem. Nevertheless, his group did succeed in placing the mountains, as a special ecosystem, in an important UN document. Even in terms of the funding recommendations, they did not come up short. Agenda 21 estimated the total annual cost necessary to address the highly controversial deforestation problem (Chapter 11) at 31.25 billion US dollars – for the fight against desertification and drought (Chapter 12), 8.73 billion; and for protection of the oceans (Chapter 17), 12.88 billion.

---

9. These motivations are inferred from judgements made by the interviewed Swiss diplomats and should be verified using other documents; a slightly different version is provided by Debarbieux/Price 2008, pp. 155–6.
10. *Neue Zürcher Zeitung*, 11 June 1992, p. 22.

The Globalisation of Perception

Mountains, the most recent historical addition, stood in second place with an annual assessment of 13 billion dollars.[11]

Much more important, however, than such classifications imprinted by administrative logic, was the text's symbolic radiance. Agenda 21 as a whole soon became such an oft-cited source that, retrospectively, it obtained a sort of constitutional character. Indeed, it can be considered the first world constitution for nature. The fact that the Mountain Chapter seemingly appeared on the global floor out of nowhere may have allowed it to develop a heightened level of influence over a period of time. Over the course of the 1990s, in any case, it caught on with countless groups who used it to elevate their positions and legitimate their activities. A high point in this colourful movement came in the year 2002, which the UN designated as the International Year of the Mountains.[12]

Global History – Many Voices

'Universality must be constructed', writes the science historian Timothy Lenoir, with reference to the production of scientific and cultural representations that make a general claim.[13] In the case of mountains, this becomes very clear. The idea of viewing these regions as a universal whole does not arise through simple observation. Even where imposing mountain scenery towers over the vicinity, still it provides only a particular backdrop. Likewise, the view from above – made possible by ascending the mountaintops, then with the help of the first relief maps in the early modern period and later through aeronautical navigation – is equally insufficient. Even when it became possible to observe the planets from outer space, the mountain zones strewn all across the continents did not readily impose themselves as a global object.[14] How and why, therefore, did this historical construction come about? This is the central question of the following chapters. In order to clarify the issue, it is not enough to simply consider the interventions surrounding Rio in 1992. The ideas expressed there were based on earlier developments. We will look at selected aspects of these from the beginning of modern times. We will see that the history of perceiving the mountains in this way played out over a long period in the sphere of general

---

11. As summarised by Grubb 1993, pp. 171–2; see also his succinct, informative comments on the history of these chapters, pp. 118, 120, 121, 128.
12. Messerli/Ives 1997, pp. 1–15, 447–66; Messerli 2004; Price 2004; examined in greater detail below, in Chapters 1.5 and 4.3.
13. Lenoir 1997, p. 18.
14. Bürgi 2007; Dech 2005.

1992: A Constitution for the Mountains

culture and scientific knowledge. Its politicisation came only in the final third of the twentieth century.

Our questions are aligned with the globalisation debate, which has been active in the historiography for quite some time. A central point in the debate concerns the plurality of voices or multiplicity of perspectives. Observers have pointed out that even recent global studies are sometimes no more than self-projections of national history or western culture on a planetary level, rather than overarching cultural perspectives about various developments that possess true relevance. In his *Pensées sur la religion et sur quelques autres sujets*, the French philosopher Blaise Pascal summarised the cultural self-centredness of the seventeenth century in a few especially appropriate words: 'Truth this side of the Pyrenees, error on the other.' ['*Vérité au deçà des Pyrénées, erreur au delà.*']¹⁵ Instead of understanding the concept of globalisation as a singular form, so closely associated with western history and expansion, one would do better to conceive of it as a plurality, which in principle would open the possibility of similar expansion phenomena to everyone. In fact, history is filled with globalisation impulses from earlier times and other cultures.

Historians cannot deny their origins, and their surroundings always make an impression on the horizons of their knowledge. Nevertheless, they can strive to acquaint themselves with other situations and perspectives and to include them consciously in the research. For the present book I have laid out the following programme and procedure: Part One provides an overview of the globalisation of mountain perceptions, primarily along the lines of a western tradition, which arose forcefully with the European expansion of the early modern period and then through imperialism. However, one should not imagine this tradition to be exclusively a product of the West – spatial expansion implies contact, which, to a certain degree, has always been multi-directional and included other influences. Parts Two and Three of the book deal with the themes of population, urbanisation, agriculture, family and mobility. The historical investigation of these subjects always returns to the mountain areas, which, for long periods of time, lay distant from the 'centres'. Part Four concerns alternative traditions and their confrontation with the 'modernity' of the West. There it will be demonstrated that globalisation is not determined or

---

15. Burke 2000, p. 55; there he also provides an example of Montaigne's similar use of mountain metaphor; from the vast literature on globalisation, see especially Perspectives on Global History 2000; Osterhammel/Petersson 2003; Raphael 2003, pp. 196–214, 266–271; on self-projection, Conrad 2006, pp. 159–60.

The Globalisation of Perception

perceived unilaterally but rather exhibits numerous variations. Now, however, let us start from the beginning.

1.2 1492: Expansion and Change in Perception

In the transition to modern times, the spatial expansion of European discoverers and conquerors proceeded, above all, through navigation. The swiftly occupied territories of the 'New World' on the American continent formed an early, and for this reason especially relevant, example of the seizure of internal spaces – which Europeans did not come to explore, and in some cases appropriate, in other parts of the world until centuries later. For a long time and for the most part, the maritime mode of expansion dominated.[16]

The early overseas voyagers were of course influenced by certain culturally coded expectations and they measured the new by that with which they were already acquainted and familiar. Through implicit or explicit comparison between the target region and place of origin, their perceptions acquired a meaning – for themselves as well as for their intended readership back at home. So it was with Christopher Columbus, who, on 3 August 1492, set out to sea from southern Spain in search of a new, westward route to India. At that time Columbus was the proud owner of a contract with the king and queen of Castile and Aragon, who also provided him with a passport and letter of recommendation addressed to the supposed rulers on the other side of the world. He had under his command one flagship and two caravels. The crew was composed of around a hundred sailors and a few higher-ranking men. In his log-book and other reports one finds numerous transatlantic references. He constantly compared the Caribbean island world, where he landed five weeks later, to the Spanish countryside, the Canary Islands and the Atlantic Coast between West Africa and England, which he knew from earlier voyages.[17]

European expansion subsequently brought a massive increase and change in the knowledge of nature and mountains. On a general level, however, these changes are difficult to describe. One can observe therein the simultaneous occurrence of contrary processes, toward the universal as well as the particular. Through integration within large-scale reference systems, local or regional knowledge came to be qualified: features that were previously considered marginal

---

16. See, for example, Bitterli 1986, p. 178; among the many new studies on the European expansion: Dürr 2005.
17. Jacob 1956, pp. 95, 102, 103, 106, 109, 112, 123, 137, 139, 148, 152 etc.; in general Bitterli 1999, p. 19.

1492: Expansion and Change in Perception

could rise in this way to become key characteristics and vice versa. Alexander von Humboldt, whose journey to South America in the years around 1800 has often been portrayed as the 'second discovery of America', was keenly aware of spatial relationships and the strength of their influence on perception. He demonstrated this through the example of volcanoes. What people believed to be true about the shape of volcanoes and the effect of their subterranean forces had been derived until quite recently, as he pointed out, from two mountains in southern Italy: Vesuvius and Etna. In fact, since Vesuvius was not only the lower and more easily accessible but also the more frequently active of the two, in this field practically just 'one hill served so to speak as the model' for mighty volcanoes in all other parts of the world. Hence insignificant details were regarded as important, whereas the essential point was entirely missed: 'It was necessary to travel in distant climates, and to compare large tracts of land in and outside Europe, in order to clearly recognise commonalities in volcanic activities and their interdependence.'[18]

Until now, the research on global environmental history has concerned itself relatively little with such phenomena of knowledge and perception.[19] Here we are concerned with a number of developments and critical points that are relevant to our mountain problem. Along with them belongs the question of changing western attitudes toward nature.

The Columbus Connection

'All these islands possess the greatest fertility', wrote Columbus after he had spent half a year exploring the Caribbean with his ships and men,

> Yet this applies especially to the last island (Haiti). On its coasts there are numerous harbours, such as would be hard to find anywhere in Europe; here many wonderful, large, and good rivers rush into the sea. High above lies the land, crisscrossed by numerous mountain ranges that rise to significant elevations, higher even than on the island of Tenerife. All these mountains are exceedingly

---

18. Humboldt 1969, p. 93 (original German); the vulcanological treatise is from 1823; Humboldt made similar statements in other places, for instance in his 1807 *Essay on the Geography of Plants* (Humboldt 1989, p. 55); for hints about the processes of universalisation and particularisation, see Osterhammel/Petersson 2003, p. 12.

19. See above all Crosby 1972, Radkau 2002 and the research survey of McNeill 2003; Grove 1995 deals with perception to some extent; for recent centuries, now see Debarbieux/Rudaz 2010.

beautiful, diverse, and accessible; they are covered with various types of trees and reach such astonishing heights that they seem to touch the heavens.[20]

Columbus mentioned mountains frequently in his writings. We need not be surprised by this, since many islands project conspicuously out of the sea, leaving such an impression of contrast that early modern seafarers often remarked upon it. Columbus even took care to mention those islands that presented a flat landscape, without any mountains.[21] What was less self-evident, however, was the fact that the navigators were allowed to set out on the western route to 'India' at all. We know that, before his ships sailed, the state commissions of Portugal and Spain repeatedly denied his requests. In particular, the experts mistrusted his hypothesis of a short travel time. This required speculations about the geography and size of the globe and available texts were sharply divided on such matters.

Columbus, who was self-educated, had collected an extensive library. He read in fascination Marco Polo's famous report on the spectacular wealth of the Far East. He applied many scholarly texts to the problems of geographical calculation. Earlier, while sailing from Lisbon to West Africa for example, he determined his geographical position by means of a quadrant after consulting the work of Alfraganus, an Islamic astronomer of the ninth century. Together with other scholars, Alfraganus had provided a new estimate of the earth's diameter and also a much-consulted summary of Ptolemy, the ancient geographer of the second century, whose original work survived only in fragments. Quite generally, Islamic geographers were the leaders in the Middle Ages; they profited from the expansive reach of their rulers and merchants – a true surge in globalisation – and from the fact that pilgrimages to Mecca gave rise to long journeys. In the fifteenth century, as some people in Renaissance Europe searched for new routes and as Columbus launched anew an older Italian project for a western route, geographical concepts arose from various Ancient, Islamic and Christian sources in a 'hybrid' Mediterranean culture.[22]

---

20. Our translation is based on Jacob 1956, pp. 202–3 (German) and Varela/Gil 1992, p. 221 (Spanish); Kohler 2006 provides an introduction to Columbus in the perspective we are interested in here.
21. Grove 1995, e.g. pp. 43–6, 323–4; Jacob 1956, pp. 92, 95, 101, 109 etc.
22. Varela/Gil 1992, p. 90; Kohler 2006, above all pp. 41–6; there is no consensus about the specific importance of the different traditions, see Sezgin 2000 and Stückelberger/Graßhoff 2006; a classical study on the Islamic contribution is Miquel 1967–1988 (also with hints about mountain representation); the hybrid character of Mediterranen culture is stressed by younger researchers, e.g. Kahlaoui 2007.

1492: Expansion and Change in Perception

As he stood before the examination committees, Columbus took care to cite those authors who estimated the earth's circumference as small. This reduced the presumed travel distance and allowed him to set the chances of success for this bold undertaking in a good light. Then, after his return from the Caribbean, he sought to describe the results of his achievement in the most positive terms. According to his reports, one region in his 'India' was more fertile than the other; the inhabitants appeared submissive and were undoubtedly ready to become good Christians and subjects of the Spanish crown; above all, however, there was the prospect of coming across immeasurable quantities of gold. With respect to nature and the mountains, he was similarly enthusiastic: 'The Spanish Island (Haiti) is a true miracle. Its mountains, hills, meadows, fields, and land are so beautiful and rich that one can plant and sow, breed cattle of all kinds and erect villages and cities.' In another passage, again with reference to the Canary Islands, he wrote:

> Everywhere in this region, towering mountains rise up so high they seem to reach the heavens. Compared with them, the height and beauty of Tenerife's mountains fade completely into the background. Everything is green, completely covered with trees; it is a wondrous thing. Lovely valleys separate the mountains from one another.[23]

Columbus's enthusiasm also touched on other natural phenomena and the historiographical tradition has all too willingly made it out to be a special case. If one views positive attitudes toward the environment in western history as an exclusively modern phenomenon, associated with the Enlightenment and Romanticism, then earlier expressions of nature's beauty appear only as precursors so that the famous navigator, as one says, 'was way ahead of his times'.[24] Actually, Columbus provides us with an especially good vantage point from which to thematise one of history's great junctures, a turning point whereby various cultures came together and gave rise to something new. Before one agrees with the verdict, however, the sweet-sounding general tone of his travel reports, especially the first one, should be taken into account, for he wholly favoured superlatives. Still more important is the question of whether nature, and the mountains as one of its manifestations, were really held in such generally low esteem, and portrayed so negatively in the older European tradition, as these judgments would suggest.

---

23. Varela/Gil 1992, pp. 172, 221 (original Spanish).
24. Henze 1978–2004, vol. 1, p. 616 (original German); this interpretation seems to reach back not least to Humboldt; Bitterli is more cautious: 1999, pp. 19, 61, 89.

The Globalisation of Perception

Interesting signs of this are found, among other places, in Marco Polo's famous travel description, which was not only a key text for Columbus but also one of the most widely read books in early modern Europe.[25] The Venetian merchant travelled in the second half of the thirteenth century through Central Asia to China, where he stayed for a long time and undertook diplomatic missions. His reports, directed at a courtly audience, contained nearly fifty references to mountains and mountain regions. These passages provide not a uniform picture but rather a colourful profusion of attributes. According to Marco Polo, some mountains were harsh and cold whereas others were fertile, with such good water and healthy air that he thought they might possess healing qualities. Mountains could also be places of refuge and they sometimes offered valuable gemstones and precious metals – in short, he did not view these places as generally inhospitable, especially not in comparison to deserts, which came out much worse in his judgment.[26]

The traditions of perception on the threshold of modernity, therefore, may have been more diverse and less stereotypical than some historians have assumed. Perhaps Columbus did not stand alone but was actually quite integrated in Renaissance society with its situationally activated images. In fact there was, as Antonello Gerbi has shown in detail, a great variety of opinions even within the small circle of early authors who had transatlantic contacts and some of them were just as enthusiastic about nature and the tropical island world as Columbus was in the report from his first voyage.[27]

The Spanish and English Questionnaires

Soon after 1500, Spanish rule in the 'New World' really began to take hold. In the motherland they kept track of which conquistadors in America had received privileges to a share in land and Indian labour. For the purpose of counselling the king and for the administration of colonial affairs, a body was formed in 1524 that came to be called the *Consejo de Indias*, or 'Indian Council'. Spanish rule now extended to the mainland and, by the middle of the century, it reached over vast stretches of land from California across Mexico to present-day Chile and Argentina. The enormous distances posed difficult problems for the gradual organisation of government organs. When King Philip II ordered a review of the

---

25. Kohler 2006, pp. 88–98.
26. Hambis 1955; detailed positive judgements e.g. on pp. 22–3 (altitude, water, fertility), 55–7 (gemstones, fertility, healthy air).
27. Gerbi 1978, above all pp. 25–34, 37–8, 41–3, 50–4, 87–91, 105–7, 149–50, 298–9, 311–3.

1492: Expansion and Change in Perception

Indian Council's work around 1570, the examiner insisted that, although the council did in fact stand above all the overseas territories, it possessed neither knowledge of them nor information about their affairs. In order to remedy this, it was decided to install an official cosmographer [*Cosmógrafo cronista mayor de las Indias*], who was supposed to produce a complete description of Hispanic America and continually update his work to reflect the latest conditions. The king also strengthened the long-established practice of collecting comprehensive information from the entire area through special questionnaires.[28]

In the spring of 1577, for example, Philip II sent a printed form letter with fifty questions to the overseas district officials. It ordered them to provide written information about each individual point, for the promotion of 'good government'. One of the first questions asked them to describe 'whether this land is even or uneven, flat or mountainous; with many rivers and springs or only a few, rich or poor in water resources; fertile or deficient in pastures; abundant or lacking in cereals; and anything else relating to subsistence'. The nature of the soil and of the mountains came up another five times in the king's questionnaire. He wanted to know if the routes connecting the place in question to the nearest administrative centre led through mountainous terrain and over long, tortuous ways; also whether routes to the nearest Indian or Spanish settlements crossed mountainous areas; where exactly each of these settlements was located, whether in the mountains or in the lowlands; whether any prominent mountains or mountain ranges were located in close or distant proximity; and finally, the king announced his interest in 'volcanoes, caves, and all other noteworthy and admirable things that may exist there'.[29] In each case where the shape of the land came under observation, therefore, the questions primarily concerned the possibilities for agriculture and animal husbandry as well as for official and commercial transportation routes; in addition, there was a certain amount of curiosity about unusual mountains, especially those that breathed fire.

In the Spanish Kingdom, the state's collection of information through such questionnaires [*cuestionarios*] began in the first half of the sixteenth century, much earlier than in most other European lands. One should not imagine that the systematic questioning produced uniform responses and descriptions from overseas. Reactions varied from non-observance to evasion and misinterpretation, as well as to the over-provision of information in order

---

28. Solano 1988; Brendecke 2009; about the older ecclesiastical tradition and different genres of questionnaires: Burke 2000, pp. 75, 126, 130; Bitterli 1986, pp. 189–94.
29. Solano 1988, pp. 81–4; Rassem/Stagl 1994, pp. 146–51 (original Spanish).

to attract favour from the king and the Indian Council.[30] Yet for our purposes, the Spanish questionnaires are especially well suited. They were renewed at irregular intervals all the way into the early nineteenth century, which means they can be subjected to a serial reading. The fact that the Spanish motherland and especially its American viceroyalties were pronounced mountain lands also makes them extremely relevant for our topic. Which forms of mountain perception distinguish these sources over time? Roughly, one can describe and arrange them chronologically under four basic categories.[31]

1. *Economy (questionnaires from 1548 to 1730)*: soil quality and land conditions for agriculture and livestock.

2. *Politics (questionnaires starting in 1577)*: land conditions and roadways; mountains as boundary markers and as factors of geographic localisation.

3. *Science (questionnaires starting in 1577)*: volcanoes (at length around 1730), elevation-specific climate phenomena (at length in 1777) and geology/mineralogy (especially 1777 and 1812).

4. *Romantic interest (questionnaire 1812)*: picturesque views, waterfalls and the echo effect of mountains.

In sum, the interests expressed in these questionnaires display great fluctuations. Over the course of the early modern period they also tended to become more extensive and detailed. In the eighteenth century, as scientific attentiveness grew, specialised measuring instruments began to appear in the documents, such as the thermometer (from 1777) and the barometer (1812). Now the officials were expected to describe exact distances and in the early nineteenth century they were additionally required to determine the height of mountain peaks. With the questions about their aesthetic and acoustic qualities, even a romantic perspective found its way into bureaucratic practice for a time. This leads us back to the problem of periodisation. One can take these questions as a sign that the new, emphatic patterns of perception quickly became stereotypes. This, in turn, had longer-term consequences for the regressive interpretation of history: if western 'modernity' was characterised in its schematisation by a romantic attitude, this could easily lead to older forms of natural perception

---

30. Brendecke 2009.

31. 33 questionnaires from 1533–1812 with an instructive introduction in Solana 1988, pp. 1–219; some questionnaires are very short and/or thematically limited (e.g. only on tributes); my treatment of the mountain issues is based on sixteen questionnaires from 1548–1812.

1492: Expansion and Change in Perception

being crudely measured by its standards, thus appearing gloomy in comparison. These days, it appears more realistic to recognise a greater spectrum of possible attitudes in the 'premodern' period.[32]

It is also interesting to compare these Spanish sources with another scientific questionnaire from 1666, published in the journal of the newly formed English scholarly society, the 'Royal Society of London for Improving Natural Knowledge'. It was the idea of Anglo-Irish founding member and later president, Robert Boyle. Here, too, one of the first questions concerned topography:

> As far as the earth itself, can its extent and position be described with respect to the East, West, North, and South; also its contours, its plains and valleys and their dimensions; its hills and mountains and their highest elevations, in relation to the surrounding valleys and plains as well as to sea level; and further, whether the mountains lie scattered or connected in chains, and if these run in a North–South or East–West direction; also whether or not the land exhibits any foothills, fire-breathing, or smoking hills.[33]

Boyle was not only a respected gentleman naturalist – he was also a member of the royal 'Council for Foreign Plantations', which was concerned with colonial matters. The questionnaire was intended primarily for sailors who set out on long journeys, then also for the genteel 'Curious Traveller'.[34] The background, as in the Spanish case, was the early modern expansion movement. However, the impetus here was already determined much more significantly by science. According to the introductory text, the questionnaire was meant to serve the objective of providing a natural history, for a place either small or large, as well as to furnish the basis for theoretical knowledge – a 'Solid and Useful Philosophy'. Significantly, the first question Boyle raised about the mountains concerned their elevation. He had already occupied himself for years with this problem, in connection with his highly regarded studies of the air and atmosphere.[35]

In contrast to the Spanish questionnaires, which in principle remained a state secret, the English text was published. Its publication proved to be exceedingly successful and led to lively discussions as well as to reproductions and imitations both in England and on the Continent. One person who took

---

32. See Mathieu 2005 and below, Chapter 4.1.
33. Hunter/Davis 1999–2000, vol. 5, pp. 509–10; for the context of the 'New Science' and the early Royal Society: Hunter 1989.
34. Hints in an announcement of 1665 and in a reprint of the questionnaire in book-format in 1692: Hunter/Davis 1999–2000, vol. 5, pp. XLII, 508; see also Hunter 1989, pp. 93–4.
35. See also Chapter 1.3 below (altitude measurement).

up the idea with enthusiasm and turned it to his own purposes was the Zurich physician and naturalist Johann Jakob Scheuchzer. In 1699, under the title 'An Invitation to Explore the Natural Wonders of Switzerland' [*Einladungs-Brief, zu Erforschung natürlicher Wunderen, so sich im Schweitzer-Land befinden*], he produced a printed questionnaire in both German and Latin versions. The questions, nearly 200 of them, were directed in this case toward informants in his own country and especially in its mountainous regions. This text can be seen as the beginning of an intensive Alpine research movement, dominated in the following two generations by the well-known Swiss personalities Albrecht von Haller and Horace-Bénédict de Saussure.[36] Through their activities and those of countless other nature lovers, eighteenth-century research on the European Alps also became a model for mountain research worldwide.

World Map Plus Mountain System

Questionnaires provide hints about a certain group's focus of attention at a particular point in time. Other instructive indicators for the development of a globalised perception of mountains are maps, especially world maps, which existed long before the modern era. Although they were generally produced in two dimensions, many early maps indicated the three-dimensionality of the earth's surface through distinctive markings. Mountains appear to have been so useful for orientation and for the imitation of nature's outward appearance that they figured as basic elements in the cartography of many cultures and sometimes served even in small maps of large territories. The great care put into them is demonstrated in the instructions for their representation. In the so-called Ma'mun geography – an Islamic map project from the early Middle Ages, handed down mainly through late medieval fragments – a set of instructions provided guidance for the exact localisation of mountain ranges (coordinates of the start and end positions) as well as for the alignment and colouring of the peaks, with more than thirty possible hues and certain shading options.[37] The significance of mountains in the mental world of mapmakers emerges especially in the depiction of unknown lands. In an Italian world map from the 1560s, for example, there is a large southern continent recognisable as *terra incognita*, outfitted on the one side with animals and fabulous creatures and

---

36. Scheuchzer's questionnaire mentions the model of the Royal Society, to which he established close relationships; see Kempe 2003, above all pp. 73–109; Boscani Leoni 2005; earlier forms of Alpine research started in the sixteenth century, see Boscani Leoni 2010.

37. Sezgin 2000, part 1, p. 121.

1492: Expansion and Change in Perception

covered on the other by an absolutely systematic network of mountain chains – for cartographers, these were evidently part to the earth's basic inventory.[38]

Over the course of the early modern period, European cartography experienced important advances with respect to dimensions, precision and specialisation. Of particular interest for our purposes are those schemes that portrayed the mountain world as a coherent system and drew geographical or historical–philosophical conclusions. The two following examples come from the second half of the eighteenth century, as scientific development was accelerating; they also come from two countries that played a central role in this development: France and Germany.

Philippe Buache, who from 1729 was the 'king's primary geographer' [*premier géographe du Roi*] and was at the same time the first geographer with a seat in the Royal Academy of Sciences [*Académie Royale des Sciences*], made a name for himself, above all, as a cartographer. He was best known for his submarine map of the English Channel and for another work showing the mountains of the world as one continuous and sustaining system. He presented it to the Royal Academy in 1752 under a title whose first part read: 'An Essay in Physical Geography, in which a General View is Proposed Concerning the Nature of the Earth's Scaffolding, Composed of Mountain Chains Traversing the Oceans as well as the Land' [*Essai de Géographie Physique, où l'on propose des vûes générales sur l'espèce de Charpente du Globe, composée des chaînes de montagnes qui traversent les mers comme les terres*].[39] Intercontinental relationships among mountains were evident along certain sea passages, such as between Siberia and Alaska, and even more so for submarine routes such as the long mountain chain in the Atlantic between West Africa and Brazil, which Buache derived from the existence of an archipelago. Some of the terrestrial mountain ranges on his map were also derivations, based on river courses, which in the absence of elevation measurements indicated the direction of the slope, the altitude and the contours of the watershed; he invented, for example, a highland running east to west across South America that later proved to be nonexistent. What reviewers noted posthumously about the king's 'armchair geographer' must be of special interest to us here: he possessed a conceptually inflated view of the world's mountains. An especially tangible, material expression of his vision was

---

38. Paulo Forlani, *Universale descrittione di tutta la terra conosciuta fin qui*, 1565; reproduced in Klemp 1976, no. 13.
39. Buache 1752 and 1753.

presented in a globe, designed under his command in relief, with a diameter of almost three metres.[40]

A comprehensive world-historical view stimulated the German poet and philosopher, Johann Gottfried Herder, as he consulted a map while working on his *Ideas for a History of Humanity* [*Ideen zu einer Geschichte der Menschheit*]. 'The mere sight of a world map confirms it', he wrote in 1784: 'Mountain chains are that which do not merely cut through solid ground but rather seem to provide the skeleton on which the land is built.'[41] He viewed the arrangement of the first mountains as decisive for the formation of the landmasses and the plants that covered them and he understood it as a kind of conglomeration process. The philosopher attributed to mountain regions a very important role, not only for natural history but in human history as well. In fact, in many ways they were for him a central focus of world history: they had served at one time as humanity's birth place and first home, then as a place of refuge for the oppressed but above all they were 'revolutionary workshops', activated by the rugged mountain folk, which imprinted the broader course of history with their stamp. According to Herder these people received their spirit of courage and freedom from the mountains, which also served as a water source for the entire world. In closing he reflected, therefore, that 'it would be nice if we had a mountain map, or better still a mountain atlas, in which we could consider these fundamental pillars of the earth in their various respects, and it would be noted how they promote the history of the human race'.[42]

Herder's wish was to be realised in the following generation. One person was especially important for this and when he set out on a research undertaking that took him to many lands, he was influenced – among other things – by Herder's *Ideas*. This man was Alexander von Humboldt. With his generation there began a new phase in the globalisation history of natural observation and especially mountain perception. He and his contemporaries developed concepts that provide interesting clues for our question about the historical genesis of a 'mountain world' stretching all around the globe.

---

40. Kish 1976; Debarbieux 2009; in the perspective of the late nineteenth century, see Penck 1894, vol. 1, pp. 139, 162, 345.
41. Herder 2002 (1784), part 1, p. 35; according to the editor, Wolfgang Preuss, the world map used by Herder could have been a work of E. A. W. Zimmermann (1777); Preuss deals also with the metaphor of 'scaffolding' and mentions Buache's studies but does not demonstrate an actual reception (*Ibid.* part 2, pp. 103–104).
42. Herder 2002 (1784), part 1, p. 47 (original German); hints about the authors Herder used: *Ibid.* part 2, pp. 101–12.

1.3 Alexander von Humboldt

On 23 June 1802 Alexander von Humboldt and two travel companions attempted to summit what was then believed in Europe to be the world's highest mountain, the Chimborazo in the Andes. The daring naturalists climbed within a few hundred metres of the summit. Although the ascent ultimately failed, Humboldt was now (mistakenly) counted as the one among mortals who had reached the highest place on earth. Not without pride, he informed his Prussian king of this accomplishment upon his return to Europe.[43] Almost 200 years later, on 15 December 1998, a memorial ceremony took place at the foot of the Chimborazo. A group of scientists from around the world, accompanied by politicians and media representatives from throughout the region, unveiled a commemorative plaque listing the famous explorer's merits and making him out to be the founding father of global mountain ecology: 'In addition to his many other contributions, it was in this tropandean landscape, beneath the eternal snows of our majestic volcano, where he laid the foundations of "mountain geoecology", or "montology", that continues to mold world society.' The plaque then elucidated the influence of this science on global events, with reference to the success of the Rio de Janeiro Earth Summit of 1992 and to the UN's recent adoption of the International Year of the Mountains.[44]

Modern historical research does not see much truth in such origin stories. Scientific disciplines are complex institutions and relationship networks that undergo continual change. A family model, which places the singular act of a 'founding father' at the centre, does not do them justice, and Humboldt himself might have been surprised by the 'montology' this group spoke of in the 1990s. Nevertheless, the reference to him may not have been completely arbitrary. The mountains in their global dimensions did in fact belong among the major themes of his life. Many of his contemporaries and immediate successors also recognised this, which is to be highly estimated, because it is not only his own achievements but also and above all their social reception that possess historical significance.[45]

---

43. The standard biography of Humboldt is still Beck 1959–61; among the many popular biographies, Krätz 2000 is especially worth mentioning; there on p. 182 a partial facsimile of the letter to the king; for climbs to higher mountains before 1800, see Chapter 4.3 below.
44. Sarmiento 1999.
45. A detailed version of the following paragraph with somewhat different questions in Mathieu 2010; for 'Mountain Geoecology' and 'Montology' see Chapter 1.5 below.

The Globalisation of Perception

'Humboldtian Science'

Alexander von Humboldt was born in 1769, a noble from Berlin or thereabouts, where he died ninety years later. He spent much of his life outside Germany: from 1799 to 1804 he undertook his journey to South America, after which he mostly stayed in Paris, the scientific metropolis of that time, until 1827. He left behind an extensive body of scientific work, much of it written in literary style. In the decade 1790–1799 he published over 140 journal articles and eight stand-alone works; from 1810 to 1819, at the height of publishing activity for the material from his South American trip, another 62 independent works appeared; the high point in this category came in 1850–1859, thanks to the success of his later work, *Cosmos*. In sum he produced an enormous amount of text, with easily a thousand independent and dependent titles in print. This was due, to be sure, not only to Humboldt himself but also to a kind of Humboldt industry. To it belonged scientific and technical assistants, independent publishing agents, translators and intermediaries of all kinds.[46]

The fact that this was not without public effect can be read in the awards he received from learned societies and other institutions, passed down as part of his private library, the 'Humboldtiana'. All these honours and certificates amounted to around 180 in number and they were widespread in geographic origin. Around three-fifths came from Germany, Italy, Great Britain and Russia; the rest were from numerous countries in Europe and North and South America. The objects named after Humboldt were and are also widespread: villages and cities, mountains and rivers, parks, caves, streets, economic and scientific foundations; also minerals, plants, animals and many more. Humboldt received his first namesake when he was 21 years old. Today there are around a thousand appellations deriving from his name, found on all the world's continents.[47]

It was the South American journey that made this cosmopolitan noble, ever committed to the Enlightenment, truly famous. The trip had taken him among other places to the Amazon and to the highest reaches of the Chimborazo. One should not assume, however, that he had to make do in the New World without any European-style infrastructure. By 1800 there were already more than twenty universities there, run by Catholic orders or under bishops; they often exhibited archaic library collections but in some cases they could look back on a long history. Of course, Humboldt's South American expedition also had its forerunners. Ever since the conquest and occupation by Spain and

---

46. See the attempt at quantification in Mathieu 2010; it is based on bibliographical inquiries by Horst Fiedler, Ulrike Leitner and others.
47. The Humboldt Library 1863, pp. 333–51; Oppitz 1969.

Alexander von Humboldt

Portugal in the sixteenth century, the continent had been explored repeatedly by travellers. In the eighteenth century they increased in number and in scientific orientation, which also served Humboldt well. In 1802, for example, he spent some time in Lima and gained entry to the state archives, where he was able to study and excerpt, among others, the unpublished manuscript of the Bohemian scientific explorer, Thaddaeus Haenke, who wrote about a region in present-day Bolivia that was then little known in Europe. Haenke, like Humboldt, was interested in botany and many other fields. In the years 1790–93 he had been a member of a great Spanish research expedition, which in turn was able to build upon previous undertakings.[48]

What characterised Humboldt was less the route he chose than his way of travelling and subsequently processing the findings. For this style, the history of science has proposed its own term – 'Humboldtian Science' – with two main traits. First, Humboldt's interests covered extremely broad fields of knowledge, which he often investigated from a spatial perspective as well as with regard for their deeper relationships. Second, he valued exact measurements, especially on the global scale and produced a 'science of measuring worldwide variables'.[49] This scientific approach had its historical preconditions. Humboldt was born in a period when long-distance traffic increased rapidly and ship passages became substantially more affordable and easier to arrange than before. At the same time, however, he was also influenced by many older scholars. Particularly important in our context is his relationship with the Genevese naturalist, Horace-Bénédict de Saussure. This man quickly rose to fame, for being (mistakenly) regarded as the first to climb the highest Alpine summit (Mont Blanc) and for his scientific and literary work, *Voyages in the Alps* [*Voyages dans les Alpes*], which first appeared between 1779 and 1796. The introduction to his highly regarded book pointed out that, above all, it was the study of mountains that could accelerate progress in the scientific theory of the earth. Humboldt was well acquainted with this text. In June 1798, he wrote to a colleague in Geneva that he should disclose to 'the illustrious Saussure' that he had recently read his work again, word for word, and taken note of all his proposed experiments, because he loved to walk in the footsteps of a great man ['*J'aime à marcher sur les traces d'un grand homme*'].[50]

---

48. Weber 2002, pp. 82, 143, 170; Kühnel 1960; Henze 1978–2004, vol. 2, pp. 428–30.
49. Cannon 1978, pp. 73–100, quote p. 96.
50. Jahn/Lange 1973, p. 635; Saussure 1779–96, vol. 1, p. ii; Saussure reached the peak of Mont Blanc in 1787, one year after the first ascent by Jacques Balmat and Michel Paccard.

The Globalisation of Perception

The significance Humboldt ascribed to the mountain world can be discerned in diverse fields. Important throughout his life for his relationship with nature was the subjective side, which is to say the emotions, feelings and moods that nature could bring forth in people. Here the mountains were certainly not to be overlooked. Thus, in 1808, as Germany stood under Napoleonic rule, he dedicated his *Views on Nature* [*Ansichten der Natur*] to all those 'afflicted souls', who followed him as readers from the daily events into the South American countryside, along the lines of a Schiller drama: 'In the Mountains is Freedom! / The whiff of the grave / Rises not into the pure air; / The world is perfect everywhere, / Where no man treads with his despair.' What he emphasised more often than the comfort to be taken in harmonious nature, however, was the pleasure it bestowed. The subjective side played an important role even in his monumental *Cosmos*, which appeared in its first volume in 1845 (when he was over seventy years old), with a subtitle stating its subject as a *Sketch of a Physical Description of the Universe* [*Entwurf einer physischen Weltbeschreibung*].[51]

Several references to the mountain problem also arose with his 'Establishment of World Laws', as Humboldt called it – on the objective side, that is. According to one biographer, the young Humboldt had three research objectives in mind: a 'History of the Plants'; a study of the 'Dips and Strikes of the Ancient Mountain Strata'; and a 'Pasiography', or language of characters, for the demonstration of genetic aspects. In all three cases, the vertical dimension played a special role.[52] Examples of his interest in mountains are likewise found in his unrealised plans, as in 1798, when Humboldt flirted with the idea of joining the French expedition to Egypt that accompanied Napoleon's military campaign. In order to gain acceptance among the scientists, however, he first wanted to carry out research in the Atlas Mountains, since up to that time 'not one mineralogist had investigated Morocco's high mountain ranges, which rise to the boundaries of perpetual snow'. After that, he journeyed not to North Africa but to South America. Hardly had he arrived back in Paris, in 1804, when he decided to supplement his experience in the Andes with a journey to the East, one that would lead him eventually into the highlands of Tibet. This plan occupied him for years before he first embarked upon it, in a partial way, with a trip to Asian Russia in 1829.[53]

---

51. Humboldt 1969, p. 6 (the motto from Schiller's 'Bride of Messina', original German); Humboldt 2004.
52. Beck 1982, pp. 88–9; for the 'Pasiography' also Beck 1959–61, vol. 1, pp. 106–7.
53. Krätz 2000, p. 62; Biermann 1983; Beck 1959–61, vol. 2, pp. 5, 29–34, 42–52, 88–154.

Alexander von Humboldt

Wanted: The Highest Mountain

The measurement and calculation of altitude belonged to the constant elements of Humboldt's scientific practice. On a trip across Spain to Madrid in 1799, he made such zealous use of his barometer that one historian qualified it as a 'barometric measurement tour'. Through the positioning of orientation points, he was then able to establish a land profile with mountain ranges and high plateaus over a distance of 1,000 kilometres. He used a similar technique in other places, and later went on to calculate (or have calculated by others) the average elevation for each continent, along with the relationship between highlands and lowlands. If he once forgot to open his barometer at a prominent location, he would find it worth mentioning years later.[54] However, the success of his South America expedition was soon overshadowed by the fact that during the early nineteenth century, the Chimborazo in present-day Ecuador was eclipsed in the horizons of European knowledge as the world's highest mountain. Other peaks had already suffered this same fate, as a brief review will show.

In the mid-seventeenth century, the scholar Bernhard Varenius enumerated the most famous mountain ranges and highest peaks in his *General Geography* [*Geographia Generalis*]. His list of mountain ranges began with the Alps and their extensions; then it went on to the Andes and to other unnamed mountains of the 'New World'; only then, in fifth place, did he turn his view to the East (the Taurus and Caucasus among others). The list of highest mountains looked somewhat different: first came Tenerife Peak (now Pico del Teide, 3720 m.), second a peak in the Azores, third the Andes (without further specification), fourth Etna in Sicily, fifth Hekla in Iceland and finally, in sixth place, an Asian mountain, namely the legendary Adam's Peak in Ceylon (Sri Lanka), previously mentioned by Marco Polo. As a North German, Varenius never saw a great mountain in his life. Still, perhaps for that very reason, his book is not uninteresting – for its conceptual classification of the mountain world. Later Isaac Newton took care to have it reissued and the new edition became a true classic.[55]

Tenerife Peak, which Varenius placed at the top of his list, had been regarded as being very tall ever since European seafarers began to frequent the

---

54. Beck 1959–61, vol. 1, p. 122; see also Beck 1982b; Humboldt 1843, vol. 1, p. 181; Berghaus 2004, pp. 60–1; Humboldt 1969, p. 145.
55. Varenius 1664, pp. 92–9 (first edition 1650); Hambis 1955, pp. 271–4; Varenius is located at the transition from an earlier 'philological' school of geography to one increasingly interested in natural facts; moreover, he classified the mountains and other 'major ecosystems' with general – and not only regional – geography; see Kastrop 1972.

group of islands in the fifteenth century. It was said it could be seen from a distance of sixty miles and more and some even believed it to be just as tall: a hundred kilometres high.[56] This, however, suggests in turn that during the transition to modern times, height was not yet any kind of important, precisely measured or measurable criterion with which one could make large-scale spatial comparisons. There were few grounds or possibilities for the critical comparison of estimates circulating from far and near. Noteworthy in Varenius's list is the fact that almost all of his highest mountains were visible from the sea. Also relevant for the classification, however, were political and cosmological ideas. All around the central Alps, for example, St. Gotthard Pass or Mountain was regarded as unusual because it was there that the Rhine, Rhone and other rivers began. Swiss authors also placed the region at the centre of the world for patriotic reasons. St. Gotthard was therefore held to be especially high; indeed, around 1800, some still considered it the highest mountain in the Alps.[57] On the other hand, early reports arriving from Asia and America naturally spoke of very tall mountain ranges. Often cited and translated was the text of a Spanish Jesuit who, in 1590, portrayed a pass in the Andes as 'one of the highest places in the universe', with very thin air and completely forsaken, where there was not one bird and the people became 'seasick on the land' (in other words, they suffered from altitude sickness).[58]

In the seventeenth century there followed, in the words of one French researcher, the 'Birth of Altitude' [*naissance de l'altitude*], with an increasing awareness of the summit regions driven primarily by scientific motives.[59] The invention of the barometer provided technical facility and motivation in the 1640s. Whereas previous elevation estimates had been based on watercourses, or measured with simple trigonometric instruments, air pressure now became a possible indicator of altitude and this spared the tiresome labour of large-scale levelling. On the other hand, barometric measurements long remained imprecise. Nevertheless, around 1650, naturalists and philosophers began to

---

56. Cajori 1929, pp. 493–4; Jouty 1998, p. 19; usually, however, the peak's altitude was given as 15 miles; Robert Boyle also lowered this figure substantially: Hunter/Davis 1999–2000, vol. 6, pp. 98–100.
57. Bertrand 1753, p. 24; Marchal 1992, pp. 41–3; since the terms for 'mountain' and 'peak' were interchangeable in both German and French, designations such as 'Gotthard Mountain' cannot be localised exactly, see Körner 1996, p. 275; Farrington 2000, p. 51.
58. Gilbert 1983, pp. 329–32.
59. Jouty 1998; older works on the history of mountaineering overlook the fact that the perception of altitude changed over time, e.g. Ziak 1956, pp. 266–7.

Alexander von Humboldt

collect as much reliable information as possible from various mountains and to compare them critically against one another. Scientifically, questions about the atmosphere, air pressure and respiration thereby became important.[60]

These research interests not only made altitude an important criterion – at the same time they also ensured a repeated reshuffling of rank order among the 'highest' mountains. At first, Tenerife Peak retained its dominant position. The aforementioned Robert Boyle, who was an active naturalist and researcher in this area, published a critical discussion in England, but without proposing any alternative hierarchy. It came to this only in the mid-eighteenth century, after a French expedition of the 'Royal Academy of Sciences' noted rather casually the height of the Chimborazo while taking general earth measurements in the Andes.[61] In the following decades, this extinct volcano south of the city of Quito indisputably held its position of superior rank in the minds of the European intelligentsia. The period in which elevations came to be routinely measured also began in the years around 1780. When Humboldt published his *Essay on the Geography of Plants* [*Ideen zu einer Geographie der Pflanzen*] in 1807, he was already able to put together a list of 125 mountains along with their elevation statistics. Two decades later, the number of surveyed mountains reached into the thousands; a physical dictionary from 1829 named 4,600.[62]

This rapid spread of measuring activity was not, however, evenly distributed around the globe and this offers us objective clues about the development of mountain perception. In Humboldt's 1807 list, 42 elevation points came from the Alps (nearly half of them measured by Saussure), and 47 were from elsewhere in Europe; from America he collected thirty data points (which he had mostly measured himself) and from the Oceania, Africa, and Asia combined he provided a mere six. More than two thirds of the worldwide list fell therefore to Europe, with a full third from its Alpine region, which in terms of territory made up only a minute portion of the global mountain surface. This dominant position of the Alps in western culture is confirmed by other indications. Humboldt and his contemporaries often made comparisons to them, for example, when they wanted to clearly describe the mountains of other continents in their writings. Conversely, in the eighteenth and nineteenth centuries, the Alpine concept became a global export. In the end one spoke of

---

60. Hunter/Davis 1999–2000, vol. 6, pp. 95–100, 236–8; Cajori 1929; Jouty 1998.
61. For Boyle see note 56; for the Chimborazo: Bouguer 1749, pp. L, CVIII (with an elevation profile of the region); for the expedition: Kertz 1999, pp. 71–2, 76–8, 130–1; for the reception: Buache 1753, p. 588; Humboldt 1989, pp. 75, 155.
62. Humboldt 1989, pp. 155–61; Cajori 1929, p. 504.

The Globalisation of Perception

the Japanese Alps, the Sichuan Alps in China, the Australian Alps, the New Zealand Alps, the Canadian Alps, the Pontic and Transylvanian Alps and so on. Some of these historically transferred designations are still in use today.[63]

As one can see, the history of European mountain perception has in many ways followed the history of colonial and imperialist expansion. This is evident already in terms of periodisation and general orientation. First the European observers looked to the West, where, above all, the sprawling mountain system of the Andes drew their attention. In Asia, territorial dominance came only later and with greater difficulty. This was an important reason why the highlands of Central Asia became objects to be surveyed only in the nineteenth century. The earliest (for Humboldt not exactly pleasant) news reporting the elevation of certain mountains in the Himalayas appeared in Europe during the decade after 1810. At first the Daulaghiri became the world's highest peak but then, from the 1850s, the position of world dominance was claimed by a successor, known by many today as Mount Everest.[64] Even then, some doubt remained. In the first half of the twentieth century, for example, an expedition was organised to evaluate a candidate in China for the status of world's highest mountain. Soon, the criteria for determining elevation were also refined and diversified. Currently there are five or so major methods: based on sea level, Mount Everest is the first; measured from the earth's centre the highest is, ironically, the Chimborazo – the fact that the earth is widest at the equator gives it an advantage of no less than two kilometres.[65]

Profiles and World Mountains

Humboldt was a pioneer, not only with his many measurements but also in his representation of mountains through elevation profiles. It is believed that he received stimulus in this direction during his time in the Prussian mining administration, from the designs that were common there. Subsequently he indicated in profile form not just individual mountains, mountain ranges or lands; instead he set the mountains from various continents side by side, in order to display global comparisons of the landscape's three-dimensional composition. Famous was the large tableau in his 1807 *Essay on the Geography of Plants* – a cross-section of the Andes, with numerous tabular explanations and

---

63. For the comparisions: Mathieu 2010; for the globalisation of the term 'Alpine' some hints in Medicus 1795, p. 10 and Debarbieux 1997; the matter would merit a thorough historical study.
64. Wyder 2004, pp. 151–3; Isserman/Weaver 2008, pp. 13–7.
65. Imhof 1995, p. 148 (China expedition of 1930).

Alexander von Humboldt

intercontinental references – as well as his later *Geography of the Lineaments of Plants* [*Geographiae plantarum lineamenta*], a colour chart showing a series of elevation-specific vegetation zones in the Andes, Alps, and Pyrenees, as well as Lapland (see Plate 3).[66]

At that time, however, such models were not even necessary in order to spark the visualisation of advances in measuring the earth's vertical surface. Several known initiatives were inspired by nothing more than the newly arriving information from South America and elsewhere. In 1806 the engraver Christian von Mechel published in Berlin an etching that was almost one metre in length, under the title *Tableau of the Principle Heights of the Globe, Founded on the Most Exact Measurements* [*Tableau des Hauteurs principales du Globe, fondé sur les mesures les plus exactes*]. It presented these 'principle prominences' in an abstract juxtaposition. Although the publisher emphasised the precision of the data, he did not fail to also advertise the presentation's visual appeal: 'Nothing has been spared in its beautiful execution and illumination, so that this sheet, under glass, can make a lovely prospect for a room's adornment, just as an admirer's portfolio alongside coloured views.' Independently, that same year in London, a Scottish landscape painter presented a work composed of many of the world's famous mountains. The dimensions of his canvas were even larger than the Berlin version (130 x 90 cm.) and he wanted to offer in its arrangement an 'agreeable picture' as well. Within the next year, it stimulated a geographer to bring to market the first volume of a comprehensive world mountain encyclopaedia.[67]

A very successful representation in this new genre came from Johann Wolfgang Goethe. It was brought about by the fact that he received from Humboldt a personally dedicated copy of his *Essay on the Geography of Plants*, sent immediately on publication in 1807, so that it lacked the later famous illustration. 'I devoured the book, and wished to make it fully enjoyable and useful for myself and others without delay', Goethe later wrote. Using the book as a guide, he sketched the mountains of the New World on the right side of a page and then, using the same scale, put the mountains of the Old World on the left. The painted trees conveyed an impression of the altitude-specific vegetation belts described in Humboldt's text. In addition, he indicated the

---

66. Humboldt 1989, pp. 314–5 and the reproduction in the Appendix; Fiedler/Leitner 2000, pp. 274, 276, 308; in general also Uhlig 1984b.
67. Wyder 2004, quotes pp. 144, 154 (original German); Wilson 1807–10 (short alphabetical description of over 4,000 mountains, with indications of known altitude measurements).

The Globalisation of Perception

snow line and the daring researchers: under the summit of the Chimborazo, Goethe drew a small figure representing Humboldt; on top of Mont Blanc, he put a second one for Saussure. Together, the two symbolised the heroism of worldwide mountain conquest. When the finished drawing, which was initially intended for private use, was published in a journal in 1813 under the title *Heights of the Old and New World, An Illustrated Comparison* [*Höhen der alten und neuen Welt bildlich verglichen*] (see Plate 4), the level of demand was so high that it promptly appeared in a separate printing. It was not long before publishers in Paris and London snatched up Goethe's illustration and came out with their own versions; soon it served as a model for the illustration in a *Picture Book for Children* [*Bilderbuch für Kinder*].[68]

A little later, however, these representations were likewise overtaken, as reports from Asia multiplied and the measurements of the gigantic mountains in the Himalayas became known. The publishers, who depended on providing the most current information, had to adapt their strategies to this finding. For economic reasons, the giants first appeared only near the margins of the page, to avoid having to redesign the entire composition. Then, however, truly new representations of the global ensemble were designed and made accessible in many different versions. The public could now obtain individual sheets in various formats and combinations – alongside the world's longest rivers, for example. With time, three-dimensionality gained entry to the emerging atlas works. Fierce competition arose among publishers, who wanted to collaborate with Humboldt and use his name for advertising purposes. Officially, Humboldt cooperated with the atlas producer Heinrich Berghaus (1845–48), but Traugott Bromme (1851), F. G. L. Gressler (1853) and others used him too. Many of these atlases went through several editions and made an impression on the perceptions of the late nineteenth century.[69] The world's mountains now presented themselves as some kind of scene composed of staggered mountain systems, or as one elongated mountain chain reaching from the Andes all the way to Lapland, or even as an island, on which the peaks of almost all the continents crowded together into one world mountain (see Plate 5).

---

68. Goethe 1813; Wyder 2004, pp. 142–143, 150–151, 155–160.
69. Examples of single sheets: Tableau comparatif 1820–1829; for atlas versions: Berghaus 2004.

1.4 Scientific Departure

With the industrialisation and modernisation of state and society in the nineteenth and twentieth centuries, entirely new conditions arose for scientific development. Among the central characteristics belonged a growing specialisation, particularly in the form of newly established scientific fields or disciplines. It is not entirely easy to describe scientific disciplines in general terms. They were marked by an ever-changing ensemble of institutional and personal connections. If one understands science and research as a 'cultural practice', then an entire bundle of characteristic features can be seen in disciplinary organisation, appearing in different forms according to particular historical circumstances. They ranged from university institutes to academic societies and special bibliographies (classical literature, standard books, specialised periodicals), as well as to the previously indicated career patterns, motivations and forms of perception.[70]

The formation of disciplines would have been inconceivable without 'boundary-work' – that is, without the active engagement of the concerned parties in the demarcation of certain territories where they could establish their competence. The multiplication of such territories was strongly favoured by the fact that the sciences unfolded in a previously unknown growth dynamic, especially after 1850, accompanied by a new phase in the general economic and social division of labour. Of course there had long been specialisation in the world of scholars and from the eighteenth century its growth quickened; in the nineteenth century, however, the phenomenon rose to an entirely new level. The differentiation of various scientific cultures, each with their own priorities, now generated a sort of grid through which the world presented itself in new ways. For us the question poses itself: how did this process change mountain perceptions?[71]

In the rapid growth of the available literature it appears that the scientific departure in the West led to a tremendous increase in the knowledge of mountains from all parts of the globe. Yet one should not regard this accumulation entirely in terms of 'progress', under whose spell European society stood for quite some time. For, through innovation, the disciplinary dynamic also brought about enduring losses: when the focus of investigation shifted, it could result in the dethematisation of previously recognised and discussible

---

70. In praxeological perspective: Lenoir 1997, pp. 45–74; Bourdieu 1976; based on systems theory, yet stimulating: Stichweh 1984 and 1994; see also Blanckaert 2006.
71. The expression 'boundary-work' from Gieryn 1983, here above all p. 792; historical studies: Cardwell 1972, pp. 249–56 and Weber 2002, pp. 154–234; on early modern specialisation: Burke 2000, pp. 81–115.

subjects in academia. Elements of older phases vanished from the libraries or retreated into non-academic areas. 'The elevation of mountains has, by some, been deemed a subject of mere curiosity, or as one to which it is impossible to give the requisite precision', wrote a British geographer in 1807, though, on the contrary, with the advanced state of natural science research at that time, he thought it could contribute substantially to the illumination of the various theories. In fact the calculation of altitude had belonged, as mentioned previously, to the distinguishing characteristics of an advanced research practice ever since the late eighteenth century. Only a few generations later, however, scientists would hold themselves aloof when listing simple mountain elevation data in their specialist publications. Even where the shape of the earth's surface was absolutely central to the investigation, one found in the late nineteenth century only synthesised data, ordered according to specific criteria. For individual values, it became necessary to look elsewhere.[72]

Specialisation and Globalisation

As a starting point for the following overview of the effects of specialisation, we will use a selection of major works from the nascent disciplines. Table 1 presents ten disciplines that exhibited a general connection to mountain themes, listed according to their modern designations. In each case an early work is cited, to which one can ascribe a certain authority within the field. Below, the table provides references to later publications in which the status-attributes are verified. Against such a synthetic procedure several objections can be raised. Naturally no single work is sufficient to characterise an entire research direction and sometimes two or more books held similar rank in a particular field, so that decisions are almost completely arbitrary. Nevertheless, the compilation allows us to come closer to the issues, above all by stressing the multiplicity of perspectives on the theme that prevailed since the nineteenth century. In each of the cited disciplines and works, only particular aspects of the mountain world became evident, and in reality this 'diversification' was even greater, because the list could have included some other disciplines and subdisciplines.

The oldest of the cited publications comes from 1817 (Alexander von Humboldt), the most recent from 1934 (Jules Blache). Between them lie nearly 120 years, suggesting that specialisation is to be understood more as a process than as a precisely defined historical period. With regard to content too, both works are quite significant for the scientific handling of the topic: whereas the

---

72. Wilson 1807–10, vol. 1, p. xv (quote); Penck 1894, for example, offers only a short list of the highest peaks, arranged by latitude (vol. 2, p. 333).

Scientific Departure

Table 1: Major Scientific Works Pertaining to Mountains, 19th/20th Centuries

1.	Botany/Plant Geography: Alexander von Humboldt, *De distributione geographica plantarum secundum coeli temperiem et altitudinem montium, Prolegomena* [*Prologue on the Geographical Distribution of Plants According to the Climate and Altitude of Mountains*], Paris 1817.
2.	Cartography: Heinrich Berghaus, *Physikalischer Atlas oder Sammlung von Karten, auf denen die hauptsächlichsten Erscheinungen der anorganischen und organischen Natur nach ihrer geographischen Verbreitung und Vertheilung bildlich dargestellt sind* [*The Physical Atlas: A Series of Maps Illustrating the Geographical Distribution of Natural Phenomena*], Gotha 1845–48.
3.	Climatology: Julius Hann, *Handbuch der Klimatologie* [*Handbook of Climatology*], Stuttgart 1883.
4.	Geology: Charles Lyell, *Principles of Geology; being an attempt to explain the former changes of the earth's surface, by reference to causes now in operation*, 3 vols. London 1830–33.
5.	Geomorphology: Albrecht Penck, *Morphologie der Erdoberfläche* [*Morphology of the Earth's Surface*], 2 parts, Stuttgart 1894.
6.	Geophysics: Johann Müller, *Lehrbuch der kosmischen Physik* [*Principles of Universal Physics*], Braunschweig 1856 (with atlas volume).
7.	Glaciology: Albert Mousson, *Die Gletscher der Jetztzeit. Eine Zusammenstellung und Prüfung ihrer Erscheinungen und Gesetze* [*The Glaciers of the Present Time. A Synthesis and Examination of Their Manifestations and Laws*], Zurich 1854.
8.	Human Geography: Jules Blache, *L'Homme et la Montagne* [*Man and the Mountain*], Paris 1934.
9.	Hydrology: Nathaniel Beardmore, *Manual of Hydrology*, London 1862.
10.	Medicine/High Altitude Medicine: Paul Bert, *La pression barométrique. Recherches de physiologie expérimentale* [*Barometric Pressure: Researches in Experimental Physiology*], Paris 1878.

Geography can serve as an overarching discipline for several fields and is therefore not specifically mentioned. On the status of the cited works: 1. Mägdefrau 1992, p. 122; 2. Troll 1962, p. 225; 3. Schönwiese 1994, p. 14; 4. Ciancio 2005, p. 15; 5. Beck 1982, p. 204; 6. Kertz 1999, p. 206; 7. Heim 1885, VII; 8. Mathieu 2006, p. 306; 9. Biswas 1970, p. 314; 10. Simons/Oelz 2001, p. 92.

former dealt with the geography of plants, and so with a natural phenomenon, only the latter considered humankind. In fact, the human dimension remained ever secondary in the emerging field of disciplines involving mountains. As this dimension is located at the core of the present study, we will have reason to return to it later. Finally, the table reflects the centres of scientific activity. The works come from France, England, Germany and Switzerland. With five out of ten works, the German-speaking regions assume first rank and almost all of these were products of the second half of the nineteenth century – the great golden age of German science, which brought forth a new type of research university that soon spread to many countries.[73]

The specialisation in limited segments of external reality facilitated and promoted an expansion of the geographic field of observation all the way up to a global orientation. This can be demonstrated in detail for various strands of tradition. The cited glaciology work of 1854 by Albert Mousson, whose title *The Glaciers of the Present Time* [*Die Gletscher der Jetztzeit*] underlines the contrast with the then-dominant interests of the newly formulated Ice Age theory, was still anchored entirely in the Alps. According to Mousson, the glaciers were the 'most outstanding characteristic' and the 'most amazing feature' the Alps had to offer the researcher. Only in his conclusions did there follow a brief outlook at other mountain systems and continents. Albert Heim, who was asked as a young geology professor in the 1880s to write a *Handbook of Glaciology* [*Handbuch der Gletscherkunde*], rendered his thanks to this predecessor. Heim, however, obtained his information from a considerably broader geographical range and sketched a preliminary mountain panorama of the entire world. In doing so, his own Alpine experience was sharply relativised: not his own mountains but rather Greenland and the Karakoram now offered the mightiest glaciers and he found that the formation of glaciers was generally determined more by the distribution of precipitation than by temperature, as previously assumed.[74]

In the particulars, of course, each research direction had its own history. In high altitude medicine, for example, many significant initiatives came from Latin America. Denis Jourdanet, a French doctor residing there, became deeply involved in the physiology of human life at high altitudes; he published an extensive comparative work on this topic in 1875, before appearing – also for certain political reasons – as a sponsor for an elaborate laboratory in Paris, which helped the young researcher Paul Bert to write his aforementioned standard work on this topic. Other physiologists mistrusted the laboratory results coming out of this metropolis and began conducting open-air experiments in the Alps. In the late nineteenth century, permanent research stations were also established there for high altitude medicine and other disciplines, so that the Alpine region became a sort of 'laboratory landscape', as Philipp Felsch has stated. The science of high altitude medicine concerned itself, however, not only with the limiting properties of mountain climates but also assumed that they produced healing effects. This direction served as the ideal foundation

---

73. Clark 2006.
74. Mousson 1854, quote p. 4 (original German); Heim 1885, pp. 426–7, 490–4.

Scientific Departure

for altitude health resorts, which attracted numerous patients during a certain phase and so turned into a branch of tourism.[75]

Altogether, the views represented by various sides confirm that the mountain world – and above all the Alpine region – played a significant role for a series of natural sciences as an 'experiential space' and 'natural laboratory', because the environmental conditions there differed clearly from the European norm.[76] In our context, however, the central finding is that it was the specialised research fields themselves that for the most part produced the lens through which an area was observed and laboratory work undertaken. Research limited itself to certain specific aspects, which were handled with increasing systematic and spatial coverage. To some degree, the mountains were subject to a disciplinary grid that continually altered and shifted, producing new findings and dismissing older ones from the corpus of legitimate academic knowledge. The details of how this took place and how interdisciplinary counter-movements arose will now be illustrated with two noteworthy researchers from France and Germany.

Jules Blache (1893–1970)

What moved the French geographer Jules Blache in 1934 to publish the aforementioned study, Man and the Mountain [*L'Homme et la Montagne*] and how did he proceed? In the book's preface, the well-known founder of the Institute of Alpine Geography in Grenoble, Raoul Blanchard, emphasised that, with this text, Blache ventured into the unknown. No one before that time had attempted to examine the relations between people and mountains in a worldwide perspective. Blache had to start from scratch and he accomplished a pioneering feat. His willingness to take risks did not go unrewarded – the book became a success. By 1950, the Parisian publishing house had Gallimard issued it no less than seventeen times. For an entire generation of young geographers and historians in France, 'le Blache' was required reading. And although the text was also directed toward a larger audience, it found its way into many scientific works.[77]

The idea of making the work's central theme the relationships between people and mountains around the world most likely came, not from the author,

---

75. Jourdanet 1875; Bert 1875; Felsch 2007; see also Simons/Oelz 2001; Vaj 2005 and 2006.
76. Cardwell 1971, pp. 90–5; Stichweh 1984, pp. 45–6; Felsch 2007, above all pp. 55–87.
77. Blache 1934; biographical notes in Veyret 1970; for his place in the history of French geography: Claval 1998, above all pp. 142, 168, 204–6; in greater detail on Blache and his book: Mathieu 2006.

The Globalisation of Perception

but from a colleague in Paris, who launched a series with Gallimard in 1933 entitled *Human Geography* [*Géographie Humaine*]. *Man and the Mountain* was a commissioned work and it appeared as the third book in the series, following *Geography and Colonisation* [*Geographie et Colonisation*] and *Man and the Forest* [*L'Homme et la Forêt*]. In an introduction, the editor outlined geography's development into a science as well as the genesis of a new research direction, human geography. For his planned series the mountains appeared as an almost unavoidable theme, the treatment of which could not wait. That the editor went directly to Blache with the project was no accident. For this man had just published a major thesis on the mountain massifs surrounding Grenoble and he was regarded as the crown prince of the institute, founded in 1907 as the first of its kind.[78]

Blache's problem was the unequal distribution of available information. As he set about his work, the institute had already acquired considerable research experience in the western Alps; other European mountain regions were accessible through an astonishingly large selection of periodicals, most of which had come into existence since the late nineteenth century. The situation was altogether different in the regions outside Europe, where 'colonial geography' had not yet made much headway and 'tropical geography' was still in its infancy. Knowledge of the mountains on other continents therefore had to be gathered from heterogeneous and in some cases dubious sources. This is one of the reasons why the world's mountains are represented so unevenly in *Man and the Mountain*. Whereas the task and objective were global, it could not be so in practice. The small regions within the horizons of the Grenoble Institute were treated in detail, but vast mountainous regions of Asia – in China, Russia and the South-east – received no mention.[79]

With regard to content, Blache decided upon the following procedure. First he composed the picture of a traditional Alpine landscape and produced from it a model of 'Alpiculture' (*économie alpestre*), defined by the dominance of the pastoral sector with its seasonal migrations of animals and people. In a second step, he distinguished those mountainous regions of the world that were losing this 'classic' characteristic. He emphasised the difference thus: 'From the Alps to the mountains of the Far East, then to those of Africa and America, the

---

78. Mathieu 2006, pp. 308–9; about the Institute of Alpine Geography: Favier 2005 and Fourny/Sgard 2007.

79. A detailed account of Blache's bibliographical foundations in Sgard 2001, pp. 110–3; shortly afterward, the unequal information density was also conspicuous in the mountain study by Peattie 1936.

Scientific Departure

picture changes several times in its entirety.' The Alpine model could be found in most of the northern mountain regions, from the Atlantic to the Himalayas, in a zone with mostly temperate climates and predominantly inhabited by the 'white race'. The areas outside this zone were characterised, according to Blache, by other economic and social forms. Thus he saw the Far East as strictly separated between the 'wild' populations of the mountain regions and the densely settled rice-growing regions in the flatlands, without any migrations between the mountains and valleys as in Europe. It is interesting that at this point the author also shifted his argument into a different register. Whereas for him the Alpine economy explained itself primarily through environmental factors, he thought that other forms across the vastness of Asia, Africa and the Americas were often culturally based.[80]

For Blache, however, 'culture' frequently meant 'race'. There were qualitative differences in his view between 'white', 'yellow' and 'black' and there were also many ethnic sub-groups. In this, the author did not find himself alone: it was the language of the time, especially in geography with its emphasis on spatial classification. Then, only a few years after the appearance of the book, Blache would go on to deal intensively with racist ideas. During the Second World War, he joined the French Resistance against the German occupying forces. He went into hiding and toward the end of the war sought refuge in a monastery. In those years he found stability through his work on a political text containing a differentiated analysis of racism (German and in general), which he published in 1945. In the epilogue, he expressed his pleasure that 'the air over the land was clear again'. Now he could finally take the manuscript of his book out from under the floorboards where it had been hidden, 'during the time when the Gestapo paid me the honour of searching me at my home'.[81]

Yet even before this dramatic period, Blache did not completely separate the colourful world of mountains into Alpine and non-Alpine parts. In the conclusions of *Man and the Mountain,* he also sought common characteristics. He saw these less in the high-altitude climate, which varied with geographical latitude, than in the rugged mountainous terrain, which brought forth the same effects across the globe: it made communication more difficult and costly, thereby favouring isolation; it also hindered agricultural work, especially arable farming, which therefore promoted pastoral ways of life. This was seen to have held less weight in the past than in the present, because the development of modern means of transportation forced traditional mountain ways of life into

---

80. Blache 1934, quote p. 11 (original French); Sgard 2004, pp. 45–51.
81. Blache 1945, p. 246 (original French); Mathieu 2006, pp. 307–8.

the margins, postponing modernisation there. Whereas the mountains had played a crucial role in the early settlement period, now people seemed to be turning away from them.[82]

Carl Troll (1899–1975)

In 1934, as Blache's pioneering study appeared in Paris, a somewhat younger German geographer found himself on a research trip in the mountainous areas of East and South Africa. Carl Troll hailed originally from Bavaria and it was neither his first nor his last expedition to the mountains of the tropical and subtropical zones. As early as 1926 he joined a research trip to the Andes, concerned mostly with morphology and plant geology, which lasted in the end for over three years. In 1937 he was a member of a German Himalaya expedition, an opportunity he used, among other things, to visit Ethiopia on the return trip. Later too, as a well-established geography professor and institute director at the University of Bonn, he loved to carry out his various investigations 'above the tree line' around the world. Carl Troll belonged among the most successful, internationally respected researchers of the German post-war era. He was often compared to Alexander von Humboldt, not least because of his early trip to South America. Yet he too was born in a period when new transportation methods again sharply reduced travel times and it is quite possible that he was the first scientist systematically to visit mountain ranges all around the globe.[83]

In any case, he paid great attention throughout his life to the three-dimensionality of the earth's surface. Troll involved himself in a whole series of work areas and he was also known for his holistic, interdisciplinary approach. That the comparative view of the mountain world was especially important to him was evident on the occasion of his retirement in 1966, with the publication of his *Selected Contributions* [*Ausgewählte Beiträge*] in three parts. Part One, on 'Ecological Landscape Research and Comparative High Mountain Research', contained thirteen essays and references to another 49 of his publications. The other two parts were entitled 'Aerial Photography and Regional Studies' and 'The Spatial Differentiation of Developing Countries in Their Significance for Developmental Aid'; together they contained only nine articles and references to another 28 works.[84] A central message Troll developed on the basis of his studies concerned the old idea of altitude-specific climate belts or the

---

82. Blache 1934, pp. 163–81.
83. Bio-bibliographical notes in Lauer 1970, pp. 11–42 and Richter/Böhm 2003; some of his early diaries are published: Troll 1985.
84. Troll 1966.

Scientific Departure

analogy between altitude and polar position. Troll rejected this simple idea, which had gained popularity in the nineteenth century, as too imprecise and he demonstrated that it made better sense to understand high-altitude climates in the context of the surrounding climate regions. Thus the mountain areas of the tropical latitudes were influenced by that zone's generally prevailing daily climate, which distinguished them fundamentally from mountain areas in the temperate zones with their seasonal climate fluctuations.[85]

As an engaged science politician, Troll was also interested in the general course of research. Against the background of his broad understanding of landscape ecology, he stood critically against certain specialisation processes. He spoke repeatedly about the losses of knowledge associated with them. Thus, in one article from 1962, 'The Earth's Three-Dimensional Landscape Structure', he placed a series of research tasks on the agenda and offered an introductory review of the development of large-scale landscape studies since 1800. In sum, the connections between climate, vegetation and landscape, which had interested Humboldt in his time and now occupied Troll, had more or less been shelved in the research. 'Looking back today, we must recognise that such broad comparative viewpoints were again mostly lost in the following period, in the plant geography of A. Grisebach [1872], but also in the handling of other natural phenomena in geography and biology – no doubt an effect of the ever more specialised alignment of nature research.' Elsewhere he wrote: 'It is no misconception of the great upswing of the earth sciences in the nineteenth century when we establish that with the general onset of specialisation, also in the earth sciences, one lost sight of A. v. Humboldt's consciously pursued goal of comprehending terrestrial features in a three-dimensional, truly spatial sense.'[86]

In our context, the science policy activities Troll developed in his older age are of special importance. He had always been active and energetic: during the years of National Socialism he conducted himself, in his own words, as if he were a tightrope dancer;[87] after the war he became a prominent speaker and advocate for German geography to the Allied Powers. Then he quickly attained a number of important posts in science policy, including international positions. From 1956 until 1968 he was vice president and president of the International Geographical Union (IGU). When he stepped down from the board of directors in 1968, he founded within the IGU a special commission

---

85. E.g. Troll 1941, pp. 136–43 and 1955, pp. 173–6.
86. Troll 1962, pp. 222–5 (original German).
87. This period has been discussed recently, see Böhm 2003 (with reference to the metaphor of the tightrope dancer on p. 6) and the reply of Butzer 2004.

for high mountain research, or 'High-Altitude Geoecology' and later 'Mountain Geoecology', as it was now called in English ecological discourse. In quick succession, between 1966 and 1974, he organised various highly acclaimed symposia on this theme and there he was able to energise younger researchers with his prestige and his engaging manner. These meetings brought together those individuals who would later found the 'Mountain Agenda' and bring the mountains of the world, as a distinct and major ecosystem, into Agenda 21.[88]

1.5 The Politicisation of the Environment

During the course of the seventeenth century there began in European culture a process that can be characterised as the 'Birth of Altitude' and, in the following century, naturalists and philosophers from various viewpoints began to grasp the world's mountains as a system. Both these things took place against the background of the expansion movement and general scientific development. In the Middle Ages and in the transition to modern times there had naturally been discussions of the mountains, their properties and origins;[89] the appropriation of territories in the 'New World' then sharpened the view of similarities and differences in the geographical features on both sides of the ocean. Then, with the awakening of scientific interest in the measurement of summit elevations, the vertical dimension was further accentuated and at the same time bound into comparative relationships: of special interest was one peak's height with respect to others.

The search for the highest mountain on earth developed into an undertaking marked by many historical accidents and temporary attributions and, perhaps for this reason, people were ever more enthralled by it until the mid-nineteenth century. Now representations emerged that united all the mountains of the earth into one world mountain, crystallising the globalisation of mountain perception as in a photographic snapshot. From the nineteenth century the process of scientific specialisation also made its contribution, for its concentration on limited segments of reality became a stimulus for the handling of such segments in a broader and wherever possible global field of observation. As an 'experiential space', the mountains played a role for an entire series of natural sciences. There was no absence of criticism about the obsession therein with detail and lack of coherence, however. The criticism came on the one side from researchers such as Carl Troll, who proposed new syntheses, and on the other

---

88. Lauer 1970, pp. 12, 39–40; Richter/Böhm 2003, p. 102; Messerli 1984.
89. Brunschwig 2005; Prete 2010.

side from the public, who sought to control the rapidly growing scientific sector. Another reason behind the loudening calls for interdisciplinarity was the fact that, around 1970, the environment and the mountains became a truly political topic. As we shall see, this unleashed a variety of organisational efforts.

In addition to this intellectual lineage in large-scale mountain perception, there also derived from it a younger branch in the Alpine movement. In 1857 the English 'Alpine Club' was founded in London as the first of its kind, in order to promote through exchange the mountaineering culture that was then in its early stages. Fifty years later, similar Alpine associations could be found in many parts of the world: from New Zealand to Asia and from Africa to the United States of America. In the German and Austrian Alpine Association [*Alpenverein*], which at that time boasted by far the most members, international initiatives were undertaken before 1900, and a little later the desire was even expressed for a worldwide mountain association. Such a plan would not be realised, however, until the interwar period – by others and in a different form. On the occasion of an Alpine meeting in 1932, with delegates from almost twenty countries, it was decided to call into life the *Union Internationale des Associations d'Alpinisme* (later known in English as the International Mountaineering and Climbing Federation). Well into the 1960s this union, based in Switzerland, remained almost a family affair. Then, however, there began an astonishing growth, which accelerated yet again around 1990. Currently more than a third of all the world's nations are represented in the union. This lightning-speed expansion came in a period when intercontinental tourism achieved an entirely new magnitude, also in the form of 'high-altitude tourism'.[90]

Transitions to Organisation

That the global environment became such an important political focal point in the years around 1970 had to do with various short- and long-term developments. It was certainly significant that, since the end of the Second World War, the United Nations provided a forum for policy debates on a global scale. The expansion of the industrial economy and the associated environmental problems, evoked by population growth and by new, potentially dangerous technologies, triggered certain fears and strengthened the feeling that things could not continue in this way much longer. In the same direction there arose an international protest movement, emanating particularly from the United

---

90. Mackintosh 1907; Ziak 1956; Bossus 1982; Gidl 2007; further indications on the history of Alpinism in Mathieu/Boscani Leoni 2005; Hoibian 2008; Isserman/Weaver 2008; Maurer 2009b.

States, which rocked the self-assurance of the West and managed to bring together many demands for change. In 1968, Swedish diplomats recommended that the United Nations should take greater care to address environmental problems and in 1972 the first great UN environmental conference took place in Stockholm. With the 'United Nations Environment Programme' (UNEP) an administration was established to ensure continuity and ten years later the activities were reviewed in a report known by the name of the commission chairman and Norwegian Prime Minister, Gro Harlem Brundtland. The report succeeded in anchoring the ideas of 'sustainability' and 'sustainable development' in the public political discourse.[91]

In Stockholm they discussed the threat to the rainforests, the problems of desertification and other ecological themes – the mountains, however, did not belong at that time to the international agenda. This would change in the following years and decades, first at the level of communication. In 1975, for example, the well-known scientific magazine *Science* published an alarming report entitled 'The Deterioration of Mountain Environments', which addressed the environmental situation based on the example of mountain regions in Asia, Latin America and Africa, with emphasis in each case on soil exhaustion, deforestation, erosion, flooding, desertification and other catastrophic symptoms. Its depiction of Nepal, a land still counted as one of ancient culture and majestic nature, made an especially dramatic impression. 'All in all, little hard data are yet available on the true scale and the nature of environmental deterioration in the mountains', the author concluded. Yet he maintained that among various scientists and government agencies, there was a broad consensus about the negative direction of development.[92]

Against the background of this engaged atmosphere, it now came to numerous initiatives and organisational alliances that also handled the mountain problematic in terms of environmental and developmental issues. Table 2 names those involved on the continental or global level. Purely scientific initiatives and the more technical developmental programs are not considered in this context. Even so, in view of the colourful diversity of the emerging international 'mountain scene', the table cannot make any kind of systematic claim. Judged by the number of entries, the politicisation of the environment developed in this case an increasing momentum, with the number of initiatives and alliances rising from one decade to the next. Many of them came about through an

---

91. McCormick 1989; Grubb 1993, pp. 3–7; Osterhammel/Petersson 2003, pp. 13, 26, 104–5.

92. Eckholm 1975, quote p. 769; see also Radkau 2002, pp. 313–4.

The Politicisation of the Environment

Table 2: Continental and Global Initiatives for the Mountains, 20th/21st Centuries

Year	Initiative, *italic = global*
1971	International Potato Center (CIP), Peru (since 1997 with *Global Mountain Program*)
1973	*Man and Biosphere (MAB) Programme, Project 6*, UNESCO, Paris
1974	Euromontana, Belgium
1977	*Highland-Lowland-Systems Programme*, United Nations University (UNU), based in Japan
1981	*Mountain Research and Development (MRD)*, USA (Journal, based in Switzerland since 2000)
1983	International Centre for Integrated Mountain Development (ICIMOD), Nepal
1986	African Mountain Association (AMA), varying countries
1986	*The Mountain Institute (TMI)*, USA (Woodlands Mountain Institute until 1994)
1988	Centre for Development and Environment (CDE), Switzerland (with emphasis on mountains)
1990	*Mountain Agenda*, Switzerland
1991	Andean Mountain Association (AMA), varying countries
1992	*UN Earth Summit in Rio de Janeiro*, Agenda 21 Mountain Chapter
1993	*Food and Agriculture Organization (FAO)*, Italy (Task Manager for the Agenda 21 Mountain Chapter)
1995	*Mountain Forum*, initially in partnership with CIP und TMI, then with ICIMOD Nepal and with regional networks: African Mountain Forum (AMF), Asia-Pacific Mountain Network (APMN), European Mountain Forum (EMF), InfoAndina (Latin American Mountain Forum), North American Mountain Forum (NAMF)
1995	*Global Environment Facility (GEF)*, with the Mountain Ecosystems Programme
1996	*Mountain Culture at The Banff Centre*, Canada
2000	*World Mountain People Association (WMPA)*, France
2000	*Global Mountain Biodiversity Assessment (GMBA)*, Switzerland
2001	*Mountain Research Initiative (MRI)*, Switzerland
2002	*UN International Year of the Mountains (IYM2002)*
2002	*Mountain Partnership*, FAO Italy (in the follow-up process to IYM2002)
2004	*Journal of Mountain Science*, China (with support, as for MRD, from United Nations University)

Year: Foundation or start of an explicit interest in mountains; many of the initiatives and organisations emerged through a process and the table tends to date them in their early phase. Major sources: Bandyopadhyay/Perveen 2004; Debarbieux/Price 2008; Messerli 2002; Messerli/Ives 1997, pp. 448–449; Price 1995; Price 2004.

interaction between UN activities and collective, practice-oriented research. This was true, for instance, of UNESCO's comprehensive 'Man and Biosphere Programme', which, from 1973, made the actors in this field known to one another and enabled further developments. The United Nations University also supported international mountain initiatives almost from the outset, among other things with contributions to incipient journals (*Mountain Research and Development* 1981, *Journal of Mountain Science* 2004). The small, informal group known as the 'Mountain Agenda' became especially important and succeeded in a short period of time in expanding the programmatic Agenda 21 at the UN Earth Summit of 1992 to include a Mountain Chapter (see Chapter 1.1 above). With this, the mountain objective also obtained representation in the UN system, through a so-called 'Task Manager', who was to pursue the topic further and who was situated within the Food and Agriculture Organization (FAO). At the same time, many potentially interested parties were encouraged to join the movement. This was increasingly the case in 2002, with the second representative event at the level of the United Nations: the International Year of the Mountains.

The activities were distributed unevenly between the participating nations and some shifts marked the course of the three decades. From the 1980s, for example, Switzerland often played a special role, with its diplomatic efforts and particularly also through its financial support for many initiatives. Still, the Swiss placed value on receiving agreement or at least moral support from other countries. With a view toward the International Year of the Mountains there began a new alliance in 2000, the World Mountain People Association, this time initiated in France and strongly oriented around grassroots organisation. After 2002 the Chinese also announced their interest with the *Journal of Mountain Science*.[93] The internet, which came on the international 'mountain scene' around 1996, contributed to the expansion and transformation of communication; considering the spatial diffusion of the actors, this had perhaps an especially revolutionary effect. Some initial difficulties were surmounted through the support of the US 'Mountain Institute',[94] and soon the medium was anchored in the everyday work life of most places. International 'networking' was now easier than ever before; still, no one could guarantee that the rapidly erected networks would also possess endurance.

---

93. See Debarbieux/Gillet 2000; *Journal of Mountain Science* (internet version).

94. The Institute provided the server for the exchange within the 'Mountain Forum', which was planned in electronic format right from the start (information from Oliver Chave, 26 April 2006).

The Politicisation of the Environment

'A Global Priority'

'The extent to which the Rio Earth Summit has proved itself a watershed in growth of mountain awareness is literally breathtaking. After spending a quarter century in the intellectual wilderness, this apparent success is still ringing in our ears', wrote Bruno Messerli and Jack D. Ives, the spokespeople for the Mountain Agenda, five years after the great conference: 'United Nations and national governmental agencies, private foundations, universities, non-governmental organisations world-wide, are proclaiming the importance of mountains as vital to world security. But caution is needed. To what extent is this a band-wagon happenstance?' The work that recorded this sentiment and posed this critical question in 1997 carried the title *Mountains of the World: A Global Priority*. Produced for the Rio follow-up process, it was consciously designed to be representative and to become an emblem of the movement.[95]

From the critical question raised therein, it can be construed that the leading protagonists were surprised to a certain degree by their own success, that they also knew how unstable and dependent upon individuals the various organisations and networks were and that they hoped to summon their people not to rest on their laurels. Actually the number of initiatives could disguise the fact that there were not overly many truly active fellow combatants but rather a few, who were simultaneously engaged in several places and cooperating with one another in various combinations. So, in any case, ran the self-assessment that also sounded in publications from time to time. In the introductory report from a large-scale research initiative in 1999, it was said that this was no temporary affair, resulting as it did from a process of awareness building 'that lasted several decades and was carried through by a fairly small number of visionary scientists'. Other indicators also suggest that the influence of a general mountain awareness should not be overestimated.[96]

The *Global Priority* publication was also a call for a new, comprehensive mountain science, a 'montology', which could provide the framework for a global discussion of sustainability issues. The new science therefore had to be stout-hearted and capable of mediating between the particular and the universal, the local and the global, the past and the future. In this way montology would belong to many fields, to cultural and social sciences, natural sciences, political

---

95. Messerli/Ives 1997, p. 457 (this chapter was also co-authored by Robert E. Rhoades).
96. Becker/Bugmann 2001, p. 8 (the foreword with the quoted sentence dates from June 1999); Rudaz 2006 examines the question of 'awareness' on the example of partnerships concluded by Swiss mountain communities; he shows that the mountain motive plays a considerable role here but not the global motive.

science and indigenous knowledge (folk science): 'It will be interdisciplinary, intercontinental, intersectoral.' Elsewhere the aspired-to montology would be described as a further development of 'mountain geoecology' and placed in the tradition of Alexander von Humboldt and Carl Troll.[97] An editor of the 1997 publication made the comparison with other major ecosystems and remarked that, in the last decade, the mountains had achieved the status of a global issue equivalent to tropical rainforests, deserts, and oceans. On the level of institutionalised science, however, the situation could have been portrayed differently. Namely, whereas 'mountain geoecology' or montology had taken hold in only a few scattered institutes, oceanography, for example, had already been a discipline for several generations and although it was highly heterogeneous, it was nevertheless officially recognised, especially at universities located near oceans.[98]

The political organisation of the mountain problematic exercised an interesting effect over questions of definition. In geographies of the early modern period, one does find quite a few descriptions of landscape expressions such as 'mountain' or 'mountain range' but for a long time the discussion seems to have been rather limited. This changed in the nineteenth century, as above all the flourishing German science searched with great intensity for an objective boundary between highlands and lowlands. Proposed limits, among others, were set at 1,300, 500, 330, and 200 metres above sea level. One should keep in mind that, in the meantime, parts of the vocabulary had changed, because the growing examination of high mountain areas by naturalists, mountaineers and military personnel led to the creation and popularisation of new expressions for landscape description. Then, in the twentieth century, the search for a uniform definition of mountains was, according to important exponents, regarded as difficult, if not failed. For example, Raoul Blanchard wrote apodictically in his 1934 preface to *Man and the Mountain*: 'Even a definition of mountains, that would be clear and comprehensible, is almost impossible to deliver.'[99]

With the politicisation of the environment there later arose, however, a pressure that the mountains – in order to be an identifiable, general subject – were to be defined in a unitary and, if possible, quantifiable way. In the years around 1970, very different values were proposed for the share of the earth's surface occupied by mountains. An ironic side effect of this attempt at

---

97. Messerli/Ives 1997, p. 464; Ives 1999.
98. Messerli/Ives 1997, p. 67; Schlee 1973; Weber 2002, p. 218.
99. Kastrop 1972, pp. 51, 120–4; Penck 1894, vol. 1, pp. 138–40, see also vol. 2, pp. 146–50 for the discussion about the general validity of landscape expressions; Farrington 2000; Blache 1934, p. 7 (original French).

The Politicisation of the Environment

objectivity was the fact that the sheer range of variation in the estimates (from twenty to 36 per cent) indicated how dependent on the selected criteria and ultimately subjective they remained.[100] The discussion intensified during the Rio conference and the follow-up process and, finally, in the year 2000, forest scientists made a serious proposal. This required the antecedent of a developed information technology, which first became available only in the 1990s. Since the definition was founded pragmatically as well as converted into cartographic terms, many came to accept it. The new standard was based on three criteria in a fixed sequence (height, slope, local elevation range); the estimated portion of the earth's surface covered by mountains was 24 per cent, or 36 million square kilometres.[101]

On the basis of these data the Mountain Agenda produced a world map for the UN Sustainability Summit at Johannesburg and the International Year of the Mountains in 2002, which classified all countries according to their share of mountains. With its quantitative background and the focus on mountain areas, both in their national distinctiveness and on a global scale, the map was a very precise expression of the efforts for public recognition (see Plate 2).[102] The mountainous regions, made in this way into a decisive criterion, found themselves to no small degree in remote and poorer areas, so that the acknowledgement also had a social aspect.

The Regions Under Study

For historical analysis, the precise spatial delineation of mountain regions is particularly useful in those cases where there is a statistically documented process at stake, the investigation of which requires a territorial basis. This applies, for example, to the understanding of population developments. Equally important for historical studies, however, is to leave the boundaries of mountain regions open and to place them consciously in the context of surrounding areas. The specific course of history obviously cannot be derived from geomorphic differ-

---

100. Kapos 2000, p. 4; a striking example of the variability of mountain definitions, provoked by politics, is the Bavarian Alps; in the Alpine Convention of 1991, they were presented as three times larger than in the classical definitions (Bätzing 1993, pp. 24, 31).
101. Kapos 2000, p. 8; Debarbieux/Rudaz 2010, pp. 226–9; at an altitude of over 2,500 metres, the other two criteria are dropped; between 1,500 and 2,500 metres, the definition requires a certain degree of slope; below this limit the local elevation range is considered as well; the UN environmental programme adapted the definition in 2002 in a modified form (reduction of mountain share to 22%).
102. Mountain Agenda 2002, pp. 28–29.

ences; instead, it reveals itself first through a thematically relevant comparison. At the same time, contextualisation opens the possibility of bringing into view the interactions between mountains and plains, which can be of great consequence for cultural developments.[103]

The following parts of this book are concerned with the themes of population and urbanisation, then with agriculture, family and mobility and finally with cultural diversity and modernity. Attention will be paid to certain periods since the beginning of modern times, as well as various samples of mountain regions. The spatially dispersed and highly differentiated world of mountains, therefore, will not be treated uniformly. Rather, the study regions are selected from case to case, each according to the subject of inquiry and the state of research. Since an entire series of themes are addressed, the overall result, in fact, presents quite a broad distribution. The overview map provides a geographical orientation (see Plate 1).

---

103. See Mathieu 2009, pp. 9–11.

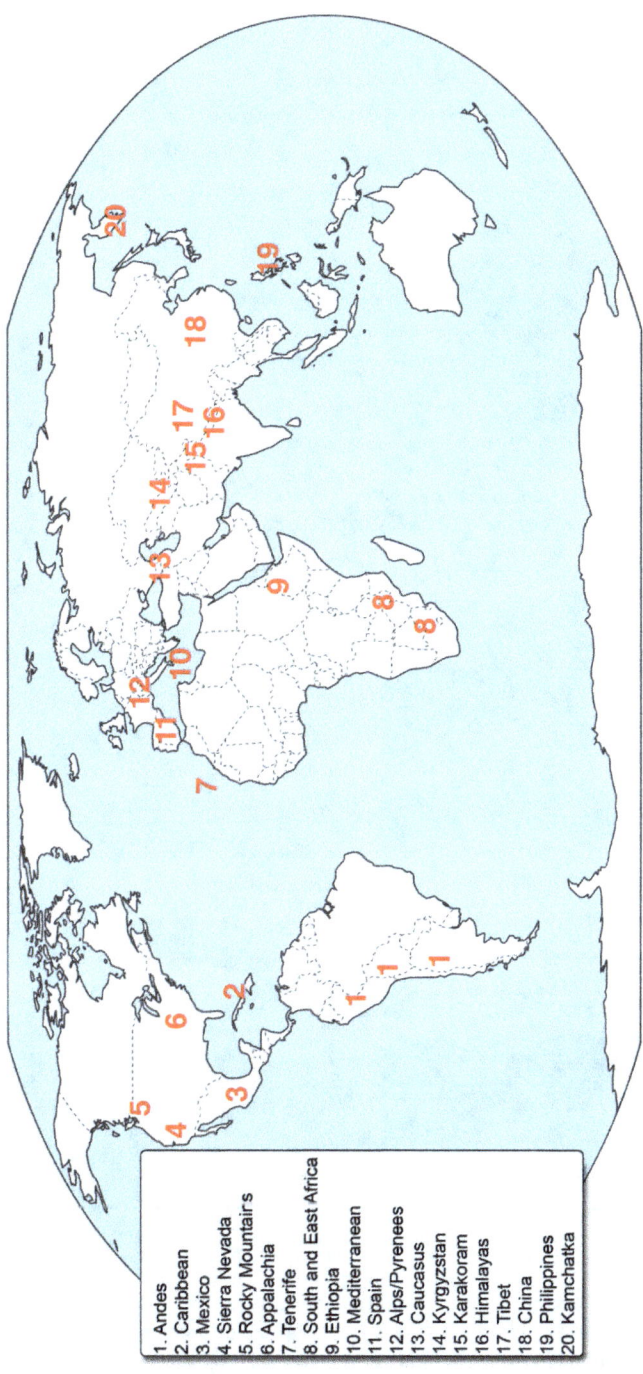

Plate 1. Regions Under Study: Mountain areas specifically examined in this book

Plate 2. Countries of the World with Mountain Percentages: Map from 2002

For the UN Earth Summit of Johannesburg and the 2002 International Year of the Mountains, the 'Mountain Agenda' published a world map with national comparisons: red indicates the countries with mountain shares of 50 to 100%, orange 25 to 50%, light green 10 to 25%, and grey 0 to 10%. The quantifications are based on a mountain definition from 2000. Source: Mountain Agenda (ed.): *Mountains of the World. Sustainable Development in Mountain Areas. The Need for Adequate Policies and Instruments*, Berne 2002. See Chapters 1.1 and 1.5.

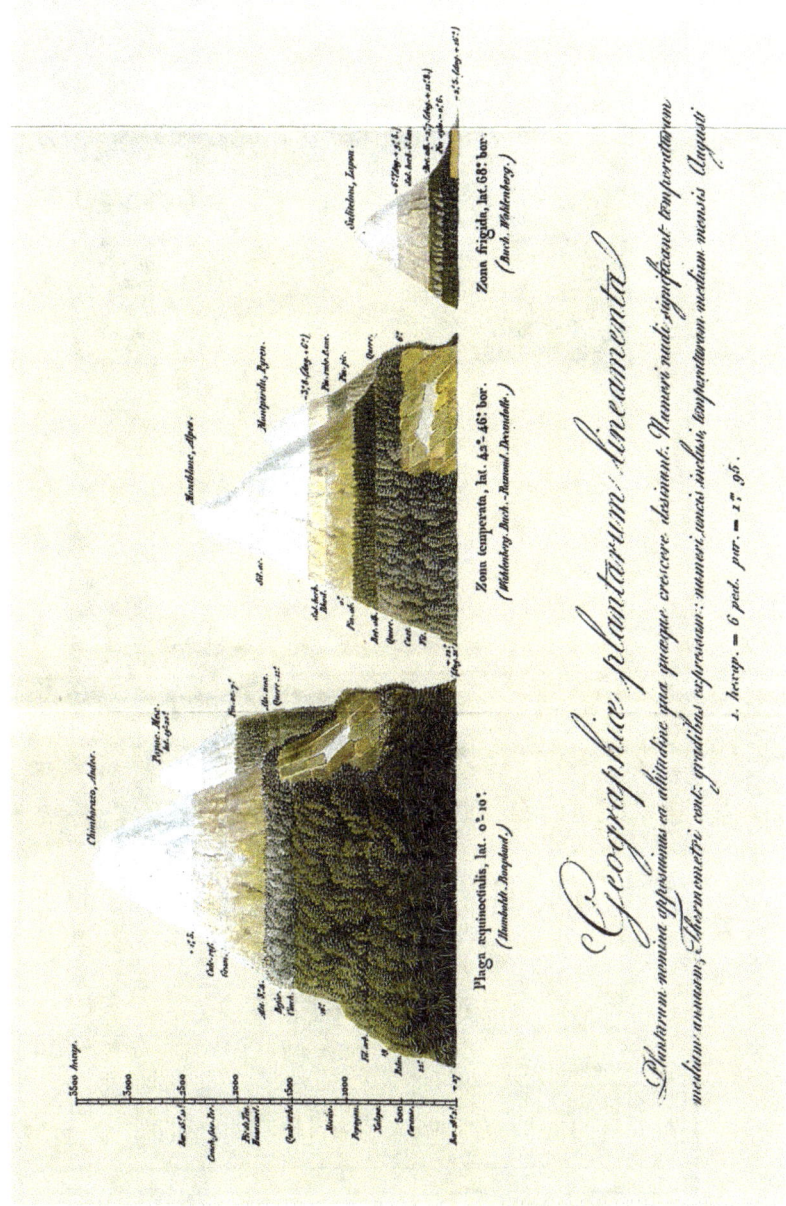

Plate 3. Altitude-Specific Vegetation in Three Climate Zones: Illustration from 1817

For purposes of comparison, in his 1817 plant geography Alexander von Humboldt exhibited mountains from various climate zones next to one another with their altitude-specific vegetation belts. From left to right: the Andes with the Chimborazo, the Alps with Mont Blanc and the Pyrenees, Lapland with the Sulitjelma. Source: Alexander von Humboldt: *De distributione geographica plantarum secundum coeli temperiem et altitudinem montium, Prolegomena*, Paris 1817. See Chapter 1.3.

Plate 4. 'Heights of the Old and New World, An Illustrated Comparison':
Drawing from 1813

Inspired by Humboldt, Johann Wolfgang von Goethe portrayed the mountains of America and Europe as a contiguous mountain landscape. On the right are the Andes with the Chimborazo and Alexander von Humboldt (indicated as a small figure), on the left are the European mountains with Horace-Bénedict de Saussure on Mont Blanc. Source: 'Höhen der alten und neuen Welt bildlich verglichen. Ein Tableau von Hrn. Geh. Rath v. Göthe mit einem Schreiben an den Herausg. der A.G.E.', in: *Allgemeine Geographische Ephemeriden* 41 (1813), p. 3–8. See Chapter 1.3.

*Plate 5. Summits of the World as a Mountain Island:
Illustration from 1875*

Worldwide comparisons of mountains became common in various scientific disciplines in the nineteenth century. Represented in this illustration, from high altitude medicine, are peaks from the Andes, Ethiopia, and Mexico, the Himalayas, Karakoram, Ararat, Caucasus, Pyrenees, Alps, Altai Mountains, Iceland, Scandinavian Alps, Norway and Spitsbergen. Source: Denis Jourdanet: *Influence de la pression de l'air sur la vie de l'homme, climats d'altitude et climats de montagne*, 2 vols. Paris 1875. See Chapter 1.3.

*Plate 6. Miao Warriors in Guizhou, South China:
Illustration from the nineteenth century*

Parallel to the integration of the mountainous province of Guizhou into the Chinese Empire, there arose numerous ethnographic reports including the illustrated 'Miao Albums'. Pictured here are 'wild' Miao warriors with crossbows and spears. Source: *Album 'Miao zhong tu shuo'*, n.d. [nineteenth century], Collège de France, Institut des Hautes Etudes Chinoises © 2008, Paris, Manuskript SB 2522/1. See Chapter 2.2.

Plate 7. Cherokee Indians on the Qualla Reservation in Appalachia, 1888

After the forced resettlement of the Cherokee in the early nineteenth century, only a small reservation remained open to them in the Appalachian Mountains. Pictured here are young women performing a dance prior to the men's ball game. Photo: National Anthropological Archives, Smithsonian Institution, Washington DC. See Chapter 2.2.

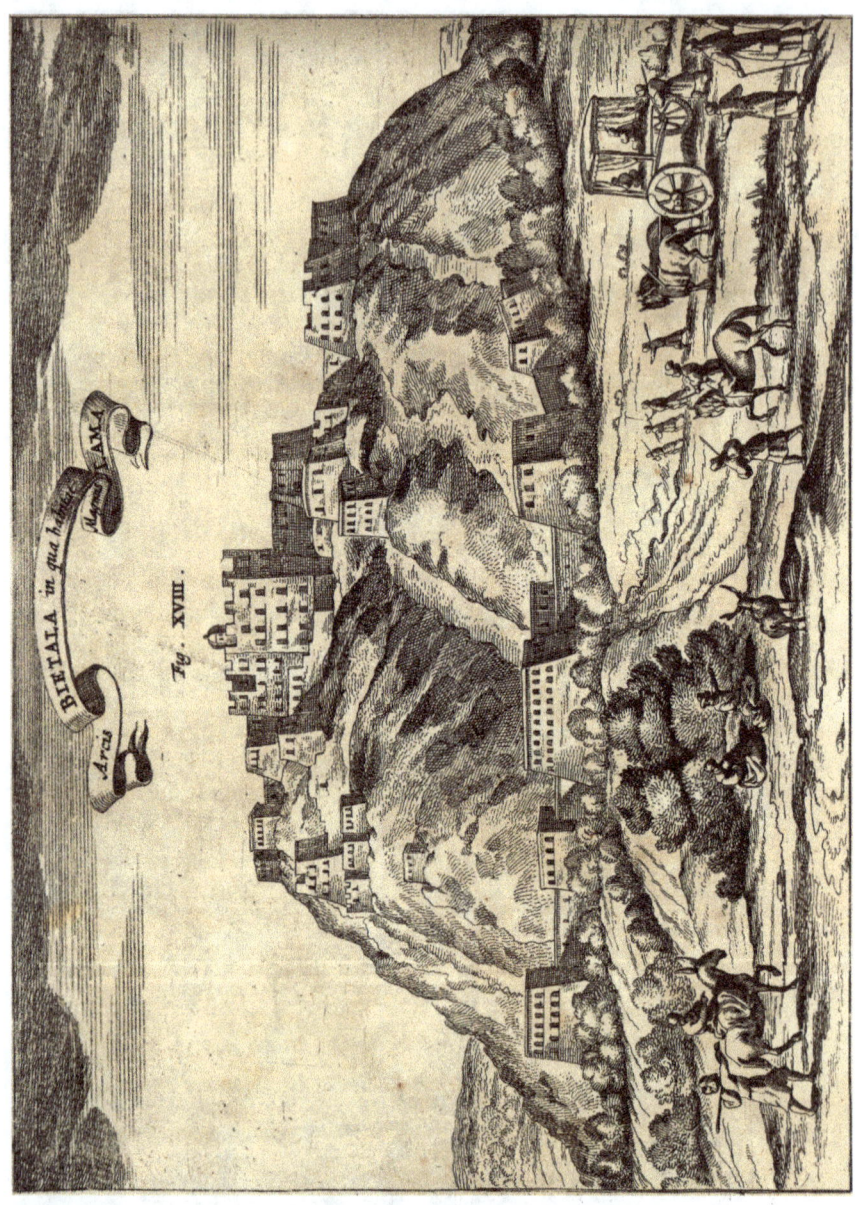

Plate 8. The Potala Palace in Lhasa: Illustration from 1667

The famous seat of the Dalai Lama was built in two stages: the 'White Palace' from 1645 to 1648 and the 'Red Palace' from 1691 to 1694. The illustration, based on the drawings by Jesuit Johannes Grueber, shows the Potala in the intermediate phase and is the earliest representation of this symbol of the rise of Tibet. Source: Athanasius Kircher: *China [...] illustrata*, Amsterdam 1667. See Chapter 2.3.

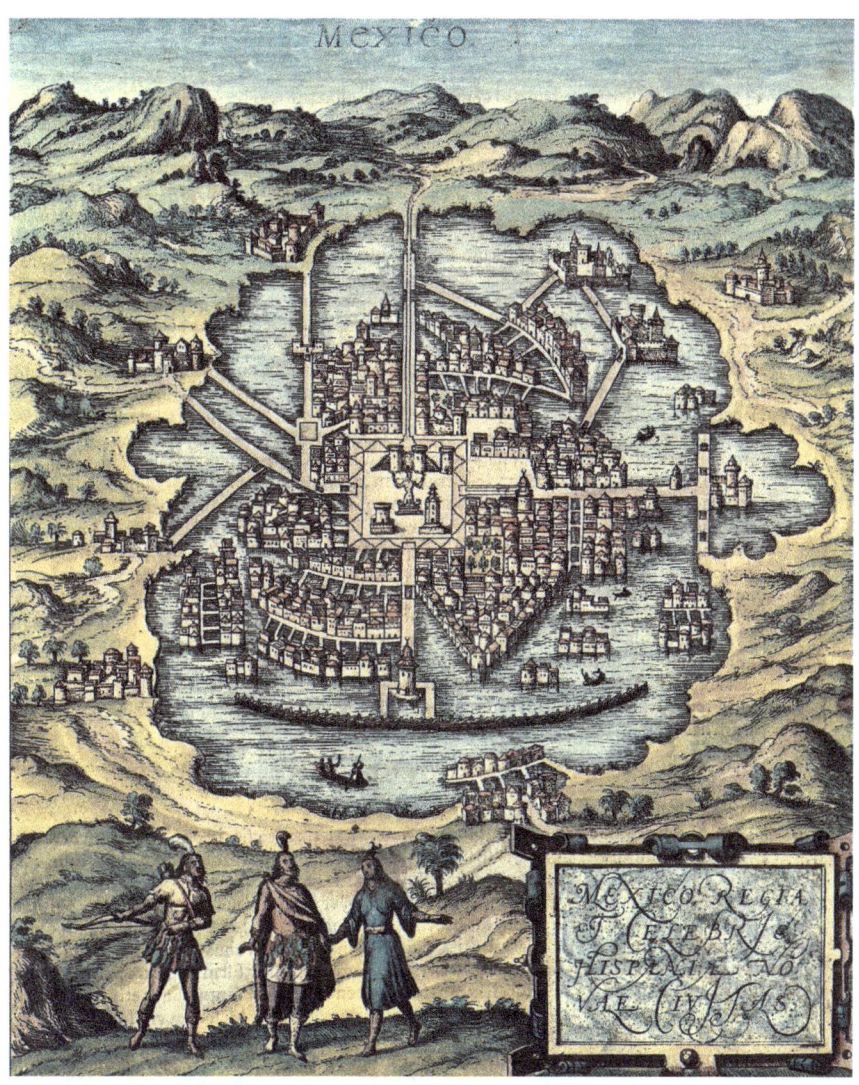

Plate 9. Tenochtitlán, Later Mexico City: View from 1617

The view is based on earlier models and ultimately on a map by the Spanish conquistador, Hernán Cortés. It shows the Aztec capital Tenochtitlán, erected on an island, with its central temple district and the surrounding lake and mountain landscape as they appeared before the conquest. Source: Georg Braun / Franz Hogenberg: *Civitates Orbis Terrarum*, Cologne 1572–1618, vol. 6. See Chapter 2.3.

Plate 10. Potato Cultivation in the Andes: Illustration from 1615

The potato originated in the Andes and was grown there especially at high elevations – between 3,500 and 4,000 metres, for example, in regions that are now part of Bolivia. The drawing by Guamán Poma shows the farming technique with digging sticks. Source: Felipe Guamán Poma: *El primer nueva corónica y buen gobierno*, Manuskript 1615/16, Det Kongelige Bibliotek, Kopenhagen, GKS 2232, drawing 397. See Chapter 3.1.

Plate 11. Field Cultivation in the Highlands of Ethiopia, 1852

In the northern part of the Ethiopian highlands there dominated a form of agriculture known in the research as the 'ox-plough complex'. The scratch plough was mostly drawn by a team of oxen.
Source: John Martin Bernatz: *Scenes in Ethiopia*, London 1852, vol. 2, plate XIV. See Chapter 3.1.

*Plate 12. 'Wild Haymaking' in the Alps:
Dramatised engraving from 1862*

In the Alps, animal husbandry involved stockpiling fodder reserves for winter stall-feeding. A few regions even went over to the collection of 'wild hay' in distant and sometimes dangerous places, as dramatised in this engraving. Source: *Die Gartenlaube. Illustrirtes Familienblatt*, Leibzig 1862. See Chapter 3.2.

Plate 13. The Rocky Mountains with Lander's Peak: Oil painting by Albert Bierstadt, 1863

The painter Albert Bierstadt took part in governmental expeditions to the North American West. His famous images nourished the hope that there, too, one might find 'European' mountain landscapes. Photo: The Metropolitan Museum of Art, New York, Rogers Fund 1907. See Chapter 4.1.

Plate 14. 'Image of the True Form of the Five Peaks': Chinese inscription, circa 1614

The five holy mountains of the Confucian-Taoist tradition were often represented in China as an ensemble, and in this form they also served as a talisman. The illustration shows a print from the stone column on the middle mountain (Song Shan), engraved around 1614. Source: Edouard Chavannes: *Le T'ai Chan. Essai de monographie d'un culte chinois*, Paris 1910, graph 56. See Chapter 4.2.

Plate 15. 'To the Most Holy Mountain in the World' by Herbert Tichy: Cover illustration from the 1953 reprint

On the jacket of this book containing Herbert Tichy's adventures, Mount Kailash in Tibet is displayed with a Buddhist monk. With the many new editions since 1937, it was one of the works that led to the canonisation of Kailash in the West. Source: Herbert Tichy: *Zum heiligsten Berg der Welt. Auf Landstrassen und Pilgerpfaden in Afghanistan, Indien und Tibet*, Vienna 1953. See Chapter 4.2.

Plate 16. International Year of the Mountains 2002: 'Celebrating Mountain Women'

Among the many events held during the International Year of the Mountains there was a women's conference in the Himalayan country of Bhutan, in which representatives from five continents participated. The program also consciously included demonstrations of identity, such as a 'Mountain Costume Show'. Photo: Ujol Sherchan. See Chapter 4.3.

~ 2 ~

POPULATION AND URBANISATION

2.1 Upland Demography

In 1957 the Polish geographer, Józef Staszewski, published a study on the vertical distribution of the world's population at different altitude levels. Shortly thereafter his German colleague Hermann Hambloch produced a postdoctoral thesis on the 'Altitude Boundaries of the Ecumene' ['Höhengrenzsaum der Ökumene'], in which he calculated this distribution in a different way and placed it within a general anthropogeographical framework. These two works are the first and only ones to inform us specifically about the vertical dimension of population distribution on a global level.[1] That they were taken up in the 1950s had to do with the fact that, at that time, thanks to the newly founded United Nations, the availability of data for large-scale population studies was quickly improving. On the continental level, a similar connection between the upswing in statistics and the thematisation of variations in altitude could be observed in Europe by the late nineteenth century. Yet one should not overestimate the accuracy of the available global statistics, even for the period after 1950. The UN yearbooks invariably specified a possible error margin of five per cent and the data sometimes had to be corrected from one issue to the next.[2] Nonetheless, many of the stated figures were now based on actual collections, not just vague estimates.

As instructive as these research efforts are for a worldwide overview of mountain demography, for historical analysis they can build only a starting point. What interests us here is not just the population's vertical distribution at a certain point in time but also how this distribution developed over the course

---

1. Staszewski 1957; Hambloch 1966 (the manuscript was finished in 1960); more recent studies on the global population in mountain regions use complex criteria (altitude combined in various ways with slope), such as Meybeck 2001 and Huddleston 2003; the simple altitude analysis has been dethematised in international mountain research.
2. Biraben 1979, p. 17.

of the modern period. To that end, we must be on the lookout for additional methods and indicators.

Population Distribution

For the vertical classification of demographic data, one faces the problem that they are collected or reckoned from within states and other political units, which often extend over various altitude levels and permit therefore only approximate assignments. The smaller the survey unit, the sharper and better calibrated each settlement pattern will be and vice versa. Staszewski supported his research in many cases using older materials, whereas Hambloch undertook a systematic recalculation. All this notwithstanding, their values for the continental and global distributions are astonishingly similar. This correspondence diminishes the scepticism that could greet such broad global calculations. Here I follow Hambloch, who in his classification also differentiated among the upper elevations.[3] It should be noted at the outset that the dimension of height makes up only one aspect of the mountains as they are generally defined. Nevertheless, it is undoubtedly the single most important dimension and the one we can best lay hold of and apply to historical objectives. Besides, the slope of the terrain often increases along with its height.[4]

Table 3 shows population density according to altitude levels and by continent in the year 1958. The lower figure refers to the number of persons in the entire area, the higher figure to the so-called 'productive areas' (or 'ecumene', in Hambloch's terms). The exclusion of 'nonproductive areas' has a tradition in mountain research, yet there are also reservations against this method. One must recognise that productivity is difficult to objectify and such an approach would then call for corrections to the size of the productive areas. This is because the stated area figures resulted from a projection of three into two dimensions. In reality, the mountains, with their many slopes, exhibit a significantly greater surface area than what appears on a map and serves as the basis for quantifications. The opposition between these two objections is an argument for the simple method of using total surface area.[5]

---

3. Staszewski referred to 1945, Hambloch to 1958; their results are comparable for the three altitude levels of 0–1,000 metres, 1,000–2,000 metres and over 2,000 metres; the differences on the global scale are limited to the low figure of 0.3%; the cited overall populations can be compared to UN statistics and are also plausible.
4. Meybeck 2001, p. 38 compares the steepness of the earth's surface to altitude on a global level.
5. For this critical line of argument Staszewski 1957, pp. 44–5; Mathieu 2009, pp. 35–6.

Upland Demography

Table 3: Population Density By Altitude and Continent, 1958 (persons per km²)

Continent	Altitude in Metres				
	0–1,000	1–2,000	2–3,000	3–4,000	4–5,000
Africa	8/9	8/8	12/15	5/10	–
North America	13/15	5/6	5/12	1/3	–
South America	7/7	12/15	12/13	14/18	2/3
Asia	46/50	16/20	6/7	4/6	0/0
Europe	61/64	9/15	0/0	–	–
Oceania	2/2	1/1	0/0	–	–
Global	24/27	10/12	6/10	6/9	1/1

The lower number indicates persons per km² in the entire area; the higher number refers to the productive area (in the sense of 'ecumene') only. Regions: North America as far as Panama; Europe to the Ural Mountains. Source: Hambloch 1966, pp. 37–44.

In the aforesaid year of 1958, total population density on the six continents (excluding Antarctica) followed, as a whole, the gradations in altitude: there were 24 to 27 persons per square kilometre at 0 to 1,000 metres above sea level, declining gradually to the lowest number of one person per square kilometre at 4,000 to 5,000 metres. Above this level, very few people stayed for long periods of time. This global diminution stood out clearly but just as obvious were the intercontinental differences. In Asia, Europe and Oceania, as well as for the world overall, the highest density figures were found at the lowest level of altitude; in Africa they were found at 2,000 to 3,000 metres and in South America even 3,000 to 4,000 metres. North America also demonstrated a certain deviation from the progressive reduction of density along with rising elevation, with slightly higher density at 2,000 to 3,000 metres than at the next lower level. We can assume that this finding resulted from the fact that Mexico, with its extensive highland population, was counted as belonging to the northern part of the double continent.[6]

Table 4 lists the number of cities with one million or more inhabitants, according to altitude level and continent, in the year 2000. It adheres to the regional divisions established by the United Nations and considers Mexico as well as the smaller countries of Central America to be part of Latin America. The distributional picture is much more sharply accentuated but it shows clear

---

6. Staszewski 1957, p. 77 offers the following population densities for Mexico in 1940: 6 persons per km² in the entire area at 0–1,000 metres, 13 persons at 1,000–2,000 metres and 16 persons at 2,000 metres and more.

Population and Urbanisation

Table 4: Major Cities By Altitude and Continent, 2000

Continent	Altitude in Metres				
	0–500	500–1,000	1,000–1,500	1,500–2,000	2,000+
Africa	25	1	6	3	1
North America	40	1	0	1	–
Latin America	29	10	3	4	6
Asia	170	19	7	5	1
Europe	53	3	–	–	–
Oceania	6	–	–	–	–
Global	323	34	16	13	8

Number of urban centres with one million or more inhabitants, according to UN statistics for 2001. Regions: North America to the USA; Europe to the Ural Mountains. Sources: United Nations 2003; Google Earth and diverse statements for the altitude classification of urban areas.

reference to the population distribution just considered: 323 metropolises, representing 82 per cent of all major cities, are found at the lowest altitude level of 0 to 500 metres, with the number declining first sharply and then more gradually up to the highest level, in this case defined as 2,000 metres and above. The highest city in the world with over one million inhabitants was La Paz, at approximately 3,600 metres.[7] The intercontinental differences resemble those in the population table: Africa exhibited a secondary peak with six major cities at mid-level altitude, while in Latin America, an equal number of cities were found at the highest altitude level. Altogether at that time there were eight cities above 2,000 metres with one million or more residents, namely Addis Ababa (Ethiopia); Bogotá (Colombia); La Paz (Bolivia); Mexico City, Puebla and Toluca (all Mexico); Quito (Ecuador); and Sana'a (Yemen). All these cities lay between latitudes of twenty degrees North and seventeen degrees South – in other words, in the tropics.

That the two tables demonstrate similarities – both globally and for the individual continents – may be explained in part by the general connection between population density and urbanisation. Assuming all other factors to be constant, the chances for urbanisation in certain regions rise along with

---

7. For general problems and inaccuracies in the determination of city sizes, see e.g. Schwentker 2006, pp. 9–13; that the determination of altitude also has its difficulties can be illustrated with La Paz, where the difference between the highest and the lowest city quarters is about 1,000 metres.

Upland Demography

increasing population density.[8] This proved to be the case here also for the tropical altitudes, where in 1945, according to Staszewski, thirteen per cent of the population lived at elevations over 1,000 metres; outside tropical regions, the share was only seven per cent.[9] At that time there appear to have been only one or two cities with over one million inhabitants at this elevation[10] but then, as urbanisation soared in the second half of the twentieth century, such concentrations were more likely to develop in areas with a noteworthy demographic potential. These observations are also useful for historical analysis, because cities are much easier than population densities to identify and locate at earlier points in time. We will return later to this point.

An important outcome of the two studies under consideration, both from the 1950s, concerns the variability of the vertical population distribution across different regions and continents. Although the global average indeed confirmed the general outline of decreasing population density along with rising elevation, the deviations from the average were just as characteristic for the overall picture. Hambloch held that 'density by no means always declined gradually toward the highest limits of the ecumene'. He sought to distinguish between demographic profiles at different altitudes and spoke of a lower-level type (rapid decline), an intermediate type (decline with an intermediate peak or maximum in elevation) and a multi-level type (gradual decline). He also noted that the general population pressure in the mountains and surrounding areas showed no ascertainable relationship to the demographic elevation profile, except in negative form: where the population was extremely sparse, absolutely no profile could be recognised.[11]

Population Growth

The UN's statistical efforts not only stimulated the investigation of vertical population distribution but soon also contributed to the renewal of regressive population estimates. In the 1970s a number of studies appeared on long-term growth at the global level. Extrapolating from the more reliable data on current world population, researchers now proposed new figures for earlier periods and paid greater attention to the sources and source criticism. Lacking empirical

---

8. Boserup 1981, pp. 64–6.
9. Staszewski 1957, p. 20.
10. Staszewski 1957, pp. 88–9 gives a list of major cities above 1,000 metres for 1950; accordingly, in addition to Mexico City, Teheran could have reached a million inhabitants.
11. Hambloch 1966, pp. 48–51.

Population and Urbanisation

foundations, many of their figures remained quite hypothetical; still, they have not been revised in any conclusive manner in research since then.[12]

Table 5 shows the estimated values for world population by continent between 1500 and 2000. From it we can see that demographic growth in this period constituted the norm. Over the first three centuries before 1800, world population appears to have doubled; during the next two centuries up to 2000, there followed a six-fold increase in growth. During the first stage, the early modern period, Asia and Europe were the fastest-growing continents, while the population in Latin America fell dramatically in the sixteenth century and did not regain its earlier level even by 1800. This initial value in 1500 represents the epoch before the European expansion and occupation of the 'New World'. Its exact height is controversial in the research, partly because the extent of the decline involves central questions of historical responsibility.[13] In the following period, after 1800, Latin America went on to become a region with extremely rapid population growth. It remained second only to North America, where the population absolutely exploded up to 2000, with an estimated increase by a factor of 63.

These global and continental data give us a framework for the assessment of regional population processes in mountain regions where such historical statements are available. For a more general estimation of the particular development in the mountains and surrounding regions during the modern period, we must be initially satisfied with the more tangible indicators of urbanisation. Table 6 provides information about the numerous cities from three continents that have proven rich in contrasts and may therefore reveal a broad spectrum. Whether there were in fact twenty major cities in South America in 1500, as the table estimates, remains unknown – relatively certain, however, is the location of all these South American cities in the Andean countries, many of them in the mountains themselves. Cusco, the famous Inca capital, is found at 3,300 metres and, according to one chronicler, it comprised around 40,000 inhabitants at the time of the Spanish arrival, with several times that many living in the immediate vicinity.[14] With the decline in population following the conquest, the number of cities also fell. Only after this turning point did

---

12. At nearly the same time as the studies of Durand 1977 and Biraben 1979, which we rely on here, there appeared the atlas of McEvedy/Jones 1978 that privileged the assumption of regular, exponential forms of growth.
13. Durand 1977, p. 282; also Denevan 1992 and Sánchez-Albornoz 2003.
14. Bairoch, from whom we take the figures for South American cities, qualifies them as 'very approximate' (1996, p. 499); for Cusco: Cook 1981, p. 219.

Upland Demography

Table 5: Estimated World Population by Continent, 1500–2000 (in millions)

Continent	1500	1600	1700	1800	1900	2000
Africa	87	113	107	102	138	784
North America	3	3	2	5	90	313
Latin America	39	10	10	19	75	516
Asia	253	347	442	638	920	3,684
Europe	76	102	116	188	405	728
Oceania	3	3	3	2	6	30
Global	461	578	680	954	1,634	6,055

Regions: North America to the USA; Europe to the Ural Mountains. Sources: Biraben 1979, p. 16 and Livi Bacci 2005, p. 45; calculations distinguishing between the European and Asian parts of the former USSR based on Durand 1977, p. 256 (for 1500 and 1900; estimated values for 1600 to 1800) and UN statistics (for 2000); for the two American continents see also the UN statistics for 2000.

Table 6: Urbanisation of Mountain Regions and Surrounding Areas on Three Continents, 1500–2000

Region	Indicator	1500	1600	1700	1800	1900	2000
Andes	C20/100	20/0	7/1	11/0	11/0	28/4	–/100
South America	C20/100	20/0	7/1	14/0	19/0	82/12	–/375
	UP%	–	–	13	15	20	79
Himalayas	C20/100	1/0	1/0	2/1	4/0	6/2	–/5
Indian Subcontinent	C20/100	–/5-10	–	–/10–32	–	256/30	–/363
	UP%	–	–	11–13	9–12	9–11	28
Alps	C20/100	0/0	0/0	1/0	1/0	4/0	–/3
Pyrenees	C20/100	0/0	0/0	0/0	0/0	0/0	–/0
Europe	C20/100	95/4	117/11	130/11	182/18	1,009/121	–/737
	UP%	11	12	12	12	38	74

C20: number of cities with 20,000 or more inhabitants, including the C100 cities; C100: number of cities with 100,000 or more inhabitants. UP%: urban population as a per cent of the entire population. –: numbers not available. Regions: Andes – Bolivia, Chile, Ecuador, Colombia and Peru; Himalayas, Alps and Pyrenees – excluding cities located at the base of the mountains; Europe– excluding Russia. Sources: Bairoch 1977, 1988, 1996; Chandler 1987; Mathieu 2009; further details in Mathieu 2003, p. 22.

Population and Urbanisation

the first urban concentrations outside the Andes become visible in the South American countries; since the nineteenth century, these gained the upper hand and became an increasingly clear majority.

As the lower sections of the table show, urban development on the Indian subcontinent (with the Himalayas) and in Europe (with the Alps and Pyrenees) took a different course during the early modern period: from the beginning, the mountains here were poor in cities compared to the surrounding regions. This difference appears all the more clearly because the urban share of the total population was still similar at that time on all three continents (eleven to thirteen per cent for 1700). In the early modern period, therefore, the differences prevailed – then, after 1800, the similarities became more prominent. Namely, in all three places the number of cities in the mountain regions now rose less rapidly than in the surrounding areas, so that disparities between uplands and lowlands developed or increased. This applies also to South America with its early urbanisation in the Andean countries. Within these countries, the disparities likewise grew. Cusco had around 300,000 inhabitants in 2000, whereas the coastal city of Lima – a Spanish settlement – counted 7.6 million.[15]

In sum, it may be said that deviations from the rule of altitude, as found in statistics from the twentieth century (Tables 3 and 4), were already clear from an earlier date. Moreover, they could have been even more pronounced in the first period than later. What arguments can be made in favour of this? From the side of geography, explanations for the spatial distribution of population and cities often come quickly to hand. They are readily associated, no doubt for discipline-specific reasons, with favourable or unfavourable natural circumstances. In this way the spectrum of possible explanations narrows from the start, tending to limit itself to static factors, even though, in the modern period, one also observes striking manifestations of change. This recommends, therefore, a certain measure of restraint.

Before engaging in attempts at explanation, we will consider the processes of population change and urbanisation from a regional perspective. Here we see that the mountainous regions were characterised by diverse settlement histories at the beginning of the modern era and thus they demonstrate variable starting positions for the outlined growth phenomena. A few regions already possessed a dense, long-established population; we can designate them 'old-settled lands'. In contrast, other areas were only sparsely or not at all settled around 1500 and

---

15. For migration see the older survey of Escobar/Beall 1982; on the differential development generally see below, Chapter 2.4.

Asynchrony of Settlement

were often seen from the centres as the 'wilderness'.[16] The following chapter outlines the situation for both categories, each in two mountainous areas: South America and the Mediterranean as well as China and North America. The examples make clear that settlement processes were influenced by countless and variable circumstances and that – regarded in such a way – each had its own distinct chronology.

2.2 ASYNCHRONY OF SETTLEMENT

Old-Settled Lands: South America, Mediterranean

> That part of the New World, which is mostly oriented around midday and which the Spaniards call the fat of the land, includes Brazil and Peru. Its capital and most distinguished city is Cusco, of such size, strength, and beauty that it could rival even the most beautiful cities in all of Spain and Italy. This city has such a handsome castle, so many fine and noble people, elegant and well-built houses, and a most scenic location.

These are the words of a richly illustrated work on the 'World's Greatest Cities', the first volume of which appeared in Germany in 1576.[17] While this text used flattering words in its reflections on the indigenous population, it was also being debated in sixteenth-century Europe whether the people of the newly discovered continent could even be acknowledged as having souls. On the other hand, there were very few who failed to pay respect to the cultural achievements of the Andean people. The Spanish conquistadors too, who had assailed the region a generation earlier, were astonished by the stately settlements, the well-built network of roads and the various and sometimes artistically irrigated forms of agriculture that they found here alongside desert-like terrain and in some cases at extremely high elevations. Alexander von Humboldt repeatedly expressed similar statements, as in 1800 when he emphasised that the mountain region as a whole was 'far more cultivated than the plain'.[18]

This unique Andean cultural landscape had a very old history. The rapid and successful formation of the Inca Empire in the centuries before 1500 was

---

16. Grötzbach 1988, p. 29 proposes a similar classification from a human geographical perspective; see also Messerli/Ives 1997, pp. 17–8.
17. Braun/Hogenberg 1576–1618, vol. 1 (1576), p. 59 (original German).
18. Bitterli 1999, pp. 239–269; Acosta 2006 (1590), p. 143; Humboldt 1989 (1807), pp. 149–51; see also the classic work of Murra 2002 (collection of articles); from the angle of anthropological mountain research: *Convergences* 1985.

only possible, according to common opinion, because it could be built on demographic, technological and cultural conditions that were produced over a long series of earlier civilisations.[19] When the Spaniards arrived, according to Carlos Sempat Assadourian, the land was 'full' of people, which matches the self-assessment one can also find in the mythological tradition. More precise details make themselves available, however, only from the second half of the sixteenth century, at a time when a massive assault had already been inflicted through the introduction of new diseases and brutal exploitation. In the highlands of the central Andes, by 1570, according to the available sources, the native population was over a million strong, whereas on the coast there lived only around 250,000 people. During the next fifty years the number of inhabitants continued to fall: by 44 per cent in the mountains and as much as 65 per cent on the coast. A similar pattern can be established in the parts of the Andes now belonging to Ecuador and Colombia, though here the lowlands as a rule did not decline more sharply in population than the mountain areas.[20]

One factor that led to decisive change in many places was the Spanish imposition of mining. The most spectacular case was Potosí, a city located 4,100 metres high, which was founded in the mid-sixteenth century and counted an estimated 120,000 inhabitants in its final days; at that time it belonged among the larger cities of the world. The rapid growth resulted from the discovery of immense silver deposits and the importance attributed to this precious metal in Europe. Potosí generated a huge demand for labour, foodstuffs and capital and it thereby created for itself an extensive urban supply area. To satisfy the demand, numerous regions had to limit their self-sufficiency and produce a surplus instead. People carrying loads or leading pack animals travelled across thousands of kilometres to meet Potosí's needs.[21] Although the patterns and distribution of settlement were therefore subject to change, it should not be overlooked that the Spaniards were also – just as the Incas before them – bound by historical preconditions. The fact that they placed the viceroyalty of Peru over most of the old-settled lands is testimony to the importance the indigenous workforce possessed for the colonial power – a development best described as 'path-dependent' or dependent upon previous situations and processes.

---

19. A summary in Bonilla 2005, vol. 1, pp. 45–86: *Las civilizaciones precolombinas*.
20. Assadourian 2006, p. 276; Cook 1981, p. 253; Newson 2003; Villamarín /Villamarín 2003. A similar demographic predominance of mountains shows up in comparison to the vast Amazon region – see the estimates of Denevan 1992, p. xxiii; on the sixteenth-century population collapse in all of Latin America: Newson 2006.
21. Bonilla 2005, vol. 1, pp. 503–14; a German version in Busset 2003, pp. 63–77.

Asynchrony of Settlement

The second stage of our regional investigation leads us to the Mediterranean, whose history is the subject of Fernand Braudel's now classic study from the mid-twentieth century. It focuses especially on the sixteenth century and begins with a detailed and colourful chapter about the mountains, foothills and plains that formed the coastline or could be found at some distance from it. For the initial situation in Italy he names the diplomat, Francesco Guicciardini, who noted in the 1530s that his land had flourished prior to the great military expeditions of foreign armies (around 1490): 'For it enjoyed the greatest peace and tranquillity, its most mountainous and sterile places were cultivated just as well as the plains and its most fertile regions, and it was under no dominion other than its own; not only was it incredibly rich in population, properties, and possessions, it was distinguished also in the highest degree by the magnificence of its numerous princes and by the splendour of many noble and most beautiful cities.'[22]

Deserving of particular interest here is Guicciardini's explicit reference to the agricultural use of the 'most mountainous and sterile places' ['luoghi più montuosi e più sterili'] in Italy. For many other regions of the Mediterranean as well, there is evidence from the start of the modern era suggesting the existence of old or even very old settlements and agricultural uses in the mountains – in the Asian, European and African regions. And in the following centuries, agricultural development progressed in these areas along a completely different course from in the Andes. A study in environmental history illustrates this with settlements from five mountain regions: the Taurus in modern-day Turkey, the Pindus in Greece, the Apennines in Italy, the Sierra Nevada in Spain and the Rif in Morocco. In almost all these regions the available documentation, though not always with complete certainty, indicates a process of growth. In the case of the Taurus, the population is said to have as much as tripled between 1500 and 1800. Seen as a whole, there was in only one case during the early modern period a slight decrease in population and this was the result of an embittered conflict between the Spanish crown and the Muslim part of the population over religious rule: the settlements in the Alpujarras south of the

---

22. Braudel 1995, vol. 1, pp. 25–85; Guicciardini 1981, p. 88: 'Perché, ridotta tutta in somma pace e tranquillità, coltivata non meno ne' luoghi più montuosi e più sterili che nelle pianure e regioni sue più fertili, né sottoposta a altro imperio che de' suoi medesimi, non solo era abbondantissima d'abitatori, di mercatanzie e di ricchezze; ma illustrata sommamente dalla magnificenza di molti prìncipi, dallo splendore di molte nobilissime e bellissime città…'

Sierra Nevada suffered the loss of almost ninety per cent of their inhabitants between 1568 and 1571.[23]

Connected with the growth there was sometimes an increase in field cultivation at the expense of animal husbandry. In the Pindus this agricultural trend can be seen in the sixteenth and seventeenth centuries, in the Taurus in the nineteenth and twentieth. Moreover, the expansion of agriculture led everywhere to forest clearance; from the eighteenth century there were even signs of deforestation in various areas of the Mediterranean.[24] Similar growth processes may be observed in the Alps and, since the source material here is relatively good, we can also evaluate the development quantitatively. Population in the Alps increased in every century from the start of the modern era, summing up to an increase by a factor of 2.7 between 1500 and 1900, compared with the growth of the entire European population by a factor of 5.3 during the same period (see Table 5 above). It is interesting to note, however, that the Alpine population grew at practically the same rate as that in the European lowlands until around 1700. Only in a second phase did the Alps lag clearly and ever more clearly behind. This indicates that the intensification of agriculture at high altitudes became problematic at a certain point in development. When the peasants decided, for example, to harvest certain hay fields for fodder not just once but several times per year, their use of these lands became increasingly dependent upon the growing season – and in the mountains, this remained as short as ever.[25]

Conquest of the 'Wilderness': China and North America

In addition to the mountain regions already exhibiting a dense, long-established population at the beginning of the modern period, which we have designated here as 'old-settled lands', there were others that were still only sparsely or not at all settled around 1500. From the central places they were often associated with the 'wilderness'. Over the course of the modern era, there occurred a sharp increase in population and the appropriation of such regions in many parts of the world. In cases where other groups already used an area extensively or simply held a prior claim, this process could be highly conflict-ridden.

---

23. McNeill 1992, pp. 147–220, above all pp. 153, 162, 177–8, 180, 192–4, 203.
24. McNeill 1992, pp. 218, 272–350; the author stresses the recent age of deforestation and makes it a central issue of his study.
25. Mathieu 2009, pp. 34–43, 61–70, 115–9; Staszewski observes that the Alps were typical for Europe with regard to vertical population distribution (1957, p. 47).

Asynchrony of Settlement

A striking example of this is China, where around one quarter of the global population lived and where, besides the many river valleys and the great plains, there were also numerous mountain regions. At first they were little used by the Han Chinese and it was not until early modern times that they came increasingly to be taken over.[26] In a certain sense this was true even of the imperial court. Its capital city Beijing, located in the northern part of the empire at a mere sixty metres above sea level, underwent a strong expansion since the early fifteenth century but not until the late seventeenth century did the court begin to harness the mountainous areas. On a visit in 1681 to Jehol Province, beyond the Great Wall, the emperor was so impressed by the varied landscape, dense forests and bountiful wild game – tigers, bears, leopards, deer and others – that he decided to build a hunting ground and a summer palace there. The reserve encompassed an area of over 15,000 square kilometres and it was used for the annual 'autumn hunt', a ritual also filled with political significance. For the occasion of each year's hunt, around 12,000 soldiers were sent into the mountains to drive the animals. Since the court was also exceedingly numerous, the economic effects of this seasonal migration were not inconsequential.[27]

Observers have pointed out that in China, as elsewhere in East and South-east Asia, there was in many places a clear separation between the majority population at the lower elevations and the tribes of the mountain regions. The most commonly cited reason for this is the cultivation of rice paddies, which allowed a very high level of land productivity and population density in low-lying places. In China, this form of agriculture developed significantly both before and after the sixteenth century. Some areas also went over to two or more harvests per year. Between 1500 and 1900 the population grew by nearly a factor of five. One possible interpretation for this particular intensification strategy, which actively targeted the central area and paid relatively little attention to the peripheral farmlands, could take economic and cultural institutionalisation as its starting point. Even in its early phases, China was marked by an infrastructure of garden-like fields and elaborate irrigation systems. This seems to have had a decisive influence on subsequent development, as a growing number of people sought sources of food and employment. The

---

26. Generally for the Chinese development and also with a view to mountain issues: Ho 1959, above all pp. 145–53; Elvin/Ts'ui-jung 1998; Richards 2005, pp. 112–47.

27. Reardon-Anderson 2000, pp. 511–4; Menzies 1994, pp. 55–64 (besides this biggest hunting reserve, the emperors possessed numerous smaller reserves, some with older origins).

state certainly also played a role in this, with its tax policies and periodic bans on migration. In any case, many mountain regions were not at first directly affected by the growth of Han-Chinese agriculture.[28]

As pressure rose in the second half of the seventeenth century and the empire began an explicitly expansionist policy under the new Qing Dynasty, the settlement of mountain regions and the integration of the indigenous populations there also increased. In the mountainous province of Guizhou, in the south-western part of the empire – which covered around 175,000 square kilometres but exhibited, according to popular saying, 'not three feet of flat country' – there lived many tribal groups, among them the Miao. They settled in fortified villages on the hilltops, often practiced 'shifting cultivation' and in general maintained a warlike disposition (see Plate 6).[29] For a long time, Han China limited its rule over the province to tribute relations with the area's leading families. But immigration, the increasing contacts and conflicts and the growing tendency toward forced assimilation into Chinese culture led the court in 1726 to build a massive local military presence and put an end to Miao autonomy. The result was years of rebellion, bloody massacres and retaliatory actions. Finally the Chinese army gained the upper hand, in part by means of a split among the Miao into the assimilated, or 'cooked' [shu] and the rebellious, 'raw' [sheng] factions. Still the conflict was not laid to rest and it flared up again in the Great Miao War of 1795 to 1806.[30]

The last stop on our mountain journey is Appalachia, a mountain range extending through eastern North America for approximately 2,400 kilometres between present-day Quebec and Alabama. With peak heights around 2,000 metres the range is not particularly high, yet it was the first major mountain region on the continent to be taken over by European-American settlers. In 1790 a Methodist preacher who had travelled back and forth through Appalachia noted: 'Our way is over mountains, steep hills, deep rivers, and muddy creeks; a thick growth of reeds for miles together; and no inhabitants but wild

---

28. Blache 1934, pp. 111–26; Hambloch 1966, pp. 76–7, 101–2, illustration 42 (altitudinal belts by ethnicity); Braudel 1992, vol. 1, pp. 145–58, above all 152–5 (inspired by Blache); Needham 1991; Scott 2009; on population: Biraben 1979, p. 16 (increase 1500–1900 by a factor of 4. 9); McEvedy/Jones 1978, p. 171 (by a factor of 4. 5).
29. On the genre of 'Miao albums', interesting for the interpretation of Plate 6: Hostetler 2001.
30. Lombard-Salmon 1972; on narrower and wider uses of the term 'Miao' and on the words 'shu/sheng' pp. 117, 214, 238; see also Hostetler 2001, pp. 102, 106–7; Scott 2009, pp. 240, 284–5; on environmental aspects: Elvin 2004, pp. 216–72.

Asynchrony of Settlement

beasts and savage men.'[31] With this, the preacher conveyed the dominant view of the mostly English and gradually westward-moving settlement communities – namely that this was a wilderness where one encountered 'wild men' but not 'inhabitants' whose territorial claims were to be taken seriously. In reality, though the mountain region was indeed sparsely settled by European standards, it was by no means untouched 'virgin land'. The Native Americans of this area, who had lived there since much earlier times and belonged above all to the Cherokee, pursued an extensive agricultural practice that spread like islands across the river valleys. Hunting through the vast forests was also important to their way of life. The land was marked additionally by trade routes and other signs of human use. An estimated 30,000 Cherokee lived in a large section of Appalachia, ranging over more than 110,000 square kilometres.[32]

There had long been sporadic contacts with Europeans but the real history of conquest in Appalachia began in the 1720s, when the first settlers pushed into the region from the eastern colonies.[33] In the following decades the relationship between the two populations remained relatively peaceful but then, as settlement conditions changed, beginning in the late eighteenth century, there developed protracted, exceedingly bitter and brutal conflicts. In another region of Appalachia that was similar in size to that just mentioned, there were already 93,000 settlers by 1790 (of whom seven per cent were black slaves); by 1830 the number had risen to 593,000 (with eleven per cent slaves).[34] In that same year, the by now established United States Congress passed the 'Indian Removal Act', which sealed the fate of the remaining Native American population. A few years later, the army forcibly drove the Cherokee further west. In Appalachia they were allowed to remain on a reservation of a meagre 300 square kilometres, which was later secured for them by a philanthropist (see Plate 7).

The occupation by newcomers only continued to increase at an even faster pace. Soon after 1850 the population passed the one million mark, then in the twentieth century it reached five million.[35] In an initial phase of development, family farms, often specialising in livestock production, spread

---

31. Asbury 1958, vol. 1, p. 636.
32. On the imprint of Native American cultures on the landscape: Butzer 1990; for southern Appalachia: Davis 2000, pp. 9–90; on population *Ibid.* p. 59; Denevan 1992, p. 260 speaks of 22,000 Cherokee.
33. Bitterli 1999, pp. 381–412; William 2002, pp. 34–42, the following paragraphs are mainly based on this detailed and competent work.
34. Williams 2002, p. 111 (for the 'Core Region').
35. Williams 2002, pp. 111, 368.

across the mountains. Later there came commercial logging, coal mining and the production of hydroelectric power for the nearby urban industrial centres of the East Coast, which developed rapidly and soon assumed a leading role. Summer tourists were visiting Appalachia by the early nineteenth century. To be sure, the mountain and nature experiences of this region were eventually surpassed by the Rocky Mountains and other majestic mountain ranges of the American West that later became accessible. In contrast to most other cultural norms, the 'wilderness' idea and the conservation movement started there and spread back toward the East: national parks were first established in Appalachia in the 1930s.[36] In those days, 'backwardness' had already characterised the region for quite some time. Despite the fact that the mountain landscape had been transformed completely over a period of only two hundred years and was now being put to intensive use, Appalachia was left behind the East Coast with its explosive growth. From the early twentieth century, emigration from the mountains prevailed. The figure of the impoverished, uneducated 'hillbilly' began to dominate the image of Appalachia and, in the 1960s, the reform-minded United States government inaugurated its 'War on Poverty', especially here on this home front in the hinterland of Washington D.C.[37]

Highlands and Lowlands

The settlement processes we have outlined for the Andean, Mediterranean, Chinese and North American mountain regions were certainly asynchronous and yet each of them led also, up to the twentieth century, to what Hermann Hambloch has called a strong 'penetration of the high altitude boundary region by a cultural landscape'. In his view, this required a certain population density and corresponding land use patterns. This German geographer, whose global overview study we consulted earlier, also employed two other categories. There were mountain regions he classified in terms of the cultural landscape's pervasiveness not as 'strong' but instead as only 'moderate' or 'weak'. In this last category the population density was especially low (less than two persons per square kilometre) and the natural landscape was permeated only by isolated 'islands of culture'. Overall, therefore, the world's mountains in 1960 displayed a colourful and richly variegated picture. Seen in a dynamic view,

---

36. Williams 2002, pp. 295–301; Wyckoff/Dilsaver 1995.
37. Williams 2002, pp. 199, 312–26, 342–50.

Asynchrony of Settlement

it presents an even sharper profile of the asynchronous population process we have emphasised so far.[38]

Two observations already made in the regional portraits are worth emphasising again, because they may claim a more general validity and because they will occupy us further below. First, there is the path dependency of development: the fact that the Spanish Viceroyalty of Peru in the Andes was largely grafted onto the old-settled indigenous lands suggests the significance of previously established structures and conditions with respect to later decision-making. Such chronological causalities can certainly also be applied to the long-lasting privileges enjoyed by lowland China, prejudiced in part by early investments in irrigation systems.[39] Second, there is the problem of intensification in mountainous areas: the example of the European Alps indicates that agriculture at high elevations did not pose structural problems until a certain point in development – namely, when it was seen as necessary to fit multiple harvests into a limited time period, a practice introduced in many of the world's lowland areas over the course of the modern period. With respect to population density and the formation of central places, this handicap could also take effect in an industrial phase – as in Appalachia, which, in the midst of the breathless development of the American East Coast, became a 'backward' region in the twentieth century.[40]

In order to ascertain the distinctiveness of mountain history, we must therefore consider the history of the lowlands or plains as well. For only the comparison between them can lead to a rounded, methodically satisfactory picture. Fernand Braudel, in his great work on the Mediterranean in the sixteenth century, pointed explicitly to the fact that many lowland areas were not favourable regions to begin with but rather places that had to be positively wrested away from nature. This applied less to the small basin-like areas than to the more spacious ones.

> When they were larger, the Mediterranean plains were far more difficult to conquer. For a long time they were only very imperfectly and temporarily taken over by man. Only recently, towards 1900, was the Mitidja, behind Algiers, finally claimed for cultivation. It was not until after 1922 that Greek colonization eventually triumphed over the marshes in the plain of Salonica. And it was on the eve of World War II that work was finished on the draining of the Ebro delta and the Pontine Marshes. In the sixteenth century, then, the big

---

38. Hambloch 1966, p, 99 and illustration 41.
39. See below, Chapter 2.4.
40. See below, Chapter 2.4.

plains were not at all rich, far from it. By an apparent paradox, they frequently presented a spectacle of misery and desolation.

Braudel then turned his full attention to the difficulties confronting the settlement of the plains: flooding, malaria, high land improvement costs. He illustrated these factors especially with the historical transformation of the Po Valley and the Andalusian Plain, touching also on the contrasts between these and the adjacent mountain regions.[41]

In terms of chronology as well as substance, a history of the lowlands presents a far more variable picture when we extend our view to other continents. Two examples from Asia illustrate this. The great coastal plain in North China is a landscape that has been changed more through human activity and over a longer period of time than almost any other landscape worldwide. In an early phase, according to the research, the plain possessed an inhospitable character. Yet the containment of the Yellow River began in the last millennium before the Common Era and the continuous hydraulic engineering work led eventually, through sedimentation, to the river rising several metres above the plain – and this significantly increased the danger of a breach in the dam. Many such ruptures were so severe that chroniclers recorded them with great care. For the period of the Qing Dynasty (1644–1911), for example, 161 catastrophes of this kind on the Yellow River were mentioned.[42] Whereas the North China Plain was settled quite early and in large numbers, the plain of the Ganges – which forms the heart of Indian culture – long remained a region where the jungle extended over relatively broad stretches of land. When a powerful Mughal ruler in the late sixteenth century waged a campaign against a regional prince, his soldiers first had to painstakingly fight their way through the jungle. According to one written report, they would fell the trees one day in order to march forward on the next. Over the course of the modern period, and especially in the nineteenth and twentieth centuries, the jungle was then forcefully driven back. It held out the longest in the Terai region at the foot of the Himalayas.[43]

Asynchrony of settlement is found therefore not only in the mountains but equally in the lowlands and plains. The classic example of a very late concentration of settlement is the Amazon region, which up until our time exhibited vast forests and presented a sharp contrast to the bordering Cordillera in the Andes. Particularly noteworthy for us is the extreme divergence in opinion about the

---

41. Braudel 1995, vol. 1, pp. 60–85, quote pp. 61–2; among recent studies of the issue: Brunnbauer 2004, pp. 135–6.

42. Dakang/Peiyuan 1990.

43. Singh 1991 and 1995; see also *The Cambridge Economic History of India* 1982, pp. 4–6.

Asynchrony of Settlement

population potential of this region, in the first place as presented by European colonialism and then later by the environmental movement. Whereas on the one side emphasis was placed on the unhealthy aspects of the tropical climate and the speedy exhaustion of its soil, there were others who valued these factors differently and focused instead on the region's vigorous vegetative growth. In the early twentieth century, some came thereby to the conclusion that the tropics were destined to be 'the region with the greatest future accumulation of people' and of all the countries in the world, Brazil appeared to them as the one 'with the greatest population potential'.[44] From a historical view, these contrasting opinions are an indication of how difficult it can be to ascertain the natural favour or disfavour of a region. They also demonstrate that this discourse does not necessarily contribute to the actual settlement process. In 1500, the Amazon region appears to have averaged less than one person per square kilometre and, until the early nineteenth century, population growth held itself within narrow limits. Parallel to the discussion of the tropics, though not establishing a clear change in opinion, the population in the Amazon later rose – at an especially rapid pace toward the end of the twentieth century.[45]

At this point one could almost say it was due to chance and not necessity that there was a relatively large population in the Andean highlands at the start of the modern period and only a small one in the lowlands of the Amazon. We will later return to this multi-faceted question of regional population dynamics (Chapter 2.4). What appears for now to be hardly a coincidence, however, is that hierarchical values are bound up with population size. In South America, 'civilisation' at first made its home in the highlands and already in the Inca period the lowlanders of the Amazon were condescendingly referred to as 'wild'.[46] Conversely, in many parts of the world it was the mountain dwellers who were seen to be the 'wild' ones, because demographic growth and urbanisation in the highlands often proceeded more slowly than in lowland areas.

---

44. Penck 1924, pp. 252, 254; see also Penck 1940/41; a central argument was the reference to tropical regions with high population densities in Asia; Penck was one of the most famous geographers of his time and belonged to the '*Volks- und Kulturbodenforschung*', supporting Germany's power politics; for a sceptical assessment see, for instance, Febvre 1970 (1922), pp. 201–7; generally Ehlers 1984, pp. 57–9, 65–73.
45. Denevan 1992, pp. 205–234 and 2003; Salati 1990.
46. Bonilla 2004, p. 15; Scott 2009, pp. 131–2.

2.3 Urbanisation

Until quite recently, the urbanisation of mountain regions remained a practically disregarded theme in the standard research. For example, one historical overview of urban development that was first published in 1985 completely excluded the mountain regions – this despite the fact that they constitute between one fifth and one quarter of the earth's surface. On the side of mountain research, a similar attitude prevailed. Here, urban development was either left untreated or classified from the start as minimal. 'Mountains are obviously rather unsuitable for the development of urban centres with extensive hinterlands', observed one author in a representative publication on global mountain issues in 1997. Although this remark was later somewhat relativised, it nonetheless expressed the dominant view: cities and mountains were traditionally separate themes.[47]

In the last ten or twenty years, however, as urbanisation has advanced rapidly in many areas and received greater attention, this separation has come increasingly under fire. At the regional level there have long been informative studies on the history of individual cities, and likewise for mountain regions, but the next step was to take the research to a more general level. Various authors published relevant investigations with new perspectives and findings.[48] In fact, one must also pay close attention to urbanisation in regions and periods where few or no cities are found, because of the pull-effect cities could exercise over long distances. Owing to their population size, urban centres were predestined to promote the social division of labour and development of markets. In addition, they often formed the centres of political and religious power. Insofar as all these forces were bundled together in a lowland region, the adjacent highlands were also drawn into the urban orbit, especially if they did not possess any cities of their own. This point is particularly important for our historical account, which places temporal change, not spatial demarcation, in the foreground. Here we will first consider the smaller cities in selected regions and then outline the development of the more prominent centres.

---

47. Bairoch 1996 (first edition 1985); Messerli/Ives 1997; the quoted sentence by Erich Grötzbach, *Ibid.* p. 30; also Mathieu 2003.
48. On the geographical side one should mention above all the studies of Axel Borsdorf, Paul Messerli and Manfred Perlik; for historical perspectives see Busset *et al.* 2003.

Urbanisation

Towards Town

As 'cities' we can initially designate places of a certain size, where the population drew much of its food supply from outside rather than producing it at home. This approach suggests that, as a rule, the early formation of cities required a certain population density in the surrounding countryside in order to provide the 'surplus' necessary to meet urban demand, whereby the transportation conditions of the time were also a matter of great importance.[49] Besides these demographic and economic factors, other dimensions – political, legal and architectural – also played a considerable role. In comparative research it is best to regard certain aspects of the city concept as generally applicable, while consciously leaving others open for regional, subjective and contextual uses.[50] Especially difficult, of course, is the classification of settlements in transition between village and city. Such places characterised the early phases of urbanisation and often built a clear majority over the large cities, even in a later period. The large urban centres were of course more widely known or even famous but far more people often lived in the numerous small towns.[51]

Chetan Singh points explicitly to such problems of definition in his investigation of a region in the western Himalayas (in the modern-day Indian state of Himachal Pradesh, with a surface area of some 55,000 square kilometres). The small towns found here in the early modern period and, to be more precise, in the nineteenth century, were often no larger than villages. Around 1900 some had only one to two thousand inhabitants. The author therefore emphasises the political and economic control these central places practiced over their mountain valleys, as well as contemporary perceptions – in other words, the specific classification of settlements that was customary in the region. Since the various small towns exercised comparable functions, their outward appearance was quite uniform:

> At strategic positions were situated the raja's palace and the temple (or temples) of the presiding and other important deities of the state. A permanent and probably the largest market (bazaar) of the kingdom was located in the town and functioned as its commercial hub. Often at a short distance from the bazaar was to be found a large open space (a chaugan or maidan) where

---

49. Boserup 1990, p. 87.
50. The problem of city definition has a long history; modern research uses mainly pragmatic approaches leaving room for various views; typically, the UN statistics are based on the varying national norms for city demarcation.
51. Clark 1995, above all the introduction on pp. 1–21.

caravans transporting merchandise camped periodically, and where seasonal trade fairs were held.[52]

With few exceptions, the places in the region that qualified as urban were the capitals of principalities – that is, of small territories that struggled with one another for supremacy and grew for their part out of the competition among local ruling families. Thus political power, as well as the religious authority with which it was bound, marked the ensemble of cities. The importance of agrarian resources for provisioning these small towns reflected itself in their geographical location on the banks of the great mountain rivers. From there they also commanded the tributary streams and the agriculturally significant side valleys. Many such valleys were connected to one another only by way of the principal towns. The towns also possessed additional functions as part of an extensive trading system. Although the principalities were not among the major producers or consumers of commercial goods, their urban centres played a role as staging places and regional transfer points for interregional commerce. Parts of this trading network reached from the large cities of the North Indian Plain all the way to Tibet and Central Asia. For all the limitations of urbanisation in the region, these small princely cities nevertheless formed, according to Singh, 'the most obviously permanent man-made feature in the Himalayan landscape'.[53]

As the British colonial power strengthened its rule over the Indian subcontinent in the nineteenth century, there came a significant change in its urban character. Now there arose in the Himalayan foothills the so-called 'Hill Stations', which were initially intended as exclusive British enclaves and erected away from the traditional princes' towns. Shimla, today the capital of Himachal Pradesh, was built on top of a narrow ridge at a height of over 2,000 metres, whereas the river valleys where most of the princes' cities were located ranged between 700 and 1,200 metres. The background to this development was a period-specific mixture of military, ethno-medical and cultural motives. In the case of Shimla, the settlement began in 1822 with the construction of a summer house by a colonial official of Scottish origin. The place soon made a name for itself as a summer retreat and it grew to such an extent that, by the end of the nineteenth century, it was larger than all the other cities of the region. Another contributing factor was the fact that the British viceroy of India escaped the heat of the lowlands each summer by moving with his entire government

---

52. Singh 2003, pp. 129–130 (original French; based on the unpublished English version).
53. Singh 1998, p. 40; Singh 2003, pp. 129–133; for city formation in other Himalayan regions see the further contributions to Busset *et al.* 2003.

Urbanisation

to Shimla, where they constructed a representative building in the 1880s, the 'Viceregal Lodge'. This seasonal change in location resembled a mass migration and from the mountain region alone it required thousands of Indian porters and other servants. The colonial administration justified the expense by citing greater labour efficiency in the high-altitude climate that gave government business during these hot months a 'hearty English tone'. Indian opponents noted, however, that the colonial officials had long since acclimatised, and they dismissed the summer residence as one 'gigantic picnic'.[54]

Shimla underwent several changes in status with the political developments of the twentieth century, yet the once-established conditions would make a lasting impression on the city's history. The role of capital city fell to the former summer retreat in 1966, with the establishment of the federal state of Himachal Pradesh and this provided a new impetus for growth. Despite the fact that the settlement was located on top of a mountain ridge, it soon became home to more than 100,000 inhabitants. Consequently, some parts of the city expanded out onto incredibly steep slopes, which came at a big cost for building activity as well as the overall urban infrastructure.[55] Shimla is therefore a striking example of path-dependent development and of the variability of favourable and unfavourable factors over time: as suitable as the ridge may have been for a small summer retreat, the setting was problematic for a large city; that it developed there, despite the adverse topography, hints at the strength of its previously established function as a central place. With the necessary adjustments, this explanatory model may be applied to many other mountain cities. Another remarkable example is the setting of La Paz in Bolivia, which developed toward the end of the twentieth century into the highest metropolis with over a million inhabitants in the world. The first small kernel of settlement, Nuestra Señora de La Paz, lay in a deep basin that evidently appeared a favourable location at the time of its foundation in the mid-sixteenth century but this later made the city's expansion much more difficult. A modern urban development plan rated three-quarters of the municipality as a hazard zone and proclaimed the accomplishment of basin's settlement a 'conquest of the walls'.[56]

---

54. Up to 1947, about 80 Hill Stations developed in India; similar mountain resorts were also established in the early nineteenth century by the Dutch in Indonesia and by the Spaniards in the Philippines – see Kanwar 2003, above all pp. 35–6, 41–5, 130–1; Singh 2003, pp. 133–40.
55. Kanwar 2003, above all pp. 17, 60, 64–9, 137, 251; in 2001, according to the census, Shimla's population was 142,555 inhabitants, without the neighbouring semi-urban villages or the numerous tourists.
56. Dollfus 1991, p. 113; *Neue Zürcher Zeitung*, 4/5 March 2006, p. 9.

Population and Urbanisation

Growth Factors

Whether a given settlement should be designated as a small, medium, large or mega city depends on the context of the investigation and is subject to temporal change. For our purposes a rigorously standardised terminology makes little sense and, besides, the available data permit only certain forms of analysis: very formal, mathematical models of urbanisation seem to be hardly meaningful at this point, on the basis of the sources and for our spatially diffuse study area. In Chapter 2.1 we suggested the difficulty of assembling reliable urban growth statistics for large regions, using data from South America, India and Europe. There we considered, to the greatest extent possible, all cities numbering 20,000 inhabitants or more (Table 6). The lower the assigned minimum value, the nearer one comes to a historically relevant description – but, at the same time, this usually makes it harder to effectively capture all the settlements of a region. Thanks to the preliminary work done by Paul Bairoch and his assistants, we can try to estimate the early modern development of European cities with 5,000 or more inhabitants (see Table 7).[57] The table indicates that in relation to the lower-lying cities, the ones at higher altitudes made up only a small percentage of the total urban population in the sixteenth to eighteenth centuries. More important still are the dynamics of development, which for statistical reasons are best estimated using the values from 1600 to 1800.[58] Whereas the population in the low-lying cities grew markedly in this period (244 per cent), the increase in high-altitude locations was more modest (110 per cent).

In general, one can assume that demographic growth represents a driving force for urbanisation. In the European mountain regions, however, there were evidently factors leading to slower growth and these carried greater weight over the course of time. In the economic sphere we must consider the problem of urban supply, which required a certain level of agricultural intensity and transportation infrastructure. In the highlands, because of the broken terrain, both were often more difficult to put in place and even more difficult to increase or improve than in the flatlands. The 750-metre mark, which serves in the table to distinguish the highlands from the lowlands, may seem low at first. In fact, however, this is not the case, because in true mountain settings (with

---

57. Bairoch's database is open to criticism, yet for general views and orders of magnitude it seems sufficiently reliable.
58. Cities of less than 5,000 inhabitants can appear suddenly in the statistics with only a slight increase in population, which raises the urban population abruptly and feigns a strong growth; this distortion is especially important at the beginning of a process (with small figures); therefore, the sixteenth century is excluded here.

Urbanisation

Table 7: Population of Cities in Early Modern Europe and China, by Altitude (Based on Different Criteria in Each Region)

Region	Altitude in metres	City Population in Thousands				% Growth 1600–1800
		1500	1600	1700	1800	
Europe	750 and above	96 (2 %)	357 (5 %)	214 (2 %)	394 (2 %)	110 %
	0–750	5,131 (98 %)	7,491 (95 %)	9,566 (98 %)	18,298 (98 %)	244 %
China	750 and above	111 (6 %)	129 (5 %)	80 (3%)	301 (6 %)	233 %
	0–750	1,775 (94 %)	2,574 (95 %)	2,605 (97 %)	4,764 (94 %)	185 %

For Europe, city population refers to the population of all (known) cities with 5,000 or more inhabitants; for China, it represents cities with 40,000 and above. Regions: Europe without Russia; China without Mongolia. Sources: for Europe, Mathieu/Furter 2010 based on data from Bairoch 1987; for China, data from Chandler 1987.

the exception of the high plains), the rural hinterland rises high above the city centre. Even in the relatively small area from which the early modern cities drew the majority of their everyday provisions, one often finds the terrain in the mountain valleys to be both high and steep.[59]

At this stage in the research it seems likely that this argument could be applied to many other regions, though certainly not to all of them. Especially in mountain regions that cannot be readily classified as old-settled lands, the situation in the early modern period was undoubtedly otherwise. An indication of this is provided by the Chinese data in Table 7. China looks back on an extremely distinguished urban history, yet, due to the lack of preparatory research, we are able to identify only places with 40,000 or more inhabitants.[60] The Chinese topography, compared to Europe, may have exhibited a somewhat larger proportion of the urban population at high elevations. Yet what is interesting here is the confirmation that, between 1600 and 1800, the growth at higher altitudes was not slower than in the lowlands – on the contrary, it

---

59. For the Alps with detailed evidence: Mathieu 2009, pp. 97–100.
60. In early modern Europe there were about 30 to 50 cities with 40,000 inhabitants and more; yet none of them was located over 750 metres, so that a direct comparison seems pointless.

Population and Urbanisation

was faster. This finding is in agreement with the late opening of important mountain regions for the Chinese economy, as outlined above (Chapter 2.2).[61]

What may be said about transportation and mining, which are frequently cited as major driving forces for urbanisation in mountain regions? A comparative-historical assessment of traffic flow can begin with the areas where urban concentrations formed early. When we consider the interaction between uplands and lowlands, various patterns stand out. The regions listed in Table 6, for example, can be classified into three groups: 1. In South America the lowlands long remained without significant urbanisation, which undoubtedly limited traffic with the Andes. 2. On the Indian subcontinent, the Ganges Plain was strongly urbanised but the remote regions in the North, beyond the Himalayas and Tibet, were not; this one-sided urbanisation most likely reduced commercial exchange and traffic flow. 3. The European Alps found themselves between the densely settled city landscapes of northern Italy and southern Germany with the Rhineland; everything seems to have favoured, comparatively speaking, a high traffic volume.[62] Nevertheless, the transalpine trade probably did not have a particularly strong influence on urbanisation in the early modern period. By far the most populous city in the Alps was Grenoble, the capital of a large province that was little involved in transalpine traffic. These and many other examples suggest that one should not overestimate the transportation factor.[63]

It was a different situation with mining, which occasionally proved to be a decisive impulse for urban growth. The prime example is the silver city of Potosí, situated a good 4,000 metres high in the Andes. Its rich mountain, the 'Cerro Rico', yielded so much in the early years that the rapidly growing city counted an estimated 120,000 inhabitants by 1600; this made it nearly twice the size of Madrid, the capital of the Spanish Empire.[64] In general, this very situationally-dependent form of urban growth was particularly widespread in the mountain regions of Latin America. On other continents the historical clues are far less dense.[65]

---

61. See also Chang 1963, pp. 121, 128, 137, 139; for the problems of sources Elvin 1978.
62. See Mathieu 2003, pp. 22–3, where the historical transport technology of the three regions is also used as an indicator.
63. Favier 1993; Mathieu 2009, pp. 92–4; instructive, for instance, are the statistics on occupations such as those available for Innsbruck in the seventeenth century; they show few persons in the transport sector (Mathis 1977); for questions of traffic volume and general traffic history: Furter 2007 and Bergier/Coppola 2007.
64. Bairoch 1988, p. 18; Bonilla 2005, vol. 1, pp. 503–14.
65. See Korol/Tandeter 2000, pp. 25–37; Dollfus 1991, pp. 118–9, 158–9; Hambloch 1966, p. 95; Messerli/Ives 1997, pp. 171–98.

Urbanisation

One factor that made an especially strong impression on the larger cities, though it has seldom received much attention with respect to urbanisation in mountain regions, was politics – that is, the exercise of temporal and spiritual power. In what follows, we would like to illustrate these forces with two examples: the high-elevation city of Lhasa in Tibet (China) and the fast-growing Mexico City.

Aloft: Lhasa

In the seventeenth century, under the rule of the Fifth Dalai Lama (1617–1682), Lhasa developed into a political and religious centre for large parts of Tibet and Asia. This led to a surge in demographic growth, accompanied by brisk building activity. Prior to that time, Lhasa, located in a river valley at around 3,650 metres, had not been much more prominent than other places in this arid mountain region. It did have an important Buddhist temple in the immediate vicinity from much earlier and two increasingly successful monasteries of the Gelugpa school from the fifteenth century. Still, in terms of growth, this religious apparatus really only became relevant when numerous Mongols accepted Tibetan Buddhism and, with the help of a Mongol ruler, brought the Gelugpa tradition to political power.[66]

The construction of the great Potala Palace on a hill overlooking the city was the most visible symbol of the rise of Tibet. It came about in two stages, in the middle and toward the end of the seventeenth century. Already impressive was the 'White Palace' of the first stage, which one European visitor rendered in a sketch (see Plate 8). Together with the 'Red Palace', the seat of the Dalai Lama would come to hold around one thousand rooms. Ippolito Desideri, an Italian Jesuit missionary, described Lhasa in the early eighteenth century as a well-built, populous and cosmopolitan city. 'Lhasa is densely populated, not only by natives, but by large numbers of foreigners of diverse nations', he wrote with a view toward the merchants, who came from all over the world, as well as the students, who streamed into the monastery from afar to receive religious training. At the market in the city centre, where a bazaar was held from dawn to dusk, a person could find whatever he or she desired, according to Desideri, and the crush of people was at times so great 'that it is difficult to get across the square'.[67]

---

66. Pommaret 2003; Bronger 2001; Larsen/Sinding-Larsen 2001; in general on Tibetan history: McKay 2003 (above all religion and politics, little on economy and society); Kollmar-Paulenz 2006; an early photographic documentation: Meyer/Meyer 2005.

67. Desideri 1937, pp. 103, 133, 134.

Population and Urbanisation

Precise population figures, however, are not to be found. One author gives 80,000 inhabitants for 1700, though without citing any sources, followed by only 50,000 in 1750 and 1800. This would concur with the political situation, which led in a less favourable direction from the early eighteenth century. It is certain that monks made up a large portion of Lhasa's population; in this centre, the basic monastic structure of Tibet, where most families placed one child in a convent, was expressed with special clarity. It is also certain that the population fluctuated sharply; the many foreign pilgrims and visitors during the religious celebrations profoundly influenced the demographic picture.[68] In order to meet their needs, in addition to the intensive agriculture of the surrounding area, it was necessary to import supplies over long distances. Considering the city's distinctly mountainous setting, both these things required extraordinary effort. In 1723 the Chinese withdrew their troops, as provisioning the garrison had triggered food shortages and higher prices, sparking dissatisfaction among the population.[69]

After this the population of Lhasa seems to have stagnated for a long time. The first reasonably trustworthy estimates from the first half of the twentieth century continued to offer similar numbers in the order of 30–50,000. Another surge in growth set in only after the Chinese occupation of Tibet in 1951, with its attendant modernisation and sinicisation politics. By 2000 Lhasa seems to have grown to several times its traditional size. In the particulars, however, the numbers are politically contested and consequently they are almost as difficult to verify as the earlier values.[70] Still, this second growth surge clearly demonstrates the importance of political power for urbanisation.

Big and Bigger: Mexico City

The history of modern Mexico City began likewise with a conquest. It was in the year 1519 that the Spanish conquistadors arrived, after a long march, at the centre of the highland Aztec Empire. At a certain point, the road opened up onto an astonishing view. 'From there we saw a great number of cities and

---

68. Chandler 1987, pp. 77–9; the figure for the beginning of the eighteenth century is based on a description of the Capuchin mission, see Snellgrove/Richardson 1980, p. 224; the mentioned estimates include all categories: laypersons, monks, perhaps military troops and part of the fluctuating population (assumed as constant); on the occasion of the principal religious feasts there was a conflux of perhaps 100,000 or more persons; see Bronger 2001, pp. 1–55, here above all pp. 35, 50.
69. Kollmar-Paulenz 2006, p. 124.
70. White 1916, p. 275; Bronger 2001, pp. 55 (with qualifications in the text), 56, 62.

Urbanisation

villages in the water as well as many other large settlements on the mainland, and there was also the straight and level road across the causeway leading to Mexico (Tenochtitlán); we were completely amazed and said to ourselves, this must be some form of enchantment', one eyewitness later wrote: 'Some of our soldiers even asked themselves if this were not a dream.'[71] In fact, the Spaniards stood before a densely populated, high mountain valley with a large lake and a number of cities along its lagoons. Particularly impressive was the Aztec capital of Tenochtitlán, with its broad entryway leading across the water, its numerous channels and the temples and palaces at the centre (see Plate 9). The Spaniards held it to be equal to or greater in size than the most famous cities of their homeland. We can assume there were around 200,000 inhabitants.[72]

Two years later the Spanish had subjugated the city but large parts of it were destroyed and the population decimated through disease, warfare and hunger. Given this situation, the conquerors now spent months discussing whether to rebuild the Aztec city as the new capital or instead to simply abandon it. Some favoured the young city of Veracruz on the coast, which boasted a better connection to the motherland. Eventually, despite important counter-arguments, the opinion finally prevailed that the centre of 'New Spain' should be built on the site of the old capital. A decisive factor seems to have been that the imperial power was thereby able to maintain its claims over the Aztec subjects and their tribute payments.[73] In the early seventeenth century the discussion of location came up yet again, because heavy precipitation frequently left the lagoon cities under water, in one case for a period of several years. The high mountain valley had no outlet stream, so the project of a 'general drainage' [Desagüe General] was to be carried out only at great expense. Again they held firmly to the old location, this time mainly on the grounds of property rights.[74]

By 1820 Mexico City had finally regained its pre-Hispanic population level. Then in the twentieth century, there was a tremendous growth surge: in 1930 the population surpassed the first million, in 1960 it was already up to more than 5 million, and by 2000 there were over 17 million inhabitants.

---

71. Díaz del Castillo 1989, p. 238 (original Spanish).
72. Newson 2006, p. 147; scholars agree that the Aztec capital was very large for the period, yet the estimates differ widely; see for instance Bitterli 1999, p. 225 and Richards 2005, p. 336; generally, for this paragraph: Kandell 1988; Ezcurra 1990; Parnreiter 2006.
73. Kandell 1988, pp. 125–6.
74. Kandell 1988, pp. 197–201; there were also floods after the construction of an outlet canal and even after its modernisation in the late nineteenth century, see *Ibid.* pp. 230–1, 371–2.

Some spoke of even higher numbers. In any case, Mexico City now belonged to the largest urban agglomerations worldwide.[75] This explosive growth cannot be explained in isolation from the political centralisation that left its indelible stamp upon the land. Already before 1800 the centralisation of rule had been put in place but afterwards it became far more effective and consequential. Almost independently of the prevailing political situation, a large proportion of state investments flowed into the capital and, together with other factors, this unleashed an enormous migration from the land to the city.[76]

It seems ironic that one of the largest cities in the world thus arose right in the middle of such an 'anti-urban' mountain environment. But then, to what extent can one really speak of a mountainous location? Mexico City sits at a latitude of nineteen degrees North, at the edge of the tropics and is centred on top of the lake that was meanwhile drained – in other words, on a flat. Yet this flat is located at an elevation of 2,250 metres and, before long, the agglomeration had sprawled out into the broken and sometimes steep terrain; beyond this, the area is surrounded by imposing volcanoes. Even at the level of the city centre, the air contains almost one third less oxygen and car engines are less efficient, producing higher emissions, than at sea level.[77] The city's location is particularly high in comparison to Europe, where the highest traditional and extremely small permanent settlements in the Alpine region barely rise above 2,000 metres. We may take all this as an indication that considerable theoretical scope is required in order to interpret the historical distribution of cities.

2.4 Two Theories

In conclusion, how can we now describe and explain the demographic development of mountain regions and mountain cities? In terms of method, the two sides of the analysis – description and explanation – are obviously linked. In order to distinguish between a sound judgment and an unfounded assumption, we must first come to understand the state of the matter. This concluding chapter begins with a presentation of important trends, as far as these can be derived from the material presented thus far alongside some additional sources. It will then provide an overview of various interpretations and close with two models of explanation that are of particular historical interest.

---

75. Parnreiter 2006, p. 166.
76. Ezcurra 1990, above all p. 586; Parnreiter 2006, above all pp. 171–2.
77. Kandell 1988, p. 574.

Two Theories

Increasing Disparities

Between 1500 and 2000 the global population increased more than tenfold, though with unequal distribution and at different times in individual territories. Asynchrony characterised developments in the highlands as well as the lowlands. As we have seen, the mountain regions of the Andes and the Mediterranean belonged to the old-settled lands, where population was already dense and long-established at the beginning of modern times; in large areas of China and North America, however, the mountains were only sparsely settled before an onslaught of settlers arrived and took over, starting in the seventeenth and eighteenth centuries; meanwhile other upland regions remained nearly unpopulated even in modern times. This asynchronous growth was just as striking in the lowlands. Examples include the early cultivation of the coastal plain in northern China and the extremely late settlement in the Amazon region (see above, Chapter 2.2). Many more cases could be cited and it is imperative for research to continue focusing intensively on historical population statistics. Based on what we know so far, it is already clear that we must pay attention not only to the positive or negative qualities of the individual territories but also to the appearance of historical 'coincidences'.

Overarching regularities moved into the foreground only in a second phase. In many places the contrast between uplands and lowlands developed or intensified over time. Whereas earlier settlement patterns had been heterogeneous, systematic differences now stood out. Seen in this way, the peculiarities of mountain regions seem to have been not least a product of modernity. For example, the traditional distributions of cities in South America, the Indian subcontinent and Europe were completely distinct from one another around 1500: there were a relatively large number of cities in the highland regions of South America but the mountains on the other two continents were decidedly poor in cities. Then, after 1800, the similarities became increasingly noticeable. In all three regions, the number of mountain cities now grew more slowly than in the surrounding areas, whereby the systematic disparities between uplands and lowlands developed or increased (see above, Chapter 2.1).

The chronology and strength of this tendency toward marginalisation was extremely variable. It began in some places by the seventeenth and eighteenth centuries, in others not until the twentieth. The mountain population tended toward absolute decline in some regions, while in others it merely grew less rapidly than in surrounding areas. Fernando Collantes has investigated the chronology and modalities of this differentiation process for Europe in comparative perspective. He demonstrates in detail, using various indicators

Population and Urbanisation

and including numerous mountain regions ranging from Scotland to southern Spain and Italy, that the marginalisation and restructuring of the nineteenth and twentieth centuries could proceed in many different ways. The variations depended quite substantially upon the prevailing economic context.[78]

Even greater, of course, was the intercontinental variability, which has occasionally been the subject of controversy in recent years.[79] On a global level it can be generally assumed that there were certain exceptions to the previously cited trends. Random sampling suggests, however, that they were limited in scope.[80] Where the disparity grew rapidly and decisively in favour of the lowlands, it was often accompanied by political pressure. In the lowland provinces of Bolivia, which make up over half of the territorial surface area, the population share amounted to scarcely ten per cent of the total in 1847. Until 1950 this proportion rose only slightly (to twelve per cent). Then, in the second half of the twentieth century, the population increased markedly throughout Bolivia – but by far the strongest growth was in the lowlands, which by 2001 already accommodated thirty per cent of the population and now claimed a greater share of political power.[81]

Interpretations Over the Course of Time

The discourse around the peculiarities of mountain regions has deep historical roots. It has yielded many different interpretations, which have varied with respect to their assessments and methodologies as well as their reception and

---

78. Collantes 2006b and 2009.
79. Older indications of growing disparities in Blache 1934, pp. 179–81; Staszewski 1957, e.g. pp. 26, 57; Hambloch 1966, pp. 51, 121; in recent studies one also finds different opinions, e.g. in Bätzing 1999, pp. 4–6; Price 2004, p. 13; the growth figures can depend strongly on the chosen mountain definitions.
80. Urbanisation became an important factor for population distribution particularly in the twentieth century, so that exceptions to the mentioned tendencies are most likely to be found in countries with high-lying metropolises; in 2000, one finds cities with over a million inhabitants at the altitude of over 2,000 metres in six countries (see Chapter 2.1); according to the available, not very reliable, data, the mountain and upland population grew faster than the lowland population in two of them (Mexico and Yemen); conversely, the low-altitude location of most metropolises at the time (see Table 4) indicates that the disparities were widespread.
81. For 1950–2001: Instituto Nacional de Estadística, Bolivia (www.ine.gov.bo Accessed 16 May 2008); the lowland provinces are: Santa Cruz, Beni, Pando; for 1847: Dalence 1975, p. 182; in that period the scarcely populated province of Cobija on the Pacific Ocean still belonged to the lowlands.

Two Theories

popularity in individual epochs. Thematically, the most significant of these interpretations for our inquiry can be divided into three groups:

1. Health and Disease: the belief that the 'mountain air' is distinguished by a special quality – and that the mountain population is therefore healthier and stronger than the people down below – is old and extremely widespread. One finds it, for example, in the European encyclopaedias of the thirteenth century, sometimes with reference to much older medical authorities from the Islamic world.[82] The idea grew during the early modern period and further still in the second half of the nineteenth century. With the spread of European imperialism over Africa and Asia, the tropical situation now came increasingly into view. For the colonial lands and colonial elites, 'tropical diseases' became a subject of special importance. Yet, because malaria and other febrile illnesses arose above all in the hot and humid lowlands, and not above a certain altitude, many experts regarded the mountains of these latitudes as particularly suitable areas for settlement. Against this 'deterministic school', there appeared other experts who emphasised additional factors and called attention to the complexity of the medical topography. Disease generally exhibited so many different faces, remarked one influential text in the 1960s, 'that it is usually impossible to attribute one particular expression of it to one particular set of environmental circumstances'.[83] Supporters of this view pointed out that the effects of epidemics were also influenced by settlement density, that certain parts of the population often developed an immunity to endemic illnesses and that it was precisely in the hot and humid lowlands that important diseases such as smallpox lost their virulence.[84]

2. Natural Resources: the English population theorist, Thomas Robert Malthus (1766–1834), was the most prominent in a long series of scholars who called attention to the limitedness of natural mountain resources for agriculture. Malthus did so in an especially radical manner, since this limitation served also to illustrate his general theory, according to which agrarian intensification and demographic growth remained impossible before the introduction of technological innovations. He expressed this idea in the second edition of

---

82. Brunschwig 2005, pp. 103–7.
83. René Dubos: *Man, Medicine, and Environment* (1968), quoted in *The Cambridge World History of Human Disease* 1993, p. 474.
84. Newson 2006; *The Cambridge World History of Human Disease* 1993, above all the articles 'African Trypanosomiasis (Sleeping Sickness)', 'Diseases of Sub-Saharan Africa', 'Diseases of the Americas', 'Malaria', 'Yellow Fever'; in a limited measure, malaria was of course also a phenomenon of the temperate zone (Bruce-Chwatt/ Zulueta 1980).

his 'Essay on the Principle of Population', published in 1803, after travels and much reading about various mountain regions, from Tibet and Turkey across Norway and Switzerland and up to Scotland. His statements about the pastoral agriculture of the Swiss Alps were unequivocal. 'The limits to the population of a country strictly pastoral are strikingly obvious', explained Malthus, since mountain pastures, once filled to capacity with cows, could not be further improved. The main problem in this region arose, in his view, from the availability of hay for winter fodder, which depended in quantity on the provision of manure and this in turn on the keeping of livestock, so that the two factors were mutually limiting. For Malthus, this explained why the population increased during the eighteenth century in the lowlands of Switzerland but not in the mountain areas.[85] He, along with later neo-Malthusians, therefore saw population distribution as conforming above all to the favourability of the natural environment for agriculture.[86]

Jules Blache focused on a different aspect of the environment in his pioneering 1934 study on the relationship between man and mountain in worldwide perspective (see above, Chapter 1.4). Central for him was not only the high-altitude climate of the mountains, which varied with geographical latitude, but also their rugged terrain. According to Blache the mountain relief hindered and raised the price of communication, promoting isolation. It also stood in the way of arable cultivation and for this reason favoured a pastoral way of life. He held the isolation effect to have been less important in an earlier era than in his own time, however, because modern transportation systems were much more expensive and less adaptable, delaying development. Whereas he assigned great significance to the mountains for early humanity, it now seemed that man was turning away from them.[87]

3. Critical Reaction: against pronounced forms of environmental determinism, as advocated especially from the late nineteenth century, dissenting voices arose to emphasise the importance of human activities and historical configurations. One of the most influential was Lucien Febvre, co-founder of the famous French journal, the Annales. In his 1922 *Geographical Introduction to History,* also called *Earth and Human Evolution* in French *[La terre et l'évolution humaine: Introduction géographique à l'histoire],* he turned vehemently against the 'half-arrogant and half-shameful' nature of determinism. According to his

---

85. Malthus 1986 (first 1803–1826), vol. 2, p. 212.
86. See also Netting 1993, pp. 276–81; Viazzo 1989, pp. 42–8.
87. Blache 1934, pp. 163–81.

Two Theories

alternative concept of 'possibilism', environmental resources were only offerings; it was human actors who decided whether and how to put them into effective use. Febvre therefore saw 'nowhere necessity, everywhere possibility' and cited the observation according to which all that affects humankind is 'is coined by chance' ['*frappé de contingence*']. In his commentary on population distribution, he highlighted above all those aspects that were difficult to explain in geographical terms.[88] Later researchers put forward similar arguments. In the 1980s and 1990s, there was even support from some geographers who had specialised in mountain systems.[89] Around that time the anthropologist, Frederic Pryor, submitted the correlation between population density and the favourability of regional agrarian conditions to a global test. He came to the conclusion that environmental potential explained at most ten per cent of variations in agricultural significance and a mere five per cent of variations in population density.[90] As weak as the correlation may have always been, it could be related here to the fact that the distribution of population and cities in the tropics tended more toward higher elevations than in the temperate zones (see above, Chapter 2.1).

As already indicated in this brief overview of the three forms of interpretation, the stance taken by individual authors depended often, though not always, on their position within the scientific field. For this and other reasons the arguments and counter-arguments broke out almost continually, making their periodisation difficult. Conspicuous conjunctures had mostly to do with external political pressure. So in the late nineteenth and early twentieth centuries, colonialism stood beneath the tropical discourse; then, in light of rapid population growth after World War II, the limitedness of resources received emphasis from the neo-Malthusians; this was followed in the 1970s by the politicisation of the environment.[91] If we want to find an appropriate position for our historical analysis, we must pay attention to the dimension of time. Neither the contribution of determinism nor its counter-imitation of 'possibilism' generally poses the questions of how chronological restrictions and

---

88. Febvre 1970 (first 1922), quotes pp. 159, 257, 398 (original French), on population pp. 155–9; his possibilistic concept is limited by the 'great climato-botanical frame conditions', i.e. the geographical zones with a different 'structure of offerings' (pp. 142–51); generally on his theoretical practice: Müller 2003.
89. See Dollfus for the Andes (1991, pp. 16, 21–2, 51, 53, 56, 114, 166); Hewitt for global mountain research (1988, p. 12).
90. Pryor 1986, pp. 883–4 (without considering the cases where agriculture is impossible).
91. Clues to dating e.g. in King 1976, pp. 108–12 (for the ethno-medical debate) and in McCormick 1993 (for the global politicisation of the environment).

changing human activities have impacted on settlement patterns and whether the strength of environmental factors varied over time. Jules Blache stands out as a notable exception. His reference to the change in relations between highlands and lowlands, resulting from new means of transport, is a genuinely historical explanation. I would like to describe two such explanatory models in conclusion.

Two Theories

In recent decades a theoretical approach, which has come to be known as 'path-dependency', has spread throughout various branches of history. Path-dependency, as opposed to context-dependency, emphasises the chronological relationship between phenomena. A specific, possibly 'insignificant' and historically 'coincidental' constellation of phenomena can have a decisive influence on development, by prejudicing a direction forward that will be abandoned later only under strong contextual pressure. This implies, among other things, that synchronic relationships often assumed a suboptimal quality. As for the relationship between human society and the environment, the much cited 'adaptation' may have therefore been in many cases more improvisation and patchwork than a *fait accompli*.[92] In the foregoing investigation of settlement and urbanisation in mountain regions, path-dependency has already been mentioned on several occasions as a possible explanation for spatial distributions and settings, such as the Himalayan city of Shimla and the two high-altitude metropolises of Latin America, La Paz and Mexico City (see Chapter 2.3). So regarded, the situation would have resulted not from 'coincidence' but from an otherwise defined, namely chronological, 'necessity'.

The second explanatory model that seems useful to me has its roots in the lively development debate of the 1960s. With her groundbreaking work on the conditions of agrarian growth, Ester Boserup presented an innovative view of development potential in preindustrial, rural societies. She demonstrated that, on all continents, under the pressure of a growing population, it was often possible to raise land productivity substantially, though this might require great expenditure and even the acceptance of a decline in labour productivity.[93] The aforementioned data on population history now hint that this agrarian growth process represented an option in mountain regions as well, though only up to a

---

92. Tissot/Veyrassat 2002 provide an introduction the discussion of path-dependency in economic history; examples of a similar type of argumentation in Tilly 1992, pp. 54–66 (state formation); Dollfus 1991, pp. 23–6 (spatial formation).

93. Boserup 1993 (1965).

certain level of intensity – eventually, the mountain setting posed an obstacle. In this view, therefore, the handicap exhibited a period-specific character. It developed with greater strength in a second phase than in the first and this reinforcement of disadvantages for growth could set in already well before an eventual industrialisation, thereby influencing its specific form.[94] Thus a multi-phase model presents itself, with variable levels of intensity and correspondingly different relations to environmental conditions.

Conversely, it can hardly be claimed any longer that the historical 'limits to population' in mountain regions were so narrowly drawn as the Malthusian perspective would have them. The above data on demographic growth also raise doubts as to whether the early modern climate deterioration, often called the 'Little Ice Age', actually played much of a role in long-term development. If the climate deterioration had weighed heavily on the population, we would not expect to find a growth trend from the late sixteenth up to the late nineteenth century. In the short term, the influence was undoubtedly much greater. Unfavourable weather conditions could lead to years of harvest failures and other symptoms of crisis, which hit the population hard and left only hope for better times.[95] All in all, we can probably assume a crisis-ridden form of sustainable or at least long-lasting development. For China, Mark Elvin notes, almost paradoxically, that the population pursued ecologically unsustainable patterns of behaviour for three thousand years. Total collapse was repeatedly avoided, he believes, because the population adjusted itself to the crisis situations: a makeshift arrangement of extremely long duration.[96] This and other observations demand that we take a closer look at agriculture in the modern period.

---

94. This in contrast to, for example, Staszewski 1957, pp. 24–51.
95. Historical climate reconstruction is a very active field of research (see the clues in Richards 2003, pp. 58–85 and Price 2006); the climate effects on human societies, however, are still little investigated in detail.
96. Elvin/Ts'ui-jung 1998, p. 41.

~ 3 ~

AGRICULTURE, FAMILY, MOBILITY

3.1 Agriculture

'All farming systems are dynamic', one reads in a global overview by agrarian and developmental experts, since each agricultural system calls for a constant review of environment and technology and makes continual adjustments necessary. In this sense, all the various forms of agriculture could also be considered equally modern: innovation, invention and technology transfer were integral to the management of plants and animals. From a historical standpoint we must undoubtedly concur with this statement, yet it should not be forgotten that the strength of the dynamic also carries weight and that the modern period, in particular, cannot set new standards. The literature speaks of a first as well as a second 'agricultural revolution'. Whereas the first transformation in the early modern period involved the increased use of manual labour, the one that followed, in the context of industrial development starting around 1850, replaced labour with improved technical equipment and machinery.[1] For our purposes, the question arises as to the extent to which the agriculture in mountainous regions participated in these innovations. To that end we will first examine certain framework conditions of the social topography and the general exchange. Agriculture is understood here to include both plant cultivation and animal husbandry. Since the latter took especially interesting forms in mountain regions, it will be treated further in a subsequent chapter.

Verticality and Seasonality

Many languages have special terms for altitude levels or layers with respect to both natural and cultural phenomena. These designations express, each in its own way, differences in the vertical structure of the landscape. When the

---

1. Bairoch 1973; Turner/Brush 1987, p. 21 (quote); Boserup 1981, pp. 114–7, 163–70; Vries 1994; Lains/Pinilla 2009. The 'revolution' metaphor is critically discussed in the recent literature; for the approach adopted here the question is not crucial.

Agriculture

Spanish viceroy of Peru wrote a report on the indigenous work force in the early seventeenth century, he divided it into three groups: 'The one is called the *Yungas*, or those who inhabit the plains and hot valleys; the second are the *Chaupiyungas*, also called *cabazada* in Castilian, who live in the higher regions where the climate is temperate and tends to be cool rather than warm; the remainder are the mountain people (*serranos*), born and raised in the cold regions.' The viceroy thus identified the native people according to the vertical levels of the South American landscape, using a mixture of indigenous (*Yunga, Chaupiyunga*) and Spanish (*cabezada, serrano*) expressions.[2] Popular also in the Andean and Mexican colonial areas was the three-part Spanish terminology: *tierras calientes, tierras templadas, tierras frías* (hot, temperate or cold lands). Alexander von Humboldt, who often thematised the stratification of altitude following his South American journey from 1799 to 1804, employed these indigenous and Spanish concepts as fixed references. With the publication of his work, Humboldt was able to awaken among western elites of the early Romantic era a burgeoning interest in and enthusiasm for the worldwide exploration of the vertical dimension.[3]

In the nineteenth and twentieth centuries, the study of verticality then split off into various scientific disciplines. From cultural geography and anthropology, John Frödin and John V. Murra should be named here. Frödin, the Swedish cultural geographer, set out in the 1920s to investigate the Alpiculture [*Alpwirtschaft*] of Central Europe and in 1940/1 he published a voluminous work containing his numerous studies based on field research, the literature and primary sources. His Alpiculture concept included not only the high summer pastures but also the arable fields and meadows, which bound the mountain population to fixed settlements and provided cows with winter fodder. So defined, the concept involved an overall complex that could be differentiated from two other pastoral forms: in nomadism there was no attachment to place as in Alpiculture and transhumance was based on a combination of high pastures in the summer and lower ones in winter, without stall-feeding.[4]

The ethnohistorian, John V. Murra, became famous in the years around 1970 with his model of 'vertical control over a maximum of ecological levels' ['*control vertical de un máximo de pisos ecológicos*']. The model referred to the

---

2. Beltrán y Rózpide 1921, p. 236 (original Spanish).
3. Troll 1968, p. 15; see also above, Chapter 1.3.
4. Frödin 1940/41; nomadism can also link high-lying summer pastures to low-lying winter pastures; in order to distinguish it from transhumance, one has to add social criteria – see below, Chapter 3.2.

Andes in a particular historical situation, namely in transition from the Inca Empire to Spanish rule. In contrast to the European model, the central focus of this American model was not on animal husbandry but rather plant cultivation, which was practiced at various altitude levels in the Andes and which, together with pastoralism at the highest elevations, gave rise to complex transactions. The model of vertical control implied a subsistence economy and non-commercial transactions. Since it possessed an ideological point that accommodated the indigenous self-assessment, it also strongly stimulated the research. Following Murra, as well as independently from him, later Andean studies documented above all the diversity in vertical forms of production and exchange.[5]

Since the 1970s, anthropologists from the circle of 'cultural ecology' have also concerned themselves with the question of global similarities in mountain agriculture. They compared the models available in the literature (such as Alpiculture and vertical control) and proposed new concepts of their own, referred to as 'mixed mountain agriculture' or 'montane production strategy'.[6] Yet the climate differences of tropical and non-tropical mountain regions posed a problem for the anthropological models of verticality. This is because the mountains of the tropics experience pronounced temperature variations throughout the day but barely any seasonal fluctuations, thus exhibiting general stability throughout the year. In Quito, which, as the capital of Ecuador, stands almost directly on the equator, the average seasonal temperature variation amounts to less than one degree Celsius. Whereas patterns of vertical mobility in non-tropical mountains can be related to the seasonal rise and fall in temperature and snow levels, there are no such fluctuations in the tropics. There, the *tierras calientes*, *templadas* and *frias* remain practically the same year round.[7]

Nevertheless, vertically interwoven and integrated forms of agriculture can be found nearly everywhere. A 1966 survey of human geography, which admittedly provided only rough estimates yet relied on global research and not

---

5. Murra 2002, above all pp. 83–139 (three articles from 1972–1985); from the copious debate: Orlove/Guillet 1985; Browman 1990; Gil Montero 2004; Assadourian 2006.

6. Rhoades/Thompson 1975; Guillet 1983, Orlove/Guillet 1985; other attempts at generalisation have been made by German mountain geographers – see, for example, Grötzbach 1988; Ehlers/Kreutzmann 2000 are right in criticising the ethnocentric tendencies expressed in the unreflecting generalisation of certain notions (above all those of European Alpiculture or *Alpwirtschaft*); on a general level, they complain about a standstill in the classification debate.

7. Troll 1941, 1955, 1968; Troll was particularly efficient in investigating and communicating the differences between seasonal and daily mountain climates – see above, Chapter 1.4.

Agriculture

simply conceptual reflections, distinguished 25 economic 'structural types' for high-altitude regions. With only two exceptions, all types were entwined with lower-lying levels of the cultural landscape, whether in the form of nomadism, transhumance, Alpiculture or some other agricultural form. The two exceptions involved small isolated societies in the high elevations of Southeast Asia and East Africa, whose economies were based above all on hunting, gathering and 'shifting cultivation'. They maintained no systematic economic ties to the lowland population.[8] This can be interpreted as a clue that vertical integration often accompanied the intensification of agriculture. Where the mountain slopes were used in regular, short intervals of time, the likelihood increased that the individual altitude levels would find different agricultural uses for different crops and livestock. This in turn may have been a prerequisite for the development of vertically organised economies or, as German researchers expressed it, 'graduated systems' [*Staffelsystemen*].[9]

Beyond that, however, many additional circumstances played a role, so that a great variety of systems can often be observed even in a limited area. In the tropical and subtropical Andes, where seasonal temperature variations are hardly noticeable, important grounds for synchronous mobility fell away. Here the vertical mobility of animals had a group-specific or familial character and each followed its own particular schedule. This was determined by access to grazing rights and, especially in the dry southern areas, by the distribution of rainfall and humidity.[10] The situation remained relatively open in the Andes' important plant-growing sector as well. Of course the major plant-growing regions sat at various levels of altitude, which gave rise to a certain exchange by way of political or commercial integration. Yet the same crops could also be grown at higher and lower elevations. So in the Bolivian highlands the major zone for growing maize extended up to around 3,200 metres, with a diminished level of production reaching at least another 500 metres higher. The primary cultivation area for potatoes lay between 3,500 to and 4,000 metres but the tuber was planted from much lower elevations up to a good 4,500 metres.[11]

---

8. Hambloch 1966, Appendix 9 (fig. 42) and pp. 68, 77, 100; on Hambloch see also above, Chapter 2.1; for South-east Asia he names examples from Thailand, Laos and Vietnam; relatively isolated tribal mountain societies existed there in further regions too – see Chapter 2.2.

9. Uhlig 1984, for example, uses the term for his survey of complex vertical patterns of the Himalaya; on the relationship between intensity and mobility also Skeldon 1985, p. 242.

10. Browman 1990; Inamura 2002; Gil Montero 2008, pp. 221–6.

11. Eriksen 1984, 206; generally Dollfus 1991, p. 56.

Agriculture, Family, Mobility

How a particular system of 'vertical control' expressed itself and developed further thus depended in large measure on political and commercial factors.[12]

New Plants and Animals

The transfer of plants and animals into new areas belonged to the important mechanisms of change in regional forms of agriculture. With the institutionalisation of transatlantic contacts at the start of the modern era, this transfer increased in tempo and importance. The useful flora and fauna of the 'New World' differed sharply from those of the 'Old World'. Columbus returned from his first voyage to the Caribbean in 1492–3 with kernels of maize and other exotic goods and more and more ships soon crossed the Atlantic in both directions, loaded with cargoes of all kinds. Thus began the process that would be characterised in a now classic book as the 'Columbian Exchange' and, after only a few decades, Africa and Asia were drawn in as well.[13] In the details, the geographical diffusion of plants and animals and their introduction to new regions is often difficult to reconstruct, since it could follow many different channels and because biological and linguistic variability complicate the identification of individual organisms. Yet in broad outline, the 'exchange' is commonly known: from the two Americas, for example, maize, potatoes and sweet potatoes came to other continents; in the opposite direction, various types of grain (wheat, barley, rice) and, above all, a series of livestock (cattle, horses, sheep, pigs) arrived in the 'New World'. The changes thereby set in motion concerned the mountain regions as much as others.

The change was, for the most part, rather specific and at first remarkably slow. In a few regions of Europe, plants from the Americas came into use in the following generations but this step took much longer in most places. Maize, for example, was described as early as 1539 in 'herb books' and before long the plant was well known in medical and botanical circles everywhere. It was a good grain 'for cooking and for making bread', according to a South Tyrolean topography from 1600. Yet the rapid diffusion of maize began in many places only around 1750. The potato knew a similarly delayed career, which was particularly relevant for the mountain regions, since it originated in the Andes and could be grown at high elevations. Peasants in the Alps and other European mountain regions introduced potatoes for the most part only later, starting in the late eighteenth and nineteenth centuries. The great time differential between

---

12. Among anthropologists of the cultural ecology direction, Orlove and Guillet (1985) have particularly advocated the consideration of such factors.
13. Sauer 1969, pp. 153–5; Humboldt 1836–1839, vol. 4, pp. 217–30; Crosby 1972.

Agriculture

botanical availability and agricultural diffusion calls for an explanation that goes beyond the cultural rejection of foreign plants. Obviously the rejection could be overcome quickly when the situation called for it. An economic point is therefore important: the yields from maize and potatoes clearly exceeded those of the usual grains, yet both crops often required a disproportionate increase in labour input, so that land productivity rose while labour productivity fell. The population growth from the eighteenth century may have made this step in intensification meaningful for the first time in many regions.[14]

In China the acceptance of useful plants from the Americas seems to have proceeded differently, insofar as it often accompanied the early modern 'opening' of mountain regions (see above, Chapter 2.2). A 1574 description of the empire's south-western Yunnan Province mentioned the production of maize in six prefectures and two administrative districts . It was grown here as well as in the neighbouring provinces by the mountain tribes and by the Han Chinese, who soon pushed ever further into the hills and mountainous regions. It was this expansion that led eventually to the proliferation of maize cultivation. The second half of the sixteenth century also saw the first reference to the sweet potato, which later rose to become a staple food in China, whereas the potato was apparently not documented until the seventeenth century. Then, in the nineteenth century it became one of the most important crops grown in the high mountainous areas.[15] Parallel to these innovations, the Chinese peasants produced new rice strains with shorter growing seasons, which allowed them to harvest multiple crops per year and grow rice successfully at higher elevations. The varieties originated in Indonesia and when introduced in the eleventh century they required around a hundred days to mature (from the time seedlings were planted in the field). The growing period was then reduced by the sixteenth century to fifty or sixty days, and in the nineteenth century to an even shorter thirty to forty days. At the same time, the altitude limit for the land- and labour-intensive rice cultivation in South-west China rose to 2,700 metres.[16]

On the two American continents, the transfer of plants and animals was perhaps even more revolutionary in its effects than in the aforementioned showplaces of the 'Columbian Exchange'. The transfer was carried there by the movement of settlers and the rapidly growing animal herds soon claimed

---

14. Mathieu 2009, pp. 65–8; Steinke 1997; Mathis 1996, pp. 235–8; Braudel 1992, vol. 1, pp. 158–72; Salaman 1985, above all pp. 142–58.
15. Ho 1959, pp. 186–92; Lombard-Salmon 1972, pp. 181–2.
16. Ho 1959, pp. 169–76; Needham 1991; Xiao-Gan 1984.

extraordinarily large ranges. From the beginning, the Spaniards introduced cattle, horses, sheep, pigs and other livestock. As the conquistadors assumed mastery, especially over the mostly high-altitude stretches of land where the indigenous population was relatively dense, there arose numerous conflicts over land use and even, in some cases, environmental degradation through overgrazing. The subjects in the viceroyalties of New Spain and Peru therefore had to adjust not only to the new rulers but also to their animal companions, though, over time, the services these animals provided turned out to have benefits for native people as well. Since vast stretches of land across the American double continent were settled only sparsely, some of the recently imported animals managed to free themselves and roamed wild across the land. One such sparsely populated region was the Pampas, a gigantic plain in modern-day Argentina. In 1619 the governor of Buenos Aires reported that 80,000 head of cattle could be taken annually for their hides without diminishing the wild herds. Later, the free-ranging cattle between Chaco and Patagonia were estimated at several million, 'in numbers comparable to those of the buffalo on the Great Plains in their heyday'.[17]

Land Use Systems

According to modern surveys, almost all systems of land use identified in the agrarian research are found in mountain regions worldwide and this seems to be nothing new. Based on a global overview map, similar observations can already be made in the period around 1500: the map distinguishes five stages of land use, from 'hunter, fisher, gatherer' to 'cultures with high population densities and the plough' – for each stage, there are also examples from mountainous regions.[18] We can assume, therefore, a long-term coexistence of various systems. Since 1500 there have appeared numerous changes and transitions on a regional level that are indeed extremely relevant on the whole, yet there has been no uniform transformation on a global scale. The change was spatially differentiated. In order to gain a view of the range of agricultural systems and the modalities of change, we will consider two criteria here: the intensity of land use and the quality of technology.

---

17. Crosby 1972, pp. 75–95; Crosby 2004, pp. 171–94, quote p. 178; Richards 2005, pp. 360–6; Gil Montero 2008, pp. 213–21.
18. According to Huddleston 2003 (p. 15), one finds today in mountain regions worldwide about 42 out of 44 differentiated 'farming systems'; on the general question of classification: Turner/Brush 1987; Ruthenberg 1983; the 1500 map stems from Gordon W. Hewes and is reproduced and commentated in Braudel 1992, vol. 1, pp. 56–64.

Agriculture

The intensity of land use is measured by the 'frequency of cropping' or the number of harvests from a given area within a certain period. A four-part classification distinguishes between the following systems: 1. long-fallow (a few crops followed by six or more fallow years); 2. short-fallow (one or two crops followed by a few fallow years); 3. annual cropping (fallow limited to a few months); and 4. multicropping (two or more crops per year from the same field without fallow).[19] This sequence affects the production of food crops and stands in relation to population density: as a rule, extensive land use systems with long fallow periods are found in areas of low population density and vice versa. Producing food for animals requires considerably more space, yet it too can exhibit variations in intensity (as with hunting, pasturing and stall-feeding). Since population density also plays a role in this, the two types of production are, up to a certain point, connected. Ester Boserup, whom I follow here, defines, for example, the following pairs: long-fallow agriculture/hunting or pastoralism; short-fallow agriculture/livestock with local pastures; annual cropping/intensive animal husbandry with stall-feeding. These pairs give only typical patterns of mixed agriculture. Special environmental conditions and other grounds may account for substantial deviations, which is of particular interest in mountain regions (see below, Chapter 3.2).

The second criterion for land use systems is the quality of technology. With a view toward major sources of energy, we can distinguish between three systems. They are based on: 1. human labour power; 2. the addition of draft animals to pull and carry loads; and 3. modern machines. The quality of technology is related to the intensity of land use and population density as well. For example, there are indications that the introduction of the plough with draft animals often took the place of hoeing and manual labour, especially during the transition from long-fallow to short-fallow systems. This transition required greater control over the spread of grass and weeds, for which the plough was far better suited. Meanwhile, ploughing was facilitated in this phase by changes in the landscape (field clearance) and by the expanded basis for forage (grass propagation).[20] So much for the general conditions – the following two examples from Asia and Africa may serve to illustrate historical land use systems with differing intensities and technologies.

Mindoro is a tropical island in the Philippines, which covers an area of over 10,000 square kilometres. In significant part it consists of mountain regions, reaching 2,580 metres at the highest point. The Spaniards incorpo-

---

19. Simplified following Boserup 1981, p. 19 and Boserup 1993, pp. 15–6.
20. Boserup 1993, p. 24; Boserup 1981, pp. 24, 48–9.

rated this island into their world empire, starting in 1570, and this resulted in a series of early landscape descriptions. In addition, there is an anthropological study on the old-settled population of the Mangyans that pays much attention to agriculture. From the mid-seventeenth century there was an increasing dichotomy on Mindoro between these 'tribal' mountain people and the Christian lowland population. The Mangyans were repeatedly overwhelmed and forced time and again to retreat to the region's most inaccessible areas. Then, in the nineteenth century, there came a massive demographic change. Whereas the lowland population in 1810 was still less than the number of Mangyans, by 1990 it surpassed them by more than ten times (783,000 to around 75,000).[21]

Throughout the surveyable past, the Mangyans of the mountain regions practiced shifting cultivation (slash-and-burn agriculture). To that end they periodically put new fields into use by clearing select forest parcels, in other words: the under-storey was removed, the larger trees felled, the rest dried and burned. In these fields they planted tubers (above all sweet potatoes, cassava, yams and taro), which enabled continuous harvests, as well as certain types of grain (rice, maize), which were ripe and ready to harvest at a specific time. The most important tools were the machete, axe and dibble. On the whole, this extensive form of mountain agriculture seems to have remained productive for a long time and to have required relatively little work. Yet a rising population could shorten the fallow periods to such an extent that the system would become susceptible to crises. In the twentieth century the Mangyans' fallow periods usually lasted only six years. Whereas other parts of the Philippines went over quite early to intensive rice cultivation and terracing, agriculture in the mountains of Mindoro was, for various reasons, in decline.[22]

In the highlands of Ethiopia in Northeast Africa, there dominated a form of agriculture known in the historical research as the 'ox-plow complex'. The northern part of the country had long employed the scratch plough, drawn mostly by teams of oxen (see Plate 11). At the centre of this agrarian system stood grain cultivation, especially the native teff variety. The 'Roof of Africa' consists of a plateau averaging 2,500 metres in height, with individual mountains and rock formations rising up to a good 4,500 metres. In the many regional

---

21. Helbling 1996, pp. 7–40, 288–90, 316.
22. Helbling 1996, above all pp. 111–47; Scott 2009, pp. 162, 192; the fallow periods with shifting cultivation in South-east Asia lasted twice as long on average and could go up to 20 or 40 years – see Helbling 1996, p. 132 and Roder 1997, p. 4; on terrace culture in Southeast Asia and the Philippines: Spencer/Hale 1961; in Mindoro, the development capacity seems to have been diminished above all by World War II, which set off major flight to the mountains.

Agriculture

languages, a distinction is almost always made between three or four general altitude and climate zones.[23] A Portuguese envoy who visited the region in the 1520s stated: 'It seems to me in all the world there is not so populous a country, and so abundant in corn, and herds of innumerable cattle.' For the early modern period we have no precise figures but there are many clues that the demographic density was in fact considerable and the land use quite intensive. The fields were often cultivated in short-fallow rhythm, sometimes irrigated and also partially terraced. Certain pastures were reserved for cattle and the forests were pushed back to small enclaves. With the growth of agriculture, the highland population had to strengthen its livestock exchange with the extensively cultivated lowland regions. Interestingly, the ox-plough complex of the northern regions spread only slowly – roughly parallel to state expansion – into the southern parts of the country. The custom of manual hoeing was relinquished there only under specific circumstances. As the political centre shifted to the South, however, and as Addis Ababa, the capital city founded in the 1880s, grew into a large city during the twentieth century, it was in the South that further development occurred. In the urban supply region, the peasants switched over particularly early to a system of annual cultivation.[24]

Generally, on the steeper slopes, the advancing intensification often compelled the construction of terraces. This became particularly important in the transition from long-fallow to short-fallow systems with the plough. Hence the transition in mountain regions was, for the most part, associated with a much higher rise in expenditure than what was usual elsewhere. According to a 1961 overview map, the terraced landscape stretched all around the globe and belonged, as stressed by the author, to the 'significant marks of human modification of the surface of the earth'.[25] In a few regions the installations were extremely old and in modern times they would be simply used and maintained, whereas in other places terracing came only later, in some cases much later. Agronomists in the twentieth century often recommended terraces as a means against soil erosion. The Food and Agriculture Organization (FAO), founded in 1945, as well as numerous private and public initiatives, promoted terracing with the goal of preventing the widely feared increase in soil erosion. Much attention was paid to East Africa, from Ethiopia to the South, an area where

---

23. McCann 1995, p. 28; Burga 2004, p. 390; a geographical survey in Matthies 1997.
24. McCann 1995, p. 3 and pp. 42, 56–57, 202, 209–10, 221 (forms of fallow); McCann 1999, pp. 79–107 and Boerma 2006 (forest issues).
25. Spencer/Hale 1961, pp. 1, 33; Velthuizen 2007, pp. 13–5; for the relationship to intensity: Boserup 1981, p. 45; an illustrative example with Dangwal 2009, pp. 28–9.

hoeing still prevailed and where the population was increasing rapidly. Whereas some presumed the worst, others pointed to regions such as in Kenya, where long-term environmental improvements had been won with terracing and other methods. In Rwanda, the densely populated 'Land of a Thousand Hills', there was a mass mobilisation in support of erosion control, encouraged by the personal collaboration of that country's president. Another UN organisation, UNESCO, later became interested as well. It admitted individual terraced landscapes into the inventory of 'World Heritage' sites – as in 1995, with the rice terraces of the northern Philippines, which had long been among the most famous landscapes of this type in the world.[26]

Obstacles to Development

Against the background of demographic growth, the intensification of agriculture therefore proceeded in many areas of the world through the increased input of manual labour. This led to higher surface yields, sometimes in such a measure that one can speak of an actual 'agricultural revolution'. Then around 1850, with the onset of industrialisation, there began in some western countries a second, technology-driven agricultural revolution. Whereas the growing scarcity of land was compensated for by labour in the early modern period, the growing scarcity of labour was replaced since the nineteenth century by improved, industrially manufactured technology. As previously mentioned, it involved the transition from land use systems based on mid-level technology (human and animal labour power) to systems with modern machines.[27] This raises the question of how far agriculture in mountain regions participated in these developments.

In general, it can be assumed that participation was a realistic and in many cases realised option up to a certain point in development. In the later stages, however, environmental factors carried greater weight in mountain settings and became real obstacles. It cannot be overemphasised that the mountain setting did not pose a problem for agriculture from the beginning and in all places. As we have seen in this chapter, systems of land use in mountain regions exhibited various cropping frequencies, including multiple harvests without fallow periods. Sometimes the mountainous conditions were especially favour-

---

26. McCann 1999, above all pp. 11–2, 66–75; Tiffen 1994, pp. 5–12, 67–75, 178–201; Ford 1999, p. 58; Spencer/Hale 1961, p 1.

27. See above, note 1.

Agriculture

able, as for irrigation or fertilisation. In addition, the harvest yields for grain and tubers were by no means necessarily small.[28]

Yet, with the increasing intensity of agriculture, the influence of certain environmental factors grew. An example from the Pakistani Gilgit district in the Karakoram may serve to illustrate. As in other places, the possibility of double annual yields in Gilgit was determined by temperature-based sowing and harvesting dates for grain. According to an agronomic analysis from 1982–1984, the latest sowing date for maize and other summer grains at 1,200 metres fell between 12 July and 5 August; at 2,000 metres, the date moved up to between 8 and 30 June. At 2,000 metres, winter grains (barley and local wheat varieties) could not be harvested earlier than 20 June to 17 July. This small window left open the possibility, therefore, of two annual harvests from the same fields.

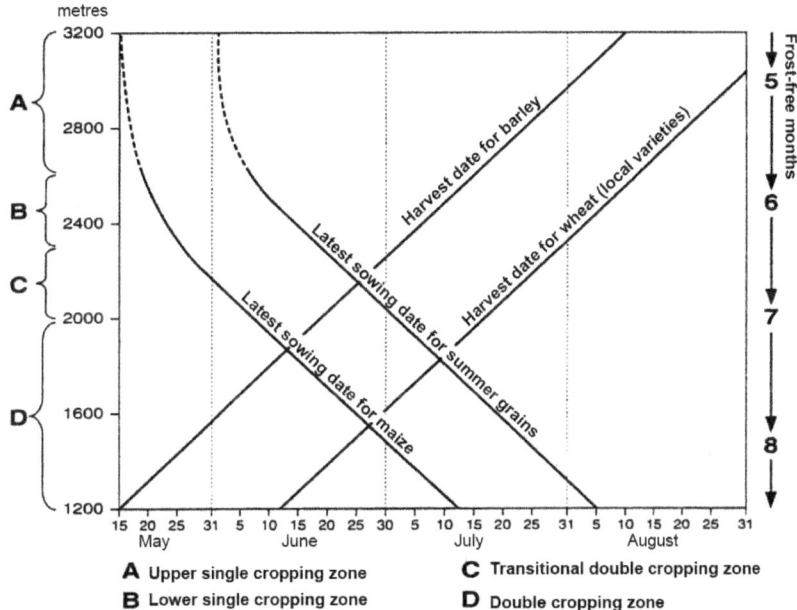

Figure 1: Single and Multiple Cropping Zones by Altitude in Karakoram (Gilgit), 1983.
Sources: Whiteman 1988, p. 66 and Ehlers 1995, p. 113.

In Figure 1, this region up to 2,000 metres is designated as a double cropping zone (D). Above it lies a transitional zone (C), up to around 2,300 metres,

---

28. In the European Alps, contrary to common opinion, one does not find systematic differences in yields between high and low altitudes before 1900 (Mathieu 2009, p. 60); the question can only be decided empirically and should be examined from case to case.

where agronomists no longer classified double cropping as reliable. Higher still are the lower and upper zones of single annual cropping (B and A). A difference of only 100 metres in altitude, according to agronomists' observations, delayed the grain harvest by five days.[29] Such obstacles could be partially overcome through the production of faster-maturing varieties and other precautionary measures and the situation varied in the details from place to place. In principle, however, the shorter growing season in high mountain settings was a factor for all crops in both seasonal and non-seasonal climates and this limitation had a much stronger influence over intensive land uses than extensive ones.[30]

The mechanisation of agriculture brought further situational disadvantages to mountain regions. This second agricultural revolution grew out of interactions with the industrialisation in western nations (above all England, the United States and Germany). The rising demand for food supplies and labour power, as well as the new offering of industrially manufactured machines, led in the late nineteenth and twentieth centuries to decisive changes. Of course there had long been certain technical improvements – but, from around 1850, with the emergence of factories producing farm machinery, the technology developed an increasing momentum. In quick succession there now appeared new resources for the cultivation, harvesting and transportation of produce to market, at first on the basis of draft horses, then with steam power and finally with internal-combustion engines.[31] Many machines were too large and heavy to be used on rough terrain. Even later, when special machines became available for mountain agriculture, technological advances led to a selection process that generally offered worse prospects in mountainous regions than on level ground. In some of the steeper areas, the mechanisation of labour proved to be difficult, expensive, or impossible.[32]

The technological selection also created a fault line between the leading industrial nations and the rest of the world. In some cases, the mountain regions were disadvantaged in a downright ideological manner. The centrally planned economy of the Soviet Union, especially in an early phase, concentrated

---

29. Whiteman 1988, p. 66; Ehlers 1995, p. 113.
30. For the 'altitude fallow' (grain cultivation only every second year) and for the relationship of grass growth to altitude, see the indications in Mathieu 2009, pp. 55–6, 59–60; a global view on altitudinal boundaries for grain cultivation in Hambloch 1966, p. 90; generally, on constraints to mountain agriculture also Huddleston 2003, pp. 17–9.
31. Herrmann 1985; Lains/Pinilla 2009.
32. An example in Darbellay 1984, pp. 423–4; increased expenditure could also result from the variegated topography, which required special equipment to cultivate only in some parts.

Animal Husbandry

solely on the flat land. In consequence there was almost no mechanisation of mountain agriculture, which came to be openly discussed and criticised following destalinisation in 1956; still, significant improvements did not appear until much later.[33] For many mountainous regions of Asia, Africa and Latin America, it was simply the prevailing market conditions that precluded or seriously delayed mechanisation. Furthermore, the rugged terrain contributed in yet another way: it made the construction of modern transportation systems more difficult and expensive, thereby hindering general market formation. In this case, too, the increasing demands of the technological culture lent greater weight to environmental factors.[34]

3.2 ANIMAL HUSBANDRY

Agriculture normally included a variety of livestock, such as cattle, sheep, goats, camels, buffalo, horses, mules, donkeys, pigs and poultry. Many of them arrived in new regions over the course of the early modern exchange process and soon they could be found all around the globe. Up until the mid-twentieth century, a few animals of the mountain regions formed remarkable exceptions: llamas and alpacas in the Andes, yaks in Central Asia.[35] As with plant cultivation, animal husbandry could also be practiced at extremely different levels of intensity. For the most part, the two spheres were functionally entwined and bound within the same dynamic in terms of the use of space. From this, one can distinguish – as indicated in the previous chapter – between certain pairs: long-fallow agriculture with hunting or pastoralism; short-fallow agriculture with livestock raised on local pastures; annual cropping and intensive animal husbandry with stall-feeding; multicropping with livestock restricted by the availability of resources. These various connections between cropping systems and animal husbandry are to be understood only as typical sequences of mixed agriculture. Specific environmental conditions and other factors could encourage different developments, combinations and processes of specialisation.[36]

Particular developments occurred specifically in mountain regions because they often possessed vast areas with marginal growing conditions. They were well suited for space-consuming forms of stock-raising, which were of

---

33. Radvanyi 1984, pp. 224, 227.
34. This aspect received early emphasis from Blache 1934, pp. 166–8 (see above, Chapter 2.4); an empirical investigation for four countries in Huddleston 2003, pp. 20–1.
35. Galaty/Johnson 1990, p. 11; Barfield 1993; Scholz 1995, pp. 51–112.
36. Boserup 1981, pp. 17–8, 22–3, 44–6.

Agriculture, Family, Mobility

great importance in many regions.[37] In fact, a survey from the mid-twentieth century shows that the cattle density per productive area at that time was disproportionately large in many mountainous regions. It was above the global average in the Mexican highlands, in European, Mediterranean and East African mountains, as well as in numerous Asian and Oceanian mountain regions, from Turkey across the Himalayas, to Japan and New Zealand. Yet the survey also reveals that the range in variation was quite substantial. Whereas each of the named mountain regions had numbers in the order of 10–25, or even 25–50 cattle units per square kilometre, there were others – especially in arid regions – exhibiting only a few units.[38]

The most important step in the intensification of animal husbandry was the transition from pasturing to stall-feeding. The conversion of pastureland into meadows and other fields had a space-saving effect but dramatically increased the amount of work: instead of merely watching over the pastures, it required the laborious production of forage crops and continuous animal care. Under preindustrial conditions, such advances in intensification often ensued against the background of a rising population and led to a scissor effect with respect to productivity. While the surface productivity increased with the intensification of land use, labour productivity often declined, because the generated yields did not rise in similar measure as the required effort. The older, extensive forms of land use offered in other words a better 'return on labour' and, for this reason, they were retained as long as the available land resources allowed (see above, Chapter 2.4). This observation helps us also in the assessment of the pastoral economy: pastoralism in mountain regions may seem archaic in the eyes of modern agricultural reformers, but its labour-saving rationality made it an extraordinarily long-lived mode of production.[39] In the next section we will illustrate the development of pastoralism with examples of nomadism and transhumance, followed by a consideration of the transition to stall-feeding.

---

37. Generally on pastoralism and on mountain pastoralism: Galaty/Johnson 1990; Barfield 1993; Khazanov 1994; Scholz 1995; Ehlers/Kreutzmann 2000; Gil Montero/Mathieu/Singh 2010.

38. Hambloch 1966, p. 89 and ill. 39 in appendix 6; in detail, the figures require precaution (due to the difficulty of delimiting the productive areas and other possible sources of error).

39. See also Galaty/Johnson 1990, pp. 2, 16–7, 26, 30 on the relatively high labour productivity of pastoralism; however, their indicator of intensity (number of animals per person in agriculture) is problematic, since it is strongly influenced by the prevailing quota of animal husbandry in the agrarian sector; even the authors point out that the indicator measures above all the degree of pastoral specialisation (pp. 5, 17).

Animal Husbandry

Mountain Nomadism, Transhumance

Measured in terms of residence, nomadism was, as a rule, the most mobile form of pastoralism. It comprised entire social groups who drove their herds across spatially dispersed grazing areas, set up temporary shelters there and broke them down again. Historically, it was especially important in the Eurasian and African arid regions that extended from Mongolia to East and West Africa. One can subdivide nomadism according to the type of migration and distinguish horizontal and vertical forms. To mountain nomadism belonged not only vertical but also horizontal mobility, which took place on the high plateaus.[40] The example I have chosen here concerns Kyrgyzstan in Central Asia, where nomadic pastoralism played an exceptionally important role and for long periods of history determined nearly the entire economic and social structure. Kyrgyzstan consists for the most part of mountainous areas: in the North it borders on the vast Kazakh Steppe and to the East and South there extend the spurs of the Tian Shan and Pamir mountains, with peak elevations of over 7,000 metres. The source material for the historical reconstruction of Kyrgyz nomadism is not straightforward, yet on the basis of early ethnographic descriptions and other evidence, its contours can be discerned for the period before 1900.[41]

The Kyrgyz made their living in former times from horses, sheep, goats, camels and a few cattle. Many followed a migration pattern, with different feeding areas for winter, summer and transitional periods. The winter camps were established at lower elevations and in sheltered places with wind protection. Horses could be kept on snow-covered pastures, since they were able to reach the grass using their hooves; other animals required grazing areas, which could be found perhaps on south-facing slopes, where the grass was clear or only thinly covered with snow. In summertime the animals were driven into the mountains where they stayed for several months, this at a distance of up to 200 kilometres and at elevations of up to 3,500 metres. The spring and autumn pastures were found between the winter and summer locations and were often identical. Each group had its grazing claims and migration routes, passed down from generation to generation. These groups comprised mainly families who shared a common ancestor. Depending on the economic or political situation, they could disperse or join together in large yurt settlements. The most difficult point in the year came during the winter months, a time

---

40. Schlee 2005, pp. 17–26; Scholz 1995, appendix 1; Scholz 2001, p. 10,651.
41. On the significance of pastoralism in this region see e.g. Khazanov in Kaufmann 2000, p. 15.

when the animals often suffered from hunger and sometimes perished in large numbers. 'After a cold and harsh winter, moving to the spring pastures meant a real holiday for all nomads', stated a report that emphasised in addition how the arrival at the summer pastures in the mountains was eagerly anticipated and celebrated with great festivity. The well-known Kyrgyz author, Tschingis Aitmatow, experienced such a summer encampment (*Dschailoo*) in his early childhood, which he describes in a colourful autobiographical text.[42]

As mobile as the Kyrgyz yurt dwellers were, their political history also fluctuated greatly. The 'hordes', which were wide-ranging yet strongly personalised and focused on military goals, could be found from the sixteenth century in this mountain region and on the steppes to the North. Over the course of the modern period there came a series of attacks and annexations, first from warrior bands out of the West (in the seventeenth century), then from the East (end of the eighteenth century) and finally from the North with the incorporation into Tzarist Russia (second half of the nineteenth century). All these attacks and attempts at political control provoked native resistance. A political centre arose in the 1870s with a Russian military settlement, which, under the Bolshevik regime in the 1920s and 1930s, became the capital city of the newly formed Kyrgyz Socialist Soviet Republic – it is known today as Bishkek. Starting in the Tzarist period, the land's nomadic pastoralism underwent a painful, sometimes dramatic and abrupt process of change. At first, a multitude of Russian settlers came to Kyrgyzstan and established residence at the lower elevations, claiming the land for themselves, which exacerbated the already difficult problem of winter pasture. Then, in 1930, inspired by western ideas, Stalinist forced collectivisation and forced settlement were put in place and, before long, the population was faced with entirely new circumstances. No matter how these measures and their long-term results may have appeared, in the shorter term this massive intervention led to a famine of catastrophic proportions: an extremely large number of people and animals lost their lives.[43]

A famous example of the system of transhumance, the history of which is particularly well documented and researched, comes from the power centre of the Spanish Kingdom in early modern Castile. As in the previous Central Asian case, the Castilian sheep transhumance connected the mountains with the lowland regions. Instead of being carried out by families and comprehensive social formations, however, it was usually performed by specialised herders who

---

42. Barfield 1993, pp. 136–45; Emeljanenko 1994, quote p. 40; Kreutzmann 1995; Farrington 2005; Aitmatov 1998, pp. 24–39.
43. Krader 1966; Olcott 1987; Shayakhmetov 2006.

Animal Husbandry

served as wage labourers for the sedentary animal owners. This meant that they could often rely on certain stable infrastructures.

By 1500, the three major attributes of this itinerant form of animal husbandry were clearly developed: the migratory routes, the political organisation and the special breed of merino sheep. In the summer, the herds lingered in the mountains of the North. As autumn approached they were led down to the villages, to graze on the stubble of the harvested grain fields. Then, along with the shepherds, they made the long march of up to 800 kilometres into the southern lowland regions, only to set out again come spring on the return trip to the northern mountains. Per 1,000 sheep, the owners generally counted on five shepherds and a few horses to transport the most important equipment. Large proprietors accumulated up to 20,000 sheep or more. They were organized in the 'Honoured Council of the Mesta' [*Honrado Concejo de la Mesta*], an influential association established in the later Middle Ages under the protection of the king. The council sustained an advantageous political-legal framework and supported the settlement of numerous conflicts, sparked by the passage of gigantic herds across the agricultural regions. The crown had a fiscal interest in transhumance because the merino sheep provided wool of excellent quality, which dominated the European market for centuries and represented Castile's most important export product.[44]

At the high point of this Castilian export industry in the sixteenth century, and even more by the eighteenth, the land supported several million transhumant sheep. Still, they formed only a relatively small portion of the total livestock population, let alone agriculture and the economy overall. Here we can allude simply to the numerous sheep raised on local pastures, which possessed a lesser quality of wool and the cattle production that thrived especially in the humid North. The less conspicuous, but greater, part of the economy consisted therefore of the 'sedentary' sectors, which were relatively subsistence-oriented and based on regional markets, providing the society and military power of the kingdom with a stable framework. For various reasons, sheep transhumance plunged into crisis in the second half of the eighteenth century and in the end it survived only in a starkly altered form: with the rising population and increasing intensification of agriculture, available grazing areas became more scarce as well as expensive; the peasants, traditionally keen to protect their land, set themselves energetically against the sheep and now obtained additional support from the modern state and economic theory of the West, which spoke of

---

44. Sanz 1994; Romero 2006; Collantes 2010; generally on (historical) systems of transhumance, e.g. Rinschede 1984; Braudel 1995; Laffont 2006.

a liberal order of property ownership and fixed spatial relations; finally, in the international market, the high-quality Castilian wool was eventually exposed to greater competition from the wool production of other European regions. The formal end point for this spectacular episode in migratory sheep husbandry arrived with the dissolution of the 'Mesta' in the year 1836.[45]

Transition to Stall-feeding

The nomadic and transhumant forms of animal husbandry based themselves on pasturing year-round. As a rule, in mountain regions too, very little fodder was available for emergencies, sick animals or those requiring special care. When feeding large herds in the highlands became impractical, they would most likely retreat to the lowland regions, accepting thereby the arduous conditions of migration, rather than producing extensive supplies of fodder at higher altitudes. Even on the broad, high plateaus that permitted hardly any vertical migration, there are many examples of year-round pastoralism. In Mongolia, with its distinctly pastoral orientation, the practice of mowing hay was still virtually unknown in 1900; for this reason, they traditionally had to count on heavy losses of animals during the harsh winters. During the first half of the twentieth century in the highlands of Tibet, at 4,000 metres or more, yak calves were fed hay and even butter oil in periods of severe weather but the majority of animals stayed out to graze.[46] This is an indication that the pastoral mode of production exhibited certain economic advantages and that the transition to stall-feeding required a specific constellation of historical factors.

Hay production and winter stall-feeding developed particularly early and with exceptional strength in the wetter areas of Europe's Alpine space. Above all, in the central part of the northern Alps, there arose from the later Middle Ages a specialised, market-oriented, and essentially cattle-raising landscape, which would be later designated a 'land of herders' [*Hirtenland*]. Formerly, this area had known a subsistence economy built on grain cultivation and the prevalence of sheep husbandry. In the transition to modern times and after, this was supplanted by cows and hay production: in summer the cows grazed in the upper reaches of the Alps, in winter they were fed in stalls and partially sold. Historical preconditions in this case were a relatively dense population with a

---

45. By the 1830s the number of transhumant sheep had dropped to one million; in a reduced volume and with changed technologies, however, transhumance has survived to the present times – see Sanz 1994b.

46. Finke 2004, p. 194; Thargyal 2007, pp. 74, 79, 112–6, 136; Barfield 1993, pp. 142, 184; further evidence from different regions e.g. in McCann 1995, 94; Inamura 2002.

Animal Husbandry

corresponding labour capacity and consumption needs and the emergence of a strong urban demand for meat and dairy products. In the North Alpine land of herders, the demand came from the exceptionally vital urban landscape of northern Italy, with its large centres such as Milan and Venice. The attraction of these markets showed itself even in the name used for the transalpine cattle trade, which was simply the 'Italian trade' [*Welschlandhandel*]. How strong the pressure could become in mountain communities to provide fodder for overwintering animals is clear from the retrieval of so-called 'wild hay' from places that were remote and steep, sometimes very steep. According to one case study from a region of the northern Alps, the collection of wild hay was particularly common in the period from the seventeenth to the nineteenth century. The procedure was sometimes so dangerous that it can be grasped historically using the documented fatalities (see Plate 12).[47]

In the nineteenth and above all in the twentieth century, fodder production and stall-feeding then extended (further) to many regions worldwide, especially in connection with the rise of cattle-raising. In the moments of transition from an extensive to a more intensive system, the danger of depleting natural resources seems to have been especially great. It is not to be assumed, however, that overgrazing is a generally inherent tendency of pastoralism. Indeed, the mobility of herders and herds, the fundamental characteristic of this economic form, demonstrates this clearly.[48] From the early modern period, the intensification process was accompanied by debates over the desirable agrarian reforms. Although numerous opinions came to be expressed, they were mostly influenced by the specifically European development. For a long time, intensive forms of use and sedentary lifestyles took priority in the scale of values of engaged intellectuals. This evaluation often corresponded also with the interests of the growing modern states, which increasingly controlled the population and sought to draw upon economic achievements. In this situation pastoralism, and especially its distinctive mobility, found itself on the defensive.[49]

In some cases the pursued modernisation strategy assumed a momentum that was disconnected from the realities of life, leading to devastating outcomes, as in the aforementioned forced Soviet collectivisation in Kyrgyzstan. A few

---

47. Mathieu 1992, pp. 108–12; Mathieu 2009, pp. 55–64, 85–92; Bergier 1997, Essay X, pp. 457–68; Blatter 2010.
48. An example of the debate on overgrazing in Richards 2005, pp. 351–66; on the problematic of transitions: Boserup 1993, pp. 36–9; for a balanced assessment: Finke 2004, pp. 200–1.
49. The propaganda for forage production and stall-feeding was widespread in Europe during the eighteenth and nineteenth centuries (Herrmann 1985, chap. 8–10).

generations later, after the withdrawal of Soviet power in 1990, the decollectivisation of animal husbandry also proved a difficult process for the Kyrgyz economy, in part because the by now established technology was geared toward the planned economy. The transition to a market economy was tied to a deterioration of infrastructure.[50] More generally, the technological and industrial age often led to a polarisation of land use in mountain regions: central zones were used more intensively and peripheral zones, by contrast, more extensively than before. Overall, this resulted in a retreat from the use of exactly those areas that had been integrated historically into the lives of human beings through animal husbandry. In the case of present-day Kyrgyzstan, large mountain areas are being abandoned almost completely to nature and there are many further examples of such tendencies. In the long term, it therefore appears that one must assume a curved trajectory of development: with the increase in population, there arose from the beginning of modern times an extension of the surface area used by peasants – even into marginal zones, thanks to pastoral agriculture; from the nineteenth and twentieth centuries, the circumstances of ever-expanding technology and industry provided the grounds, in a second phase, for these use areas to shrink.[51]

3.3 Family and Mobility

As the historical and anthropological research has shown, family structures and relationships are highly variable. They change from one period to another and, at the same point in time, they can differ from one place to another. One reason for the variability lies in the fact that families are influenced by many economic, cultural and political factors. Among the diverse aspects of historical development, the transition from a domestic subsistence economy to one of market integration and specialisation is of particular importance. In the course of this transition, private and public institutions assume duties and functions that previously fell to family groups. The shift is driven forward among other things by urbanisation, which increases the possibilities for contact. Through migration and other channels, rural families are also connected to urban centres. Until now, no society has relied completely on market integration; even in highly industrialised regions, some goods and services are produced within the

---

50. Farrington 2005.
51. For the development of extensive animal husbandry in industrial societies, e.g. Collantes 2006.

Family and Mobility

family sphere. Nevertheless, in many places the change fundamentally altered external relations as well as internal structures and interactions.[52]

Since its institutionalisation around 1970, family research has often assumed that ecological parameters in the mountains have left their mark, directly or indirectly, on family structures in the surveyable past and that these structures in the highlands therefore exhibited similarities distinguishing them from those of the lowlands. Yet as the sources opened wider and as familiarity with the subject increased, this conception has been destabilised. The investigated variables, such as rural forms of property, rules of inheritance and household succession, marriage patterns, household size and structure, the distribution of authority and the awareness of kinship ties, did not submit to a uniform geography.[53] This suggests that, if the ecological parameters had any influence, it was only over specific aspects. Starting from this idea, we will set out in this section on a trail already laid by earlier mountain explorers. In many places they have noticed that, over the course of the year, the vertically structured mountain agriculture required individual family members to be mobile, which could impact on more general social behaviour. This may be illustrated first with a case from the Pakistani Karakoram.

Spatial Organisation of Families

The Karakoram, with its arid valley climate and its steeply towering, extremely high mountains – many over 7,000 metres – belongs certainly among the most impressive landscapes in the world. The upper elevations of this rugged territory receive abundant precipitation and support an enormous sheet of ice. On the valley floor, the great quantity of snow runoff can be used for irrigation purposes, which allows for an intensive agricultural oasis. For many centuries, the Karakoram was inhabited by various groups who were experienced in using resources at diverse altitude levels.[54]

In a settlement of the Bagrot Valley, four distinct productive zones can be distinguished at altitudes between 1,500 and 4,000 metres: the main vil-

---

52. An overview is given, for instance, by Gestrich 2003.
53. A selection with an accent on the European Alps, where the discussion of family history has been intense: Cole/Wolf 1974; Netting 1981; Convergences 1985; Bernand/Gruzinski 1986; Viazzo 1989; Mitterauer 1990; Mathieu 2000; Albera 2001; Fontaine 2003; Lorenzetti/Merzario 2005; Derouet 2010.
54. The region has been investigated above all by German geographers; some of their work is also instructive from a historical perspective: Grötzbach 1984; Kreutzmann 1989, 1993, 2000, 2006; Hewitt 1989; Felmy 1993; Ehlers 1995; Herbers 1995; Ehlers/Kreutzmann 2000.

lage, above that the summer villages, and at the very top the settlements of the summer pastures; finally, down below and far removed from the others were the winter pastures. One can imagine the complexity of spatial organisation and the importance of verticality. In the 1990s, the main village and the summer villages formed the major sites of agricultural production. Winter and summer wheat as well as maize and potatoes grew there. Pastoral activities took place in the high-lying summer pastures (with dairy farming) and the winter pastures, located some days' journey below the main village (the male herd only). Throughout the year, the economy of this mountain community operated at various levels but the spatial distribution was greatest during the summer months. Between June and August, more or less simultaneously, work was performed in the three upper zones. In most cases the families divided themselves up and, besides this, many moved back and forth; foreign observers registered astonishment at the 'almost constant spatial fluctuation of man and beast' in this remote valley of the Karakoram.[55]

The region is not amply furnished with historical sources, especially for the period before the late nineteenth century when it fell to British India. Essential clues for earlier development, however, are provided by the major irrigation channels, which can be dated by local scholars. In fact, these channels were the lifeblood of the settlement and its population. With sufficient water the fields could be cultivated continuously, potentially yielding two harvests. In the wake of demographic growth, multicropping in Bagrot extended up to 2,100 metres. The agrarian structure was also tied to the transportation conditions and patterns of settlement. In the 1980s, roads connecting to the new Karakoram Highway were opened and motorised vehicles could reach the main settlement for the first time but before then everything was transported on the backs of people or animals. In earlier periods, the settlement pattern experienced considerable changes. In the first half of the nineteenth century, as wars between the rulers of small principalities laid waste to the valley and its population, the settlements were often consolidated and fortified. Following the *Pax Brittanica* and the subsequent increase in population, decentralised farmsteads spread out through the fields. In the Bagrot Valley there are many recent filial settlements and, in 1940, a new principal town was established

---

55. Grötzbach 1984, p. 312; diagrams on the organisation of space and time in Grötzbach 1984, p. 313; Ehlers 1995, p. 114.

Family and Mobility

at its lower end. From then on, since this lay on top of the traditional winter pastures, the valley residents had to search further afield for grazing areas.[56]

The population of the Karakoram belongs to various Islamic faiths. In documented times, family structure was characterised by patrilineality, patrilocality and the priority of (the elder) sons to inherit. 'Joint families' of married brothers were a common form of household management and counted together with demographic growth among the reasons for relatively large household size, on average seven to nine people according to one survey from the late twentieth century. Yet the household units were mobile and they split up into smaller groups for significant periods of time.

> As the year progresses, from spring through summer to autumn, activities change, and where they are done and by whom also changes. The onset of winter puts an end to most outdoor activities and the arena shifts indoors. The house becomes a 'space' for both genders and there is a redistribution in the use of space.[57]

The sexual division of labour was fundamental but also flexible. Temporary residence in the summer pastures, for example, counted as the special prerogative of the young men. Some of the local households delegated them and they could also work for hire, caring for other families' yaks, sheep, and goats. As emigration to the Pakistani lowlands increased, these activities were transferred more and more to the older men and they declined overall. Significantly, the decline was less pronounced in those parts of the Karakoram where women, too, were traditionally allowed to work in this 'pure' productive zone.[58]

Variability and Change of Families

Detailed investigations show that vertical mobility could vary from region to region, from place to place, and from family to family. It not only built a variable phenomenon; it was also a 'total social fact' (*fait social total*, Marcel Mauss), which was connected with many spheres. Here it might be worth naming a few of them, keeping an eye especially on the infrastructural side:

1. Population: changes in land use often accompanied population processes and included the more intensive use of old regions as well as the expansion into new ones. In both instances, the framework changed for the organisation of space. Intensification prolonged the time spent in the fields, whereas expansion

---

56. Grötzbach 1984; Kreutzmann 1989 and 2006, pp. 251–72, 329–58; Ehlers 1995, pp. 112–4.
57. Hewitt 1989, p. 346.
58. Hewitt 1989, pp. 340–1; Felmy 1993, pp. 201–6; Kreutzmann 2000.

lengthened the time necessary to reach them. In mountain regions, this change must have increased the altitude-specific differences in the intensity of use.

2. Politics: for patterns of mobility, not only the size but also the distribution of the population carried weight and this in turn was subject to political dynamics. Rulers and regimes often influenced settlement through the promotion of central places. The wars they waged could disperse an area's inhabitants or force them to crowd together in fortified places.

3. Culture: the gendered spaces in a society bore the mark not only of general cultural rules but also of local discourse and practice. 'Purity', according to Hermann Kreutzmann, was associated in large parts of the aforementioned Islamic Karakoram with yaks, sheep, and goats, as well as with the highest productive zone. 'Impurity' was associated with the village cows and with female spaces, confined to the area around the main house. In some parts of the region, however, women were permitted to use the highest altitude level, which testifies that 'contrary beliefs in purity are important and taboos determine pastoral activities'.[59]

This brief discussion of background elements to vertical mobility indicates that developments could vary between different regions and periods. As for an explanation of the general trends, one does well to begin with the population and with an additional technological point. Demographic growth, the experience of many mountain regions during the modern period, increased the likelihood and the extent of vertical mobility – among other reasons because the increasingly intensive use of land at the lower valley levels remained connected to the land at the upper levels, with both areas claimed traditionally by the same groups but used only extensively in the latter case. Subsequently and still more recently, however, as modern technology took hold in and around agriculture, the general trend turned against vertical mobility – one reason was that efficient transportation technologies reduced the basis for decentralised investments.[60] On a general level, therefore, the *longue durée* presumably knew two phases: a long phase of expanding systems followed by a short phase of contraction (see also above, Chapter 3.2).

Besides the agro-pastoral infrastructures, social and familial aspects also possessed significance with respect to vertical mobility. Two catch-phrases may suffice in illustration:

---

59. Kreutzmann 1993, p. 33; Ehlers/Kreutzmann 2000.
60. Mathieu 1992, pp. 128–32.

Family and Mobility

1. Social control: Before the era of telecommunication, social control was closely connected to space, locality and physical presence. The periodic divisions of the household, which were customary in many forms of vertical mobility, did not fail to affect the patterns of authority. So it was, for example, in the Karakoram region with women's roles in the summer pastoral economy: in an earlier period, overseeing the animals here was traditionally a concern of the respected older women, perhaps accompanied by their grandchildren; doing this, they took temporary respite from the male authority of the house. More recently, families separated along different lines but with similar results: the younger, in-marrying wives went with their husbands and children to the summer pastures. With this, they assumed large workloads but, as explicitly stated, it also enabled them to withdraw for a time from the strict age hierarchy among their kinswomen and to make their own decisions.[61]

2. Division of labour: although the sexual division of labour heeded cultural ideals, even the simple fact of household partition could have an influence on prevailing practice. In large groups it was easier to enforce strict gender rules than in small ones. In the latter case, promoted by vertical mobility, people had to demonstrate greater flexibility. In spite of Islamic beliefs about gender divisions, for example, an observer of the northern Karakoram remarked in the 1930s that the boundaries were permeable: 'A man who is able to, does every kind of men's and women's work, and a woman who is able to, does both women's and men's work.'[62]

At this point we can return to the general question raised initially, as to whether mountain regions exhibit commonalities in family structure that set them apart from other places. There is no doubt, as the examination of conditions surrounding mobility clearly indicates, that mountain regions may reveal peculiarities during certain phases and in certain respects. These resided in the vertical organisation of space and arose from the agro-pastoral dynamic, in combination with environmental factors. Yet by no means was there ever complete geographical conformity. Between the sixteenth and the twentieth centuries, mountain regions continued to exhibit variations in spatial organisation, just as flatland regions also displayed forms of pastoral mobility.[63]

Furthermore, the 'scarcity of land' did not provide for the overarching uniformity that is sometimes claimed in the literature with respect to family

---

61. Herbers 1995, p. 237.
62. Kreutzmann 1993, p. 33.
63. See above, Chapters 3.1 and 3.2.

matters in mountain regions. Here one must remember, first of all, that scarcity is a historical phenomenon and it can take effect anywhere; in marginal areas it appeared at lower population densities but not necessarily earlier than in regions with longer growing seasons. The most famous example for the scarcity argument, because of its unusual nature, concerns the polyandrous marriage patterns that have been documented in parts of Tibet and the western Himalayas. Polyandry, the marriage between multiple men and one woman, is found far less often in a global context than polygamy, the marriage of multiple women to one man. Yet in addition to these aforementioned Asian mountain regions, similar forms of multiple-partner marriage are also known elsewhere. In the Tibetan-Himalayan case, it was almost always brothers who shared one wife. 'Instances of three and five husbands are quite common', a traveller observed in the 1880s, 'but without having gone rigidly into the matter, I should say that most instances of polyandry were those of two husbands' – this for the simple fact that few families had more than two brothers. Viewed over the long term, it is doubtful whether this variant of multiple-partner marriage put land resources under less pressure than the 'joint families' of monogamously married brothers or the entirely closed forms of inheritance that have been found elsewhere. 'Polyandry was clearly something more than a rudimentary survival strategy for mountain areas with limited agricultural land', one historian concludes.[64]

Migration

In the modern period there have probably been only a few families or none at all without at least some contact, however limited, to the market. Yet for many families, external relationships were restricted. They produced most goods and services within the framework of a domestic subsistence economy. The proliferation of market contacts, stimulated also by the increasing population density, then set in motion the development of large-scale interwoven and integrated systems, in which each individual played a specific role. To a considerable degree, market integration and specialisation came about in mountain regions through emigration to other regions. Initially, this outward migration often had a temporary character and through the continuous coming and going of people and products this created a variety of connections between places of origin and destination. Older researchers saw in it a shedding movement: the meagre endowment of resources in mountain regions was seen to have led before long to overcrowding and to have made outward migration inevitable. The formula

---

64. Singh 2011 on the western Himalaya; hints about the discussion of Tibet in Thargyal 2007, p. 165.

Family and Mobility

from Fernand Braudel's work on the Mediterranean in the sixteenth century became famous: 'The mountains have always been a factory of men for other people's use' [*une fabrique d'homme à l'usage d'autrui*]. Researchers since then have delved more deeply into the topic and there are now also comparative investigations of mountains and migration in a global context. The expanded studies have contributed to the assignment of greater weight to elements other than overpopulation – such as the attraction of urban centres, the pull-effect of earlier emigrants in the context of a chain migration and the influence of village or regional elites, who could conduct the flow of labour power over large areas. Laurence Fontaine, who has concerned herself with the western Alps in France as well as other mountain regions, concludes that the emigrants were very much 'used' by others – yet not primarily by city dwellers, as Braudel had in mind, but by their own elites.[65]

The western Alps, where the author began her study, are to be seen in the context of the early urbanised regions in northern Italy and southern France. As cities and trade increased in scale there from the later Middle Ages, commercial networks soon extended into the mountains, where periodic markets were established in the sixteenth century. Some mountain villages now began to align themselves toward specialised activities for other regions. On a local level there existed a society of smallholding peasants, led by an elite of families who were able, through their wealth and innumerable lending activities, to assert considerable power over their clientele. A few of the more prosperous and larger merchants of the area succeeded in building large-scale trading networks, with contacts reaching across central Europe all the way to the coastal cities of the North Sea and the Baltic Sea. The large merchants were organised in formal family companies, and they built a basic scaffolding for the many peddlers and shopkeepers who originated in the same villages and took over the retail distribution of their wares. In this way there formed a hierarchical system based on family and village solidarities, which was in a position to push forward even into the rural areas and open the way for the sale of ever new consumer goods. The migration of individuals tended to be temporary but on the whole it developed an increasing momentum and connected life in the mountain villages with the broader economic and political landscape of Europe. Through the progressive restructuring of trade and the emergence of nation states, the situation changed considerably since the eighteenth century and this brought

---

65. Braudel 1995, vol. 1, p. 65 (the English translation changes Braudel's metaphor and speaks instead of a 'reservoir of men'); Fontaine 2005, p. 48; on migration in mountain regions seen in a global perspective: Grötzbach 1984; Skeldon 1985; Fontaine 2005.

Agriculture, Family, Mobility

new directions and dimensions for migration. In the fluctuating cycle of crisis and conjuncture migration now often assumed a definitive character, so that in the western Alps of France, which had long experienced population growth, a period of decline set in in the mid-nineteenth century.[66]

The Alpine example can be generalised only within limits. We know that there were also mountain regions in the modern period, the history of which was characterised primarily by immigration and not by emigration, as for example in China or North America (see above, Chapter 2.2). Besides, the old-urbanised surrounding regions, which decisively influenced migration in the western Alps, were not yet a widespread phenomenon in the period around 1500. Areas of urban concentration were much more common in the regions surrounding the mountains after the explosive growth of cities in the nineteenth and twentieth centuries. In general, urbanisation, with its land-grabbing dynamic, builds the best single indicator for the assessment of development. From it we can gather that the stage models of migration offered in the literature, though indeed not entirely false, are by no means precise renderings of historical reality. The simplest of these models is the thesis of 'mobility transition', which postulates a transition from practically sedentary societies to ones that were mobile, as the result of industrialisation and urbanisation.[67] It stands beyond a doubt that during the nineteenth and twentieth centuries, migration swelled enormously almost everywhere. In South America, for example, there were still no cities with 100,000 inhabitants in 1800 but by 1900 there were twelve, and by 2000 no less than 375. Indeed, migration from the South American mountain regions to the major cities increased massively from around 1950.[68] Yet mobile segments of the population had also existed there previously and in other regions the rising surge of migration could arrive earlier, as in the western Alpine case. This asynchronous development suggests that in individual locations, the phases of migration assumed their own distinctive characteristics. It should not be assumed that all mountain regions followed the same path of development, writes an international expert on migration, 'as the intensity of external pressures will vary with the distance of the mountainous region from the centres of modern influence, their strategic importance, and their resource base'.[69]

---

66. Fontaine 1991; see also Fontaine 2003 and 2005.
67. Discussion of the 'mobility transition' thesis put forward in 1971: Viazzo 1998; alternative models for mountain migration in Grötzbach 1984b and Skeldon 1985.
68. Escobar/Beall 1982 and above, Chapter 2.1 (Table 6); hints on early modern migration in the Central Andes in Cook 1981, pp. 248–51.
69. Skeldon 1985, p. 248.

Family and Mobility

To this pressure there contributed not only economic forces but also political ones. With early modern state-building and the subsequent transition to true nation states, the hierarchy of cities and the centre-periphery gradient increased in strength. At the same time, some peripheries now became boundary regions for growing political spaces and thereby came under greater control. This affected migration according to changed market structures and under conditions involving direct coercion, such as military conflict or forced resettlement. A telling example of this is provided by the history of the Greater Caucasus, that long range extending over more than 1,000 kilometres between the Black Sea and the Caspian Sea, which reaches 5,640 metres at its highest peak and belongs in its entirety among the more significant old-settled mountain landscapes. Its integration into Tzarist Russia began in the second half of the sixteenth century with the arrival of independent frontiersmen and soldiers on the plains at the northern foot of the mountains. In the eighteenth century these 'Cossacks' experienced a strong growth in numbers and obtained regular army status. Although the situation in the border region was long marked by a Russian-Caucasian exchange, the drive to expand in the distant power centre led eventually to a bloody war of subjection, which ended only in 1864. Certain forced resettlements of the mountain people to new locations on the plains began under the Tzarist army, on the eve of the nineteenth century. Yet it did not become a mass phenomenon until after the Russian Revolution, when the young Soviet Union strived for a policy of forced industrialisation and agrarian modernisation throughout the entire territory. The 'organised migration' was supposed to free the mountain inhabitants from their 'feudal' past and lead directly into the socialist future, which appeared in the form of newly established, large-scale operations in the steppe. From the mountain region of Dagestan alone, which made up only part of the Caucasus, almost a quarter of a million people are said to have been resettled to the lowlands, using covert or open force, between the 1930s and the 1960s.[70]

Relative Poverty

Overall, migratory movements contributed quite considerably to the increasing disparities between mountain and lowland regions, in a developmental process of which we have already spoken (Chapter 2.4). The chronology and strength of this trend were variable and there were certainly also exceptions on a global scale. Yet, based on the known population data, and above all the urban data,

---

70. Barrett 1999 (for the early resettlements pp. 41–2, 47); Hewsen 1978; Radvany 1984, pp. 216–20; Badenkov 1990, p. 133; Meckelein 1998, pp. 156–7, 166, 174–80.

one must assume that in the modern period this was in fact the dominant trend. Around the year 2000, more than four fifths of all major cities were found at the lowest elevations, up to 500 metres above sea level (Chapter 2.1). What did the increasing disparity mean for the mountain population's material livelihood and for the distribution of poverty and wealth?

This question has been posed repeatedly since the beginning of the great development debate in the 1960s. The background situation in this moment of departure was decolonisation and the quickening of international relations, together with rapid technological change and the growing wealth of western countries. In many cases, however, it was a rhetorical question with a fixed answer: mountain regions are poor. In both politics and science, there was broad consensus in this view. When in 1964 the president of the United States officially declared 'war on poverty' in that country, it was no coincidence that he chose a district of the Appalachian Mountains for the symbolic proclamation and also made it an important battleground in the programme. A generation later the mountains became a global theme, particularly through their inclusion in the catalogue of Agenda 21 at the 1992 UN Earth Summit in Rio de Janeiro. By way of introduction, the Mountain Chapter firmly maintained that support for these threatened natural regions was essential to humanity: 'On the human side, there is widespread poverty among mountain inhabitants and loss of indigenous knowledge.'[71] Yet critical voices could already be heard, insisting that such assertions required empirical proof. With the growing availability of data it was subsequently shown, at least on the statistically ascertainable level of states, that the poverty of mountain inhabitants was not to be verified. Countries with a high proportion of mountains could be found in all categories, from the 'least developed' to the 'developed' countries. With respect to poverty, per capita income and a variety of other developmental indicators failed to distinguish them from countries with few or no mountains.[72]

From a historical view, two observations now call for our attention:

1. The relevant unit of analysis for this subject is the region and there are many indicators suggesting that the development of each mountain region has been influenced by the lands surrounding it. There were and are, in other words, extreme differences between mountainous regions and countries at various technological and economic levels, in the North and in the South. Even within individual countries, one could generally demonstrate major differences between

---

71. Williams 2002, p. 342; United Nations 1993, Agenda 21, p. 109; see also above, Chapters 1.1 and 2.2.

72. Kates/Haarmann 1992; Parvez/Rasmussen 2004.

Family and Mobility

mountain regions; but on average they have often remained behind national standards, a situation associated with the increasing weight of environmental factors in the modern era. Insofar as prosperity is a developmental phenomenon, it stands to reason that in the world's mountains there prevailed relatively greater poverty and less wealth than in the lowlands.[73]

2. Development is a temporal process. Considered only over short periods, its background can easily elude us. Yet our knowledge of long-term changes in the living conditions and distribution of wealth in mountainous regions is currently deficient. It is important therefore to closely examine the historical evidence in many places, to determine how various generations met life's material necessities and how they were influenced in this by the existing technology and culture.

---

73. See above, Chapters 2.4 and 3.1; the argument receives further support from the investigation of the FAO, according to which an above-average part of the global mountain population around 2000 lived in developing and transition countries (92%) and in rural regions (73%), see Huddleston 2003, p. 5; however, the exact figures in such studies depend strongly on the chosen definition of space.

∼ 4 ∼

CULTURAL DIVERSITY AND MODERNITY

4.1 Western Modernisation

A basic historical question that must be asked of mountainous regions is the question of their cultural meaning. Which ideas and practices coalesced in certain areas and epochs with mountain ranges and summits? Which background should one use to interpret their emergence and transformations? In the first part of the book we have investigated the globalisation of the perception of mountains, which has progressed with the expansion, science, and politics of the West since the beginning of the modern era. In any case, this form of globalisation is only one aspect of a multi-faceted history of interpretations. The second and third chapters then presented economic and social aspects of mountainous regions on various continents over time; now the diversity of cultural forms will be discussed. Generally, one can assume that in countless areas there were more or less distinguished and self-contained representations. These indigenous representations had their own unique origins, and in the modern era they were increasingly forced to compare with other representations, especially with those introduced or imposed by the West. In the last centuries 'modernity' has become a key political cultural term in the West. The expression 'modern' has its origins in the Middle Ages and has continuously assumed new meanings ever since. The use of the term could be many things: claim, demand, reality. Despite the term's elusiveness – or precisely because of it – it began to serve as a worldwide reference point in the struggle regarding the proper world view.[1]

In this struggle, one of the especially controversial points is the relationship between secularism and sacrality: in which direction should society go – towards purely worldly perspectives, or towards a religious perspective which

---

1. Burke 1992, p. 137.

Western Modernisation

also touches on other dimensions of human existence? The various answers to such questions are laid bare in society's relationship to nature and to mountains. Here we will first examine developments in Europe and North America, before turning our view to Asian landscapes.

The Enlightenment and Romanticism in Europe

In the second half of the eighteenth century there was a marked change in the European elite's perception of nature. The change was so distinct that contemporaries thematised it again and again as a conscious experience. 'For a long time Switzerland with its many mountains did not appear to be a land that offered suitable objects to awake and satisfy the curiosity of travellers', declared the enlightened journal *Nouvelles de la République des lettres* in 1782, for example. This applied especially to France and England, where the Alps were regarded as an awesome mountain range and were only known because they constituted a hindrance on the way to beautiful Italy. Not until ten to twelve years prior to the publication of the aforementioned article had the love of natural history spread among scholarly and wealthy travellers. Before, they were only interested in ruins, sculptures and paintings, that is, in cultural goods, of which Switzerland had nothing to offer in comparison to the riches of Italy. When the natural scientists discovered the practice of observation and when the philosophers came to believe that they could rediscover the innocence and good morals of early times in this area, both became much more seriously attentive to the mountains: 'We are beginning to reap the fruits of their labours, and we can assume with great probability that in the future Switzerland will no longer be one of the least visited countries of Europe.'[2]

In fact, travels to Switzerland, above all to the Alpine landscape, became more and more popular and fashionable. Estimating based on the numbers of published travel reports, one can assume that between 1750 and 1790 these visits increased more than eight-fold.[3] The mountains of Switzerland, previously no matter for public admiration, in a short period received a great deal of attention. As the aforementioned journal pointed out, natural scientists contributed to this trend, some of them having started studying the Alps much earlier. The contributions of philosophers and literary writers were also important. In his epistolary novel of 1761, *Julie ou la Nouvelle Héloïse*, Jean-Jacques Rousseau made the new feel for nature and mountains a central theme,

---

2. Quoted by Marcil 2003, pp. 169–70 (original French).
3. Quantification based on the listing by De Beer 1949.

and with tremendous success; the book became one of the best sellers of the late eighteenth century. In historical scholarship this change has been handled many times. Here I want to indicate two points which have heretofore been given little notice in research: the question of periodisation and the tendency towards sacralisation.

Their consciously experienced difference between an old and a new perception of nature and their pride in their own modern attitude led many contemporaries to portray sharply their break with the past. A formula from the late nineteenth century gave the two periods their catchy names: after the 'mountain gloom' followed the 'mountain glory'.[4] This black-and-white view was adopted by many but it obscured the fact that there were already certain positive perceptions before the dramatic increase in attention and admiration that the Enlightenment and Romanticism brought to the mountain world. Before 1750 the mountains were not seen by everyone in all circumstances as fearsome, off-putting and ugly – in short, as *locus horribilis*. The perceptions were much more complex and dependent upon the situation. For example, an English manual of poetry from the middle of the seventeenth century recommended sixteen negative adjectives for the description of mountains: 'barren', 'desert', 'inhospitable' and so on. This same guide, however, also regarded eight neutral or positive expressions as appropriate, namely 'stately', 'lovely', 'cloud-touching' and so forth. Some intellectuals compared the mountains with 'warts' and other 'superfluous' excrescences but others fought back for the mountains and compared them with the 'King' and with 'Men of brave heroique mind, with eyes erect to heaven'.[5] Therefore the change in the late eighteenth century did not consist of a simple reversal from negative to positive but rather of a dramatic new weighting of earlier ideas and assessments.[6]

This change went along with a certain tendency towards the sacralisation of mountains within and without religious institutions.[7] Much speaks for the idea that in Christian Europe mountains (and nature in general) traditionally

---

4. The terms are ascribed to the English art critic John Ruskin (*Modern Painters*, Chapters XIX–XX, Book V, 1856); Nicolson used them explicitly in 1959 to name the two periods (Nicolson 1997, p. 6).

5. Nicolson 1997, pp. 35, 54, 255 (with many interesting examples).

6. See also Chapter 1.2 of this book and Mathieu 2005 (on periodisation, also pointing to the contradictions between competing models); an impression of the complexity of representations since the Renaissance is provided by the various contributions in Mathieu/Boscani Leoni 2005.

7. For the following paragraph see also the survey in Mathieu 2006b and the miscellany of Brunet 2005.

had little or no religious meaning. For example, there was only a very small number of peaks named after saints and the mountainous regions played no special role in the pilgrimage geography of the continent. However, in the course of the modern era there were increasing indications of a greater sacral value. One powerful sign of faith was the placing of Christian crosses on mountaintops, a practice that only began to spread at the end of the eighteenth century. Austria's erection, with great effort, of crosses on many prominent peaks, beginning in 1799, is well documented. Later countless mountains in Europe were symbolically seized for the Church and Christian values.[8]

At the time of the first placement of large crosses on mountaintops, Austria found itself at war with revolutionary, anti-clerical France. In another variation, however, the idea of sacred mountains was also widespread in France: especially at the climax of the Revolution in the years 1793 and 1794, 'holy mountains' were erected out of dirt piles and other materials all over the Republic in the public places and in the churches. In the preceding political-philosophical discussions nature had taken on a quasi-mystical status as the absolute good, with which society was to reconcile itself. Nature was the embodiment of the freedom, equality and fraternity that the Revolution had written on the flag. The artificial 'mountains' served as the public, ritualistic representation of nature, on top of which 'the superior being' revealed the laws of nature to humanity. Even Alexander von Humboldt lent a hand in building a large mound at the *Champ de Mars* in Paris.[9]

This nature and mountain cult in revolutionary France was only an especially radical expression of a Europe-wide phenomenon. 'By the later eighteenth century the appreciation of nature, and particularly wild nature, had been converted into a sort of religious act', writes Keith Thomas in his classic work on the human–environment relationship in the early modern period. Nature was then seen by the intellectual elites as not only beautiful but also morally salubrious. The mountains represented both qualities in an extreme

---

8. Martin Scharfe has worked on the history of early Austrian mountain crosses (Scharfe 1999 and 1999b; 2007, pp. 268–75). Detailed travel reports show that there have been some earlier crosses on mountains (Ebel 1793, part 2, pp. 53, 140, 163). The Spanish tradition may have been especially old, perhaps with origins in the struggle with Islam; in America the conquistadors often put crosses on conspicuous points as a sign of domination (Braun/Hogenberg, 1576–1618, vol. 2, no. 3; Varela/Gil 1992, pp. 382–3). On the later colonial practice: Mills 1997, above all chap. 9. Regarding the development in the Alps in the late nineteenth and early twentieth centuries: Cuaz 2005, pp. 72–8.

9. Harten/Harten 1989; Krätz 2000, p. 30.

measure – indeed, they were a monument to the glory of God.[10] In fact, in the eighteenth and nineteenth centuries a vocabulary developed, which originated in the nexus between aesthetic and religious experience or which used expressly religious images. One spoke of the feeling of 'delightful horror' and of the 'sublime', and the mountains were described as 'cathedrals of the earth'. Even when it was primarily about physical performance, as in mountaineering, the sacral was not entirely absent and was consciously reflected upon. In the 1910s the 'Alpine Club' in London debated very earnestly on the question of whether mountaineering was a religion.[11]

The 'Wilderness' Movement in North America

Sacral elements were even more conspicuous in the experience of nature in the United States' advance from the East Coast to the West of the expansive continent. American scholars have demonstrated this in a series of impressive studies. This emphatic turn to nature in the nineteenth and twentieth centuries is also interesting because it was connected with the creation of special natural and national parks, a practice that later spread worldwide.[12]

In an initial phase the white population was still very much in the European tradition. The Puritans regarded the 'wilderness' in biblical terms as an inhospitable place and also as one of spiritual temptation. This negative view began to change with the transatlantic import of romanticist ideas at the end the eighteenth century. Nature then became an emotional drama, which one always had to endure, if one wanted to be cultured. The script of this drama came from Europe, and the landscape model of the Alps was especially frequently cited. Yet, in the course of the nineteenth century there developed a gradual emancipation from this idea. The important circumstances for this change were the formative experience of the 'frontier' and the quest for a national identity.

The settler communities, who progressed step by step from the East Coast to the West and who wanted to prevail over the new environment and over the Indian population, initially saw defeating the 'wilderness' and introducing 'civilisation' as their mission. The aforementioned romanticist influences only had a limited impact among the pioneers. However, the white occupation proceeded faster than expected and, in the 1890s, the period of the frontier was seen as over, because the entire land between the two oceans had been accessed. The

---

10. Thomas 1983, p. 260.
11. Stutfield 1918.
12. The following is based above all on Nash 1989 and 2001; Hyde 1990; Cronon 1995; Wyckoff/ Dilsaver 1995; Turner 1997; Kupper 2009.

Western Modernisation

less the idea of the frontier was anchored in reality, the more it mutated into a new national ideology. Many regarded the frontier as a wellspring that, in the past, had allowed the young American nation to regenerate its powers in nature far from the impairments of civilisation and had allowed it to develop its own character. It was desirable, therefore, that the natural wilderness, at least parts of it, be saved from the further advances of civilisation.[13]

This appreciation of nature was also bound up in an increasingly strong feeling of nationalism in another way. Namely, it was seen as a given that America could not compete with Europe in terms of culture – but certainly could in terms of nature. It was said more and more that the American landscape and 'wilderness' not only equalled but surpassed that of Europe. For example, shortly before 1850 a travel report about the Sierra Nevada ascertained that 'the Alps, so celebrated in history and by all travelers and admirers of mountain landscape, cannot ... present a scenery more wild, more rugged, more grand, more romantic, and more enchantingly picturesque and beautiful, than that which surrounds Lake Tahoe.' Later it was less important to prove America's superiority with transatlantic comparisons, because authors increasingly developed their own models and also integrated the particular desert landscapes of the South-west in the inventory of natural national monuments.[14]

These and other factors contributed to the prominence of the sacral dimension of the natural experience in the United States. This is underlined, for example, in a study of the history of the landscape of the 'Far West' from 1820 to 1920. Certain religious components had already been inherent in the term 'sublime' but this quality was more strongly emphasised by the Americans: 'The sublime in nature became evidence of God's power and allowed humanity to stand in awe of His work.' Transcendentalism was also an influential movement in the United States in the nineteenth century, the study continues. Natural objects like waterfalls, great mountains and deep forests could be admired as expressions of a godly will.[15]

The Scot John Muir was very prominent in this movement. He was a natural scientist, a prophet of the wilderness idea and an early advocate of conservation. Starting in 1868, Muir lived for a long period in the mountainous Yosemite Valley near San Francisco. There he experienced, even more strongly than in the earlier phases of his restless life, a conversion to nature, which he

---

13. Nash 2001, above all pp. 23–43, 149–51; Hyde 1990, 215–6, 242; Cronon 1995, pp. 76–80.
14. Nash 2001, p. 74 (quote); Hyde 1990, pp. 219–43.
15. Hyde 1990, p. 18.

began to describe in a powerful and an intensely biblical language. For him, the Sierra Nevada was holy; the mountains breathed a spiritual life – indeed, they wore a halo, they were the throne of God and simultaneously an expression of His beauty. After 1906, when he was involved in protecting another valley in the area from technological assault for the sake of an urban water supply, Muir used biblical terms as powerful weapons. He struggled against the 'Prince of the powers of Darkness' and the 'temple destroyers' who were only after the 'Almighty Dollar'. He led this struggle as a representative, because it was really the 'Lord's battle' and his opponents challenged the 'God of the Mountains'.[16]

Yosemite was by then an official national park of the American federal government; in 1890 Muir had pushed the establishment of the park through Congress. Before this step, in 1872, Yellowstone National Park in the Rocky Mountains had been established; it is regarded as the first such park in the world. By 1940 the United States could already count more than twenty national parks. William Cronon has pointed out that, before World War II, the selection of parks in large part followed traditional criteria. It was about the preservation of 'sublime' landscapes with mountains, canyons, waterfalls and other romantically coded natural elements. Only later were the criteria expanded, so that a swamp, for example, could also be placed under protection.[17]

In single cases the motives were quite varied and partly contradictory. The interests of tourist promoters mixed with the national body of thought (as regards substitutions for the frontier and distinctions versus other nations) and with wilderness ideas stemming from transcendentalism; later, scientific motives made themselves apparent for some time. The globalisation of the national park movement in the first and especially in the second half of the twentieth century was similarly multifarious. Yet, regardless of the local interests in conservation in various states and continents, in the year 2000 there were 4,000 national parks worldwide, many of them in mountainous regions.[18]

---

16. Turner 1997, for example 185; Nash 2001, pp. 167–8 (quotes).
17. Cronon 1995, p. 73.
18. Kupper 2009; Chape 2003, p. 23; Velthuizen 2007, p. 53; the national parks comprised a total surface area of over 4.4 million square kilometres; in addition there were many other quantitatively important categories of 'protected areas'; it is estimated that between one third and one half are located in the mountains – see Debarbieux/Rudaz 2010, p. 210.

Western Modernisation

Mountain Sacredness – the Emergence of an Idea

The great wave of attention that has illuminated the mountain world in the West since the eighteenth century can be connected with various things: economic factors (increasing agricultural intensification and the shortage of extensive or unused lands, improvements in communications and transport); political factors (quests for national identity in natural and spatial references); and not least cultural factors (scholarly and religious developments, and social distinctions through new tastes).[19]

Normally in this context the Enlightenment would be mentioned as a period that we traditionally regard as secular, if not anti-religious. However, recently scholarly history's portrayal has changed and the Enlightenment now appears as a complex period, which was also creative in regard to religion. One can observe in the Enlightenment processes of both secularisation and sacralisation. Of course the question arises as to how broadly to define the terms 'religious' and 'holy' and how to judge the general trend in the case of the perception of mountains. It is beyond doubt that in the western perception of mountains the worldly aspects were of greater significance. However, it is also certain that the religious aspects became more important during the course of the modern era. The 'holiness' of the mountains was not an old phenomenon but rather an almost completely modern one.[20]

Many authors have pointed out that Christianity has long presented itself as a decidedly anthropocentric religion that defines a sharp division and hierarchy between mankind and nature.[21] One can regard the physio-theological movement as a first attempt at revision, which, starting in the late seventeenth century, wanted to create a connection between nature and the bible and to deduce the existence of God from the wonders of His creation. However, even at the height of this movement in the 1730s it was firmly established in the discourse of intellectuals and clergy that Christians could not derive a cult from it. Such rites were seen as pagan. 'The heathen were even given to seeing some mountains as deities', stated the German *Universal-Lexicon* and in another article it referred to similar attitudes among the 'oriental peoples'.[22] Later there were shifts in accent that brought an appreciation of nature to Christianity and

---

19. See Mathieu 2005, pp. 71–2.
20. For religious currents and aspects of the Enlightenment, for example: Outram 1995, pp. 31–46; Greyerz 2000, pp. 285–324.
21. White 1967; Thomas 1983, pp. 17–50; Nash 1989, pp. 88–95, 238 (with further literature).
22. Zedler 1732–52, vol. 3, pp. 1244–5, vol. 13, p. 378.

led to the aforementioned placement of crosses on mountaintops, for example. However, a really broad and fundamental reinterpretation seems to have first begun in the ecological discussion of the 1960s, as the human–environment relationship of Asian religions was also increasingly received in the West.[23]

Parallel to Romanticism and to these changes in religious views, in western scholarship the idea appeared that mountains were holy always and everywhere. This idea was presented in various versions and with varying determination. We can schematically differentiate three phases: in the second half of the nineteenth century a series of romantic texts appeared which presented the argument of holiness with many anecdotes and little distance;[24] in the first half of the twentieth century scholarly authors presented the argument more soberly and as an established fact but in general only briefly and with little evidence;[25] in the second half of the twentieth century, and primarily after 1980, some researchers have applied much more energy to collecting data and systematically investigating the phenomenon. The most important study is from the American religious studies scholar and mountaineer, Edwin Bernbaum, who in 1990 published his successful and well-informed work, *Sacred Mountains of the World*. For Bernbaum it was not primarily about *whether* the mountains were holy but rather *how* this holiness expressed itself. He also decidedly placed his work at the service of the environmental movement and the conservation of mountains.[26]

Generally it may be difficult to demonstrate the idea of the sacredness of mountains with the history of mountains in the West. As our account has shown, we are not faced with a constant attribution of qualities but rather with a change from the profane to a certain sacrality. However, before we present general considerations, we should discuss the history of the Asian perception of mountains, which has substantially inspired Bernbaum and other advocates of the sacredness-thesis.

---

23. Nash 1989, chap. 4, speaks of the 'Greening of Religion'. In a more detailed examination there would, of course, be many preceding currents to name. Also important is the tendency towards a re-interpretation of Christianity as a historical heir to 'natural religions'; on this, see Albert 2005.

24. Well-known examples are the publications of John Ruskin and Élisée Reclus – see Walter 2004, p. 241; Andrian 1891 collected a great number of Asian and European mountain myths that were exceptional for the period in quantitative, though not in qualitative terms.

25. Blache 1934, pp. 99–100, 174–5; Peattie 1936, p. 4.

26. Bernbaum 1997, 1997b, 2006; see also Gratzl 1990 and 2000; Grötzbach 2004; Barbero/Piano 2006; for a more critical position: Mathieu/Singh 2006.

4.2 The Spiritual Empowerment of the Landscape

East Asia

'There is no such thing as *the* Asian perception of nature', we read in an overview of the perception of nature in Asia. As in the West, perceptions in Asia are also differentiated. Within one culture there are often many, partly controversial points of view, which – together with real environmental transformations – change again and again. Nevertheless, according to the overview, there are certain general traits of many Asian societies which can be identified: in comparison to the West the distinction between 'nature' and 'culture' was usually less categorical. 'Nature' was therefore viewed more in context and had to be continually newly determined and defined. This often happened with ritualistic means and the ritualisation in many Asian societies was tantamount to a sacralisation of nature.[27] When elaborate religious teachings were also added, the landscape was literally 'empowered', as Tibet experts put it, and thereby charged with religious energy or spiritual power. In the Indo/Sino/Tibetan cultures the spiritual empowerment was widespread – albeit with different driving forces and characteristics. The Chinese variant, with which we will begin here, had a decidedly political character.[28]

In 1572 Wanli succeeded to the throne of the great Chinese Empire as the thirteenth emperor of the Ming Dynasty. He was barely ten years old at the time. Shortly thereafter, entirely in the style of earlier rulers, he addressed a prayer to the holy Eastern Mountain, Mount Taishan:

> O God, you give birth to everything which must bloom and you concentrate the supernatural energy in yourself. You are the eternally lasting glory of the oriental lands. You assure the peace of the people and of all beings. Ten thousand generations have really found help from you. Now, through the rights of heredity, I have been invested with supreme power. With deference I perform the rites; oh God, would You accept the sacrifices and listen to the prayers; stand by my dynasty.[29]

Several months before his death, Wanli's predecessor had ordered that the temple of the mystical Jade Emperor on Mount Taishan be renewed and rebuilt in such a manner that it would envelop the highest rocks of the Eastern Mountain. The mountain had long been dotted with shrines, temples, inns,

---

27. Bruun/Kalland 1995, quote on p. 4.
28. Huber 1999, p. 15; McKay 2003, vol. 2, p. 10.
29. Chavannes 1910, p. 302 (translated from the French, originally Chinese).

small shops and other buildings and monuments and now the summit would receive a religious identity, too, indicated with the temple's inscription: 'Summit of the Jade Emperor, Repaired by Imperial Order'. The Jade Emperor was the sovereign ruler of the Taoist pantheon, the members of which were assumed by the faithful to reside in the far remote Kunlun Mountains in the West of the empire. However, on Mount Taishan one could appeal to many other deities and persons who had become immortal. For example, in the vicinity of the aforementioned temple, the predecessor of Wanli's predecessor had begun with the construction of a temple to Confucius, which was then finished during Wanli's reign. Many stories circulated regarding what the great philosophical master was supposed to have said at Mount Taishan, with the effect that his cult spread further.[30]

At this famous place one could also pay homage to the deity of Mount Taishan itself. Emperor Wanli did this only from a distance and never personally took the pilgrimage. However, three of his successors visited the Eastern Mountain in the seventeenth and eighteenth centuries. They left behind numerous inscriptions, including some related to the mountain deity itself – for example: 'The Associate of Heaven Who Is the Guardian of the Empire' (1684) and 'Tai Peak Bestows Happiness upon Us as a Reward' (1731). These attributes were in keeping with the popular ideas widespread in China. In numerous cities and villages of the empire there were temples dedicated to Mount Taishan, in which written characters pointed to its godly qualities: 'His holy virtues equal those of heaven'; 'His godly power rewards and punishes'; and 'To escape His deep sight is difficult'.[31]

Just as common was the popular pilgrimage to Mount Taishan. In 1608 an author stated that all residents of the provinces north of the Yangtze River made pilgrimages to the 'Great Mountain' to donate incense. On pilgrimage the simple people would observe everything properly: the vegetarian regulations and other taboos, the correct clothing and the sense of respect. However, the prayers and ceremonies were hardly ended before they gave themselves up to profligate festivals. In fact, the pilgrimage to Mount Taishan was subject to many regulations and edicts. In 1735, for example, it was announced that the emperor was lifting the pilgrim-tax, which had been found oppressive, but he was simultaneously affirming the official rules of behaviour. After the declara-

---

30. Baker 1925, pp. 115–9, 126–7, 137.
31. Baker 1925, pp. 156–7 and Chavannes 1910, pp. 27–8 (translated from French, originally Chinese). Regarding insights into the complex religious practices on the local level and at different hierarchical ranks during the Qing period, see Feuchtwang 1977.

The Spiritual Empowerment of the Landscape

tion of the republic in 1912 the pilgrimage continued. Until the communist revolution in 1949 one could count thousands of pilgrims daily during the main months. As the People's Republic of China later began to open, Mount Taishan once again attracted many pilgrims and more and more tourists. In 1987 it was added – right after the Great Wall – to the list of UNESCO World Heritage Sites. At roughly 1,500 metres it is not high but much speaks for the assumption that this mountain has the oldest and densest cultural tradition in the world.[32]

Mount Taishan was part of a vast territorial system of holy mountains. The 'Five Peaks' of the Confucian/Taoist tradition include, besides the Eastern Mountain (the most important of them), a holy mountain in the North, in the West, in the South and in the middle of the Chinese Empire. Their heights are conspicuously modest (roughly 1,290–2,020 metres) and the distance between them quite considerable (over 1,400 kilometres from the Northern to the Southern Mountain). The 'Five Peaks' were represented with particular signs and characterised by a series of criteria. So, a stone column from the 1610s, around the end of the reign of Wanli, identified for each of these mountains the place – with prefecture and under-prefecture, two assisting mountains, the familial and given names, the officially granted titles and the mountain's main functions. Experts in toponomy tell us that the mountains had spoken names: for example, 'Tai' meant 'prosperity, peace, and tranquillity' (the Eastern Mountain, Taishan); 'Heng' meant 'endurance and tenaciousness' (the Northern Mountain, Hengshan); 'Hua' meant 'flower' (the Western Mountain, Huashan) and so on.[33] According to ancient Chinese literature, the 'Five Peaks' were early checkpoints for inspections of the empire by the emperor and his delegates. In general it was believed that the mountains ensured the stability of the Earth with their weight. In materialised form the 'Image of the True Form of the Five Peaks' represented – as a carving in stone, as a paper copy, as a metal amulet or painted on porcelain – a talisman of great protective power (see Plate 15).[34]

In the first centuries of our time-keeping, Indian Buddhism, which has an interest in nature much like that of Taoism, reached China. In the style of the 'Five Peaks', Chinese Buddhism later brought forward its own system with the four holy Buddhist mountains, also widely dispersed across the land. At the most important of them there were hundreds of small and large cloisters

---

32. Elvin 2004, pp. 407–8; Baker 1925, pp. 9, 186–7; Bernbaum 1997, pp. 32, 41.
33. Chavannes 1910, pp. 415–21; Blunden/Elvin 1983, p. 110; Yushu 2002.
34. Baker 1925, pp. 175–9; Chavannes 1910, pp. 8, 42, 415; Demiéville 1973, p. 364; for the consideration in state worship: Feuchtwang 1977, p. 587.

and temples in the modern era.[35] Buddhism and a particular political situation were among the reasons that the development of a new perception of the landscape and mountains gained entry in Chinese society from the fourth century. Paul Demiéville has described it as a veritable romantic revolution, in which fleeing from civilisation became a *leitmotiv*. The mountainous landscape was a theme in the paintings and in the literature then and would exert a formative influence, with many variations, over a very long time. Even Mao Zedong, the leader of the communist revolution, still stood under the impression of this classical tradition and wrote poems about the mountains.[36] Thus, along with the intensity of the expression, two structurally contrary phenomena were unique in the Chinese experience: on the one side, the close connection with the governmental-political structure and the systematic territorial layout and, on the other, the early criticism of civilisation and romanticisation of nature.

High Asia

Along with the two large systems of holy mountains, there were also numerous regional and local mountain cults. Generally such small-scale cults were widespread in Asia and many of them were mixed with expansionary, elaborate religions as well. One can assume that these elaborate ideas and practices were often superimposed on the small-scale cults and – depending on the situation – allowed them to continue to exist in niches, integrated them into dominant doctrines or forced them to disappear. In some circumstances the dynamic may have come from below or from the periphery. This spectrum of various possibilities provides an idea that one must reckon with considerable variability in Asian mountain cultures. The propagation of Buddhism did not lead to the same results everywhere. When offshoots of Chinese Buddhism made it to Japan in the sixth century, this led to a mixture of indigenous cults and further developments. In the highlands of Tibet, Buddhism became a force only relatively late and here again it brought about other results. Because of its wide broad resonance, Tibetan history is of particular interest to us and will be examined more closely here.[37]

---

35. Bernbaum 1997, pp. 35–40; Mullikin/Hotchkis 1973, pp. 74–142.
36. Demiéville 1973; see also Elvin 2004, above all pp. 321–68.
37. On Japan, for example, see Bernbaum 1997, pp. 56–71 and Raveri 2006; the following paragraphs about Tibet are based primarily upon Huber 1997, 1999, 2003; Blondeau / Steinkellner 1996; McKay 1998; Buffetrille 1998, 2000; for a general outline, see Kollmar-Paulenz 2006.

The Spiritual Empowerment of the Landscape

The worship of landscape elements belonged and still belongs to the basic religious inventory in many societies in the area of Tibet and the Himalayas and at the centre of their worship are mostly mountains and lakes. According to the relevant research, two main categories of mountain cults can be differentiated:

1. The cults of the *yüllha*-type ('god of the locale') were associated with local communities and their historical identity. They were transmitted orally and their periodic rituals at the foot of the hallowed mountains were primarily concerned the immediate wishes and problems of the temporal world.

2. The cults of the *néri*-type ('mountain abodes of important deities'), on the contrary, were primarily aimed at questions of death and the afterlife, whether it was rebirth or liberation therefrom. They were based in extensive textual traditions, were maintained by religious specialists and their members were recruited from larger, in part distant, groups.

These regional and super-regional pilgrimage sites were also scenes of missionary activity, of disputes between rival sects, and of the governmental interests of Tibetan Buddhism. The basic element of the multi-layered rituals consisted of physical circumambulation of the mountains in question.[38]

One assumes that the culture of the *yüllha*-mountains was superimposed, assimilated and repressed by the culture of the *néri*-mountains, starting in approximately the eleventh century. In this period the important process of the duplication and dislocation of certain religious practices from the Indian lowlands into the Tibetan highlands set in. On the social and political levels the (second) Buddhisation in Tibet led to the founding of countless cloisters, to the establishment of a basic monastic structure and, starting in the seventeenth century, to the development of an important centre in Lhasa (see above, Chapter 2.3). Just as important for the understanding of the *néri*-mountains is the transmission of the sacral geography from exclusive, esoteric traditions from India. With techniques of meditation and with the help of the Mandala-diagram, tantric hermits and ascetics in Tibet could create complex forms of a visionary religious landscape. These visionary landscapes could be fixed to the outward landscape at many points, primarily involving mountains, at which famous spiritual pioneers, using these means, brought important 'treasures' to light. The popularisation and establishment of pilgrimages then changed the character of the heroic meditation-mountains and increasingly also brought

---

38. Huber 1999, pp. 22–5; McKay 1998, pp. 6–7; Buffetrille 1998; the important Tibetan Bön religion cannot be considered in this short survey.

governmental-political interests into play. It has been pointed out that the most important *néri*-mountain districts – Kailash, Lapchi, and Tsari – are in the South of Tibet on the border with the states and tribes of the Indian/Nepalese region.[39]

Of special importance was the 'Pure Crystal Mountain' in Tsari, which the Tibetologist Toni Huber researched in an impressive historical-anthropological study. He summed up the varied process of sacralisation as follows: notwithstanding the possible preceding local cults, it was meditating tantric pilgrims who were there at the beginning and established the religious power of the mountains during an expansion phase of Buddhist sects at the end of the twelfth century. The popular lay pilgrimage began only later and their circumambulation circuits were first established in the sixteenth century. The most important pilgrimage ritual of the crystal mountain, known as the 'great ravine circuit of Tsari', developed in the eighteenth century, parallel to the consolidation of the theocratic state in central Tibet. The earlier traditions of meditation had by then largely disappeared and they were only revitalised in the twentieth century. Following the Chinese occupation of Tibet, all rituals had to be abandoned around 1960. The limited liberalisation of the 1980s eventually brought a revival in modified form.[40] Huber's reconstruction is supported in part by detailed historical sources. Especially important in this case is a text written in the years after 1570 as a mythological-topographical guide for pilgrims by a well-known aristocratic monk and intellectual. Such guides made it possible to learn to see the mountain world in its entire Buddhist complexity.[41]

Under the old Tibetan regime, there were five circuits of different elevations around the Pure Crystal Mountain, each with a specific religious use. The most spectacular was the aforementioned 'great ravine circuit', a mass procession which took place every twelve years, in the Tibetan year of the monkey, from the beginning of the eighteenth century until 1956. The conditions were dramatic and dangerous. The danger came from the necessary descent into the rutted, almost impassable jungle landscape of the South and even more from the small tribal societies who ruled this area and who were often hostile to Buddhist pilgrims. These pilgrims came from all the regions of Tibet and usually added up to approximately 20,000. Various developments and events

---

39. Huber 1997, 2003, 1999, chaps. 3 and 4; on the border position p. 24. These mountain districts carry many names; I take up the most common forms and spellings from the quoted literature.
40. Huber 1999, pp. 28–9, 72.
41. Huber 1999, above all pp. 60–72, 85. The multiform genre of 'narrative maps' for religious travels was, and still is, widespread in Tibet. See also Buffetrille 1998 and 2000.

The Spiritual Empowerment of the Landscape

fuelled the aggressive atmosphere in the early twentieth century and during the procession of 1944 an actual massacre occurred. In order to carry on the event despite it all, delegates from Lhasa took care to pay a so-called 'barbarian tribute' to tribal leaders before the beginning of the pilgrimage. With this transfer of goods, accompanied by great ceremonial effort and acknowledged by a swearing of oaths, the Buddhist elite hoped to ensure their people's safe conduct. However, even without being attacked, the procession of roughly 150 kilometres, which required about two weeks, was exceedingly demanding. Moreover, as with other rituals, only those who overcame the circuit with devotion in the spirit of Buddha could hope for the redemption of sins and religious merits.[42]

For various reasons the authorities in Lhasa invested massively in this holy mountain district and its great processions. The close connection with the structure of the state was symbolically underlined, among other aspects, by the fact that clothes of the Dalai Lama were carried in a prominent position through the ravine circuit. Religiously motivated restrictions of land use were also issued more than in other districts. The view that all life and all substances in the vicinity of the Pure Crystal Mountain were holy or divine came originally from Buddhist masters and later entered popular belief. Both served the authorities as a basis for banning all agricultural cultivation of the soil. Forbidden, too, were the clearing of pastures and the keeping of pigs and chickens, who could dig up and disturb the Earth. Naturally, hunting and the killing of any form of life were also taboo. Defecation was limited to only designated places on the circuit routes and spitting and blowing one's nose was also restricted.[43]

'To the Most Holy Mountain in the World'

The Kailash district in western Tibet had long had a more meagre number of pilgrims than the aforementioned Tsari region but for a considerable time it also had a prominent spiritual status. In the nineteenth century the 6,710 metre Mount Kailash, together with a nearby lake, was cited in an agreement between Tibet and Ladakh as a state witness.[44] In the course of the twentieth century it developed into a national symbol of Tibet and a global symbol of the holiness of mountains. The western appropriation and the related worldwide canonisation must have happened in the period between the 1930s and the

---

42. Huber 1999, pp. 128–74.
43. Huber 1999, pp. 119, 197–200.
44. Desideri 1937, pp. 83–4, 228–31; McKay 1998b; 2003, vol. 2, pp. 28, 787.

1980s. In general comments about sacred mountains by western geographers around 1935, Mount Kailash remained unmentioned. In 1990 it appeared in various works, independent of each other, as the undisputed primus and as the spiritual antithesis of Mount Everest, which, despite its prestige, had a materialistic aura because of high-level mountaineering.[45] In the beginning, popular works of travel and adventure literature were important for Mount Kailash's career. In 1937 the Austrian Herbert Tichy published a book under the title *To the Most Holy Mountain in the World* [*Zum heiligsten Berg der Welt*] which showed on its jacket the conspicuous form of Kailash (see Plate 14). Later the spread of Buddhism in the West, the political Tibet movement and other factors contributed to its rise in reputation. As an ultimate proof, the pan-religious statement that Mount Kailash enjoys a high rank in four religions (Hinduism, Buddhism, Jainism, and Bön) is often mentioned.[46]

In 2003 the various ideas of sacredness were highlighted when the Chinese authorities wanted to construct a vehicular road around Mount Kailash. State representatives claimed that the road would be of use to pilgrims on the circuits. For once, the Tibetan government-in-exile in India was of the same mind, though it warned against abusing the holy mountain as a tourist destination. The 'Tibet Initiative Germany' saw it as a colonial act that would only serve the commercial development for Chinese and would trample the religious feelings of Tibetans as well as those of 800 million Hindus in India. The organisation appealed to the governments of Germany and India and to the European Union to take steps against the plans. Supported by partners in other European countries and by the German Mountaineering Association, the Tibet Initiative organized a Mount Kailash demonstration on top of Zugspitze, the highest mountain in Germany. The number of signatures on the accompanying petition greatly exceeded expectations.[47] At the time of this protest, a third of the average of approximately 20,000 people who visited Mount Kailash in years not marked by ritual were already described as tourists and not as pilgrims. Many were from India and the West. Naturally the cultural-religious attitudes

---

45. Blache 1934, pp. 99–100, 174–5; Peattie 1936, p. 4; Bernbaum 1997 (first 1990), pp. 8–15; Gratzl 1990, pp. 9–10, 81.
46. From the voluminous literature: Korom 1997; Snelling 2006. Tichy (1937, p. 96) used a quantitative basis for the prioritisation of Mount Kailash (compared to Mount Fujiyama). Tichy was inspired by Sven Hedin, who wrote the preface to his book.
47. *Frankfurter Rundschau*, 28 Aug. 2003; and the documentation on www.tibet-initiative.de (viewed on 28 Dec. 2008). Later the Chinese authorities dropped the plans for the road.

The Spiritual Empowerment of the Landscape

at this elevated pilgrimage site had been heterogeneous before but, with the rise of modern backpacking tourism, they have become even more diversified.[48]

Cultural Diversity

What is 'sacred'? What is 'sacredness'? There are no universally accepted definitions but many would agree that some aspects of the terms can be generalised and that it is sensible to leave other aspects open for uses specific to context. First, the term 'sacred' presumes a demarcation from 'profane' and corresponding prohibitions or taboos against transgressions. Second, the holy domain is hierarchically superior: it embodies societal power and attracts public attention. The relationship of the holy to a religion or church, on the other hand, is quite open. The form of its expression in representation and rituals, meanings and feelings is also open. These variable, context-specific aspects make it clear that the sacred is newly configured in any phase, even when the actors are convinced of its timelessness. So, many Tibetans believed that a number of their mountains had been powerful and sacred forever but historical analysis brings to light that these holy mountains must be understood as what Toni Huber has called 'the cultural products of long and particular processes of social construction'. Furthermore, a certain caution in interpreting is also methodologically important. Regarding Tibet, the question was discussed of whether the mountains were deities themselves or whether they simply formed their abodes. It has been pointed out that this distinction was often unimportant in believers' minds, which also relativises the value of the scholarly question. It cannot be the task of research to further refine a religious belief system.[49]

If we remember the cultural appropriation of mountains in the West (Chapter 4.1) and compare it with the appropriation in the East as just presented, we cannot avoid the conclusion that the differences are greater than the similarities. In Asia one finds in the modern era (and before) firmly institutionalised cultures of sacred mountains implemented in ritual practices. In Europe and among the American settlers there is no parallel at hand and only in the course of the modern era has a certain sacralisation happened in connection with modernisation. We could conclude from such observations that cultural diversity is of central significance in this aspect of environmental

---

48. Snelling 2006, pp. 313–80; Burri 2005, p. 7. In the religious 'year of the horse', 2002, the number of pilgrims was much higher.

49. Huber 1999, p. 21; Blondeau/Steinkeller 1996, pp. VIII–IX, 24. For general descriptions of 'sacredness' and 'sacred places/mountains', see e. g. Colpe 1987; Brereton 1987; Bernbaum 1997, pp. XIII–XXII; Hoheisel 1998; Bendik-Keymer 2003.

perception. The 'sacredness of mountains' was a result of discourses and attributions that stood in interrelation with societal processes but it also demonstrated a considerable measure of autonomy. Thereby people 'spoke' with the mountains, rather than the mountains speaking with people. Contrary to the pronouncements that emphatically insist on a general holiness of mountains, one must defend this cultural dynamic and diversity as well as insisting on certain minimal methodological standards. Anyone who would define the sacral so broadly that virtually no room remains for the profane, for example, also causes a terminological flattening and a corresponding loss of meaning. If everything is sacred, then nothing is sacred.[50]

How varied the perceptions of mountains can be in Eurasia and elsewhere may be seen in their naming. The toponomy of mountains, the so-called oronymy, is far from providing a well-rounded picture but recently it has made progress, especially with regard to comparisons.[51] Generally one can assume that many peaks – especially in the high mountains – only received names with the inroads of governments and mountaineers in the nineteenth and twentieth centuries.[52] However, the following points to deep historical differences:

1. In Europe there were very few mountains named after religious figures. For example, in a list of over 1,300 summits in the Alps, only five names of saints appear and some of those are doubtlessly because of the transmission of a settlement's name to the mountain peak above it. Indeed, saint's names were widely used for villages and cities, such as Saint Moritz or Saint Veit. One also searches the list in vain for superior religious names, such as a 'God's Mountain' or a 'Mount Heaven'. Probably it would have been viewed as blasphemy to endow a bleak summit with such a name.[53]

---

50. Methodologically insufficient, for example, is the general claim of sacredness made by the organisers of a conference on sacred mountains in Piedmont in 2004 (Barbero/Piano 2006, above all p. 375). The conference was co-organised by a documentation centre of the '*Parco Naturale del Sacro Monte di Crea*', a modern protected area around a '*Sacro Monte*'. These 'sacred mountains' staged the Passion of the Christ or scenes from the life of Mary or a saint. They developed from the sixteenth century, primarily at the southern foot of the Alps. They can be considered a sign of the beginning of sacralisation of mountains in modern Europe (Mathieu 2006b), yet further conclusions on the general subject of mountain perceptions would be inappropriate.

51. See INST (ed.) *Die Namen der Berge*, 2002 (a project for the International Year of Mountains with contributions from more than a dozen countries and mountain regions).

52. See for example Francke 1911, pp. 6–7; Simo 2002; Scharfe 2007, pp. 116–9.

53. The list of the 'principal summits in the Alps' is from Furter 2005, pp. 269–337.

The Spiritual Empowerment of the Landscape

2. In China, on the other hand, the latter form was strongly represented. The attribute *Tian* (heaven) indicates not only the extensive high mountains in the West of the empire, the Tianshan ('Mount Heaven') but also the Tiantaishan ('Mountain of Heaven's Plate'), Tianmushan ('Mountain of Heaven's Eyes'), Tianszhushan ('Mountain of Heaven's Columns') and others. The religious dimension is even more intensely embedded and anchored in the regional culture in the case of general rhetorical categories for 'sacred mountains'. In Tibet this semantic field has also evolved, and one uses general terms like *néri* ('mountain abodes of important deities'), which *a priori* bear witness to the existence of holy mountains and differentiate them from the profane.[54]

The naming of mountains is also quite revealing as a reflection of the colonial grasp of the European powers and for the later decolonisation debate. In many cases the choice of names was no insignificant weapon of the colonial rulers in symbolically taking possession of a conquered landscape and introducing their own culture. Because they are topographically eye-catching, mountains were best suited for such strategies. In Africa the colonial partition and opening happened in the decades before and after 1900. One study mentions the following modes of European naming: various – primarily high – mountains were named after the newly created colonial states (such as 'Mount Cameroon'); occasionally one asked the native population for their name, which could lead to misunderstandings due to a lack of linguistic competence (the name 'Kilimanjaro' perhaps originated thus); a third method was the honorific naming for European explorers or leaders (such as 'Mount Stanley' or 'Kaiser Wilhelm Peak', the name of the Kilimanjaro before 1918); and finally the mountain's form served as a motif (an example is 'Table Mountain' in South Africa, where the mountainous landscape is especially thickly dotted with English and Afrikaans). With the coming of decolonisation, the criticism of the names that were viewed as imperialistic intensified, which led to alternative namings or to official abolition of such designations.[55] Of course this tug-of-war was generally only one part of an extensive exchange in mountainous regions from the beginning of the modern era. This exchange was provoked by the processes of globalisation and accompanied by claims to power and misunderstandings. This is the theme of the next and final section.

---

54. Yushu 2002; Huber 1999, pp. 13–4, 22–3. The complexity of Tibetan classifications is stressed in Blondeau/Steinkeller 1996, pp. VIII–IX.

55. Simo 2002; Horn 2002; Hansen 1996b, p. 53. On linguistic colonialism in a general (South) African context see Comaroff/Comaroff 1992, pp. 250–8.

4.3 NORTH–SOUTH CONFLICT COMMUNITY

In the transition to the modern era, there were extremely diverse forms of mountain perception. In the aforementioned case of China, for example, one found not only many local and regional cults but also nationwide, systematised forms of mountain worship; at the western end of Eurasia, in Christian Europe, it was completely otherwise, for nature and the mountains were accorded no religious significance, instead being classified as foreign and as heathen. The onset of the European expansion movement expressed the diversity in some regions with brutal clarity. In Latin America, as we shall see, traditional mountain cults, along with other forms of indigenous religions, were forbidden and systematically persecuted. Linked to western expansion, however, there also arose a new interest in natural phenomena and the development of modern science. Heightened attentiveness to the environment was among the major impulses for that cultural transformation through which the mountains assumed certain sacral traits, even in Europe. In general there was a massive intensification of global contacts and interactions in the modern period, often accompanied by quarrels and hegemonic claims. What were the effects of this emerging 'conflict community' of 'North' and 'South' in the mountain regions? Did it lead to a levelling of cultural diversity or to new forms of differentiation?

The following section sketches this process on the basis of selected stopovers. The keywords are Colonialism, Alpinism, Tourism. We will conclude with the 2002 International Year of the Mountains, a United Nations occurrence that elucidates the question of cultural convergence with special clarity.

Colonialism

The Spanish expansion into Central and South America can be seen as the beginning of modern colonialism; important here is the fact that it also led rapidly to a confrontation of various mountain perceptions. This occurred first of all in the religious sphere: it was through evangelisation that the conquistadors and their successors justified their rule and, within a few generations, they established a system for the exercise of religious power. In the Andes, where I direct my attention here, this process resulted in rich documentation that has attracted much research attention in recent decades and produced a series of important studies, including some new interpretations.[56]

---

56. The following paragraphs are based on Mills 1997; MacCormack 1991; Ramírez 2005; Duviols 1972; Wachtel 1992; Bonilla 2006; Platt 2006; Reinhard 1985.

North–South Conflict Community

Ten years after the conquest of 1532, the Spanish monarch established the viceroyalty of Peru on the territory of the former Inca Empire. At that time, the Spanish clergy's mission was often limited to mass baptisms and thus had no real influence on the culture of the indigenous population. That a more profound Christianisation would require a different approach and eventually lead to serious conflict was demonstrated in the second half of the sixteenth century. Starting with indigenous groups in central Peru during the 1560s, there spread a religio-political movement under the name *Taqui Ongo*, or 'dancing sickness'; it rejected the new faith as well as everything Spanish. Even before this, the view slowly began to take hold among foreign ruling circles that large parts of the population had become Christians in name alone, whereas in fact they continued to follow their 'heathen ways', which came from the devil and demanded eradication. In a number of councils, the Spanish clergy in the Archdiocese of Lima now applied themselves to a stricter organisation and programmatic guidelines. Still, in order to really set in motion what some intended as an 'extermination of idolatry' [*extirpación de la idolatría*], there needed to be more supervisors who would make it a priority. This came to pass in the early seventeenth century.[57]

An *auto-da-fé* on the main plaza in Lima, on 20 December 1609, marked the opening act. Members of the government appeared on horseback and from their palace balconies the viceroy and the new archbishop were able to look out over the plaza where a pulpit, two stages and a large pyre had been erected. A collection of objects and mummified bodies, which had been confiscated in a mountain region not far from the capital, were publicly burned as 'idols' of a false religion. A captured indigenous cult master was bound to a stake near the pyre. He had already admitted his 'mistakes' before but now it was time for him to hear and feel the judgment: two hundred lashes, hair shaven and banishment to a remote Jesuit college. This message about the future handling of non-Christian religious practices was directed primarily at the many indigenous people who had been summoned to the *auto-da-fé*. Forty years later there came yet another public spectacle in Lima, with which the archbishopric sought to make a further advance in what had meanwhile become the institution of rooting out idolatry. This time the drama centred not on a captive sorcerer [*hechicero*] but on a shard of wood from the true cross, just received as a gift from the Holy See in Rome. Before blessing the combatants called out

---

57. For the chronology see especially Duvios 1972, here above all pp. 99–146.

into the field against the superstitions, they were able to place the new relic ceremoniously on display.[58]

The campaigns were carried out by specially appointed ecclesiastical visitors [*visitadores*], who, along with a few assistants, 'visited' the parishes of the diocese in order to expose and punish the rampant 'errors'. In several waves, these actions lasted until the mid-eighteenth century. Important in our case is the indication that they were directed in part against popular mountain cults. When a visitor interrogated María Poma Ticlla at her home high in the mountains in 1660, for example, she reported on offerings and communal rituals that were performed for a certain deity [*huaca*] at a holy site on Mount Chanqui, as a means of bringing the maize to fruition. The promotion of the llama herd's welfare was also associated with a mountaintop. María attended to this by calling out one of its names and a few words of appeal: 'Antanama Hurco, receive this which we offer to increase the llamas. I wish for it so much.' In addition, people presented food and gifts to the mountain deities with the intention of procuring a great variety of things: material goods such as money or mules, general assistance and support, luck in love or simply 'a good life' and 'good fortune'. That the confrontation with a visitor aroused anxiety and led to evasion strategies is easy to understand. María Poma had already turned to the authorities in Lima prior to the interrogation, alleging that the visiting priest was known for torturing, imprisoning and imposing large fines on the people. She was informed, however, that the man was a 'saint' who harmed no one. This decision was repudiated only a short time later in a long, extremely detailed indictment.[59]

Most interactions between the two unequal populations unfolded schematically, yet even the most careful observers had trouble understanding them. Difficult to grasp from a western perspective was the central indigenous expression, 'huaca', which could refer to all that was holy or supernatural. Besides certain ancestors, it also applied to natural phenomena such as mountains and rock formations as well as to a great number of cult objects. 'Huaca' phenomena were often tied to oral traditions describing an indigenous group's place of origin at a particular spot on the landscape. Acts of religious consecration were not decisive for the origins of holiness as they were to the Spaniards and other Christians. A snowy mountain could be 'huaca' no less than an offering performed there. According to an expert, 'the sacred was thus inhering in things

---

58. Mills 1997, pp. 30–3, 146–7.
59. Mills 1997, pp. 64–6, 111, 115, 119, 129, 158–9 (quoted originally in Spanish and Quechua).

North–South Conflict Community

independently of human action or ritual'.[60] The Spanish clergy regarded such religiosity at first as uncivilised and heathen, in the sense of pre-Christian; then, in the wake of increasing severity in the late sixteenth century, they saw it as none other than the devil's handiwork. As a remedy the visitors combed each community, destroying all mummies and cult objects they could find and erecting large crosses on the special sites. In this way they also meant to rid the population of all that was seen as the 'veneration of natural objects'.[61]

Only much later and in a different context did the church change its attitude toward manifestations of nature and the mountains. At the end of the nineteenth century Pope Leo XIII initiated a large-scale 'Plan for Our Saviour, Jesus Christ': symbolising the nineteen centuries since the Redemption, monuments were to be built in commemoration on nineteen Italian mountaintops. At the time of this religious offensive, the future Pope Pius XI had already conquered three of the highest Alpine peaks. When the passionate mountain climber was then elected supreme church leader in 1922, the Alpine Club in London immediately made him a member. Now for the high Catholic clergy too the mountain world had become the ideal place for elevating the spirit and for religious experiences.[62]

Alpinism

Just as the confrontations in the sixteenth and seventeenth centuries began in the Spanish Empire, it is in the British Empire of the nineteenth century that we find the institutional origins of the Alpine expeditions and conquests. Mountains had been climbed in a sporadic manner for a long time and in many regions (in some places even above 6,000 metres), yet the Alpine Club, founded in 1857, was the first organisation created especially for this purpose. The foundation was an expression of enthusiasm for the self-assured and 'manly' sport of mountaineering, which took hold rapidly from mid-century and appealed above all to the aspiring and urban middle classes. At first the Alps became the 'Playground of Europe', as a book title proclaimed in 1871, but other mountain ranges later joined the ranks. Soon there were Alpine clubs on

---

60. MacCormack 1991, pp. 335–8; Mills 1997, pp. 39–74; Ramírez 2005, pp. 113–54.
61. For these assessments and attitudes, see, for example, Duviols 1972, p. 106; MacCormack 1991, pp. 8, 264–5, 394; Mills 1997, p. 27; the religiously motivated human sacrifices in the Andes were appalling for Europeans; on the other hand, many indigenous groups of that period found Christianity to be foreign and deficient (Reinhard 1985; MacCormack 1991, p. 145).
62. Cuaz 2005, pp. 72–3, 114, 122.

almost every continent and a few top climbers now began to develop certain global ambitions. This new pursuit was embedded in the colonial culture of the late nineteenth century and in the propaganda of discovery and conquest. Although 'first ascents' became an end in their own right, mountaineers often had to justify their passion. Initially the opinion was widespread, even in the countries of origin, that mountain climbing was some sort of mental illness, executed by 'persons of unsound minds', as one English travel guide described it. One could hear such doubts repeatedly expressed, later too, and particularly following major sensationalised climbing accidents. In fact, high mountain climbing soon belonged among the sports with high death tolls.[63]

Alpinism is of interest here because it resulted in many points of contact: the mountaineers were mostly accompanied by guides and/or porters from the foreign mountain populations; in some cases, general relationships with these populations also developed; and finally, it caused various mountain conceptions to collide with one another. This may be observed in many regions.[64] Yet the most dramatic showplace was undoubtedly the Himalayas and the adjacent Karakoram, not only because all fourteen 'Eight-thousanders' on the planet are found there but also because this was an area marked by intensely religious forms of mountain perception. This came to expression also in the climbing history of Mount Everest, which was considered the world's highest mountain from the mid-nineteenth century and yet was not of primary importance in the religious hierarchy of regional Tibetan Buddhism.[65]

Everest sits on the border between Tibet and Nepal, where it is also known as Chomolungma and as Sagarmatha. In order to approach it, explorers had to enter one of these countries from British India and both were long closed to foreigners. Especially with respect to mountain climbing, the meaning of which was hard to convey, the rulers harboured political and religious misgivings. In the Buddhist sphere of influence surrounding Everest there existed a type of territorial control known as 'sealing the hills and the valleys', driven since the fifteenth century by religious motives. These 'closures' or taboos assigned to

---

63. Hansen 1995, quote p. 300; Salisbury/Hawley 2007; for the globalisation of Alpinism see above, Chapter 1.5.

64. Indications in Carey 2003; for Europe, and based on folk tales, some authors have spoken of an older 'taboo' on mountain climbing (Scharfe 2007, pp. 77–92); we have to stress, however, that little is known about the social-historical significance of these 'traditional' tales, which were compiled in the nineteenth century; moreover, there is no comparative study of their distribution in upland and lowland regions.

65. A survey on Himalayanism in western perspective is provided by Isserman/Weaver 2008.

certain activities, such as the killing of living things, were enforced by various authorities with differing motivations, intensities and results. In the vicinity of some monasteries, this could lead even to the establishment of wildlife preserves. The monastic movement experienced a new upswing, particularly from the nineteenth century, and pushed increasingly for what it saw as a higher and purer way of life among the general population.[66] The British Mission to Tibet under Francis Younghusband burst into this situation in 1904, which cost hundreds of Tibetans their lives, resulted in the temporary occupation of Lhasa and also retained, with its forced agreement, the character of an invasion. The exiled Dalai Lama had not signed the agreement but now, at least in theory, mountain expeditions could obtain permission to enter his territory. The Tibetan authorities put their religious concerns aside, especially in periods when tensions with China mounted and they had to rely on British weapons and diplomatic support.[67]

The first expedition to seriously attempt an ascent to the highest point on earth took place in the spring of 1922. It comprised a dozen European 'Sahibs', or gentlemen, along with a film-maker, a Tibetan translator, a small military escort and a great number of local porters, cooks, orderlies and other assistants; in addition, there were around 300 pack animals. On 30 April the long column arrived in military formation at Rongbuk Monastery, the northern entry to Everest at over 5,000 metres. The monastery had been founded only two decades earlier and the abbot subjected the British leader to a thorough examination. Throughout all the formalities, his scepticism and repugnance toward the strange undertaking were unmistakable. The Briton promised they would kill no animals in the district. Then the abbot imparted his blessing and dismissed the expedition with the following admonition, according to his autobiography: 'As our country is bitterly cold and frosty, it is difficult for others than those who are devoted to religion not to come to harm. As the local spirits are furies, you must act with great firmness.' At any rate, the climbing attempt failed in tragedy, as did the next one two years later. Not until 1930 was it again possible to obtain official consent. In answer to the English ambassador's request, the Dalai Lama responded:

> From our point of view, almost every snowy mountain in Tibet is the seat of the gods and of the guardian deities of the inner religion [i.e. Buddhism], who

---

66. Huber 1991; 2004; Ortner 1992; 1997; 1999 (remarkable historical-anthropological studies of the Buddhist Sherpa region; also in theoretical respects, including observations on the debate about Orientalism and its limits).

67. Hansen 1996, p. 743.

are very jealous; yet, in deference to the wishes of the British Government and in order that the friendly relations may not be ruptured, permission is hereby granted.[68]

Finding themselves in a peculiar situation were the 'Sherpas', who came above all from the populations living on the Nepalese side of Everest and who were the preferred assistants chosen by mountaineers in those decades, so that soon the name also became a professional title. Aside from the very real dangers of their wage labour, the Sherpas had to overcome their Buddhist reservations against mountaineering, gain the support of their lamas and steer their foreign employers away from the most serious transgressions of religious commandments. In the mountains, therefore, they often followed the prescriptions with great scrupulousness.[69] Sherpa Tenzing Norgay, who stood on top of Everest alongside the New Zealander Edmund Hillary for the first time in 1953, after taking part in several earlier failed expeditions, was also considered a religious person. As a child he left a monastery following a bad experience, yet he subsequently remained a conscientious Buddhist. On the first ascent in 1953, he evidently found it natural to say a prayer on the peak and set an offering in the snow. Yet he had to disappoint his mother, who believed that high above on Everest there were a golden sparrow and a turquoise-coloured lion. He saw no such things, he later reported in an autobiography. Neither did he notice how Hillary left behind a small crucifix on the mountaintop, as the latter claimed in his book. As for Tenzing, he saw only a good luck charm.[70]

These and other gestures of identity – also and above all the question of national flags – were illuminated on all sides upon the descent. The two heroes were plunged immediately into a storm of politically charged interviews, honours and awards of all kinds. The first ascent of Everest was an occasion with worldwide resonance, uniting and dividing at the same time.[71] Besides strengthening all the global, national and cultural identities that were mobilised in this phase of decolonisation, there was also the question of 'modernity'. Were the spectacularly successful ascents of international Alpinism, or Himalayanism, a sign that modern society was striving more generally upward? The advanced technology and performance-based self-discipline that were applied to climbing might convey this impression. Yet from its inception, mountaineering also

---

68. Isserman/Weaver 2008, pp. 108–26; Hansen 1996, quotes pp. 724 and 743.
69. Ortner 1999, pp. 127–8; Hansen 1999.
70. Ortner 1999, pp. 112–4; Isserman/Weaver 2008, pp. 290, 494; Hansen 1997, pp. 172–93; 1999, 229; generally on summit rituals: Siegrist 1996, p. 150.
71. Stewart 1995; Hansen 1997; 2000; Maurer 2009.

North–South Conflict Community

tended to be critical of civilisation. Many of its protagonists expressed opposition to urban growth, traffic, the rush and the routines of the industrial age, displaying their passion as a choice in favour of the superior world of nature.[72]

The criticism of western modernity was reinforced by the protest movement that spread out from the United States in the years around 1970, hastening the cultural change. In 'Himalayan mountaineering', the change affected both sides: on the one hand, part of the international community of mountaineers showed a greater interest in regional traditions; on the other, indigenous people adapted western lifestyles and broadened their field of action. At the Everest base camp it now became common for foreigners, too, to perform Buddhist rituals before a climb. Even Buddhism could appear in a new light, not least because many monasteries received financial assistance from abroad. The head of Tengboche Monastery at the southern entry to Everest was quoted as saying in 1992: 'Before, the gods didn't like climbing, but everything has changed.'[73] Also with respect to the mountaintops, complex discourses about mountain ethics and the imbalance of power among the various interest groups came to expression as matters of great religious importance. When certain plans to climb the holy Mount Kailash in Tibet became known in 2001, intended as a 'political demonstration against environmental destruction', this led to widespread outrage and protest, not just from the religious side but also from mountain climbers. Many of them had long maintained that their activities transcended the materialism of everyday life.[74]

Tourism

Whereas the institutionalisation of Alpinism occurred in the second half of the nineteenth century, the upswing in other mountain sports really set in at the start of the twentieth. In 1924, at the first Olympic Winter Games in Chamonix, competitions were held in the following sports: speed skating, figure skating, ice hockey, curling, cross-country skiing, ski jumping, Nordic combined, bobsled and military patrol. Only figure skating was open to women. The Medal of Honor for Alpinism was awarded to the British members of the 1922 Mount Everest expedition (the group representative there promised to deposit the medal up on top of the highest peak). Alpinism was subsequently struck from the Olympic agenda and, in its place, soon came Alpine skiing,

---

72. Ortner 1999, pp. 36–41.
73. Ortner 1997, pp. 153; 1999, pp. 130–3, 185–216; see also Dixit 1992 on the economic and political organisation of 'Himalayan Mountaineering' in that period.
74. E.g. Bernbaum 1997, pp. 236–47.

followed later by many other sporting events. Officially, the 'winter sports' consisted of disciplines carried out 'on snow and ice'. This, however, required special natural or technical conditions that stood in the way of the Olympic movement's universal ambitions, which is one reason why the Winter Games were first institutionalised long after the Summer Games. Pierre de Coubertin, an important pioneer in this movement, recalled the concerns in his memoirs:

> We can fabricate artificial ice, it is true, but not snow, much less mountain peaks. Are we to demand that the Dutch construct a mountain chain for (the Olympics of) 1928, that it be made from secondhand materials, or custom-built from the ground up?[75]

In fact, the choice of venues for the Games generally fell to places in or near the mountains, which were characterised by a tradition of tourism and infrastructure: 1924, Chamonix, at the foot of the legendary Mont Blanc in the French Alps; 1928, St. Moritz in the Swiss Alps, famous for its distinguished clientele and its early engagement in winter sports; later Garmisch-Partenkirchen, Cortina d'Ampezzo, Innsbruck and Grenoble. Despite its global claims, the winter component of the Olympic enterprise long remained decidedly European and particularly Alpine: of the twelve Winter Games up to 1976, no less than two thirds took place in the Alpine space. Whereas North America was able to secure a number of Games for itself quite early, the rest of the globe waited almost fifty years for the Olympic Committee's first endorsement (1972, Sapporo, Japan). Similarly one-sided was the distribution of participating countries. The European share was initially a strong eighty per cent and in the late twentieth century it still ran to sixty per cent. This became the subject of engaged debate, especially as globality gained substance with the growing number of participating delegations, which eventually reached around two fifths of all countries worldwide (see Table 8).[76]

The Olympic Winter Games were, in many respects, connected with modern tourism in mountain regions and here they can provide us with an

---

75. Coubertin 1931, quote pp. 167 (original French), 189 (Everest promise); on the early period of modern winter sports and of the Olympic Winter Games: Arnaud/Terret 1993; Busset/Marcacci 2006; Gerlach 2004; Kamper 1964; Krüger 1994; Morales 2002; Pallière 1991.
76. CERSO 2002; the figures in Table 8 were, of course, also influenced by political conditions, for instance by the increase in European countries after the dissolution of the Soviet Union in 1991.

North–South Conflict Community

Table 8: Development of the Olympic Winter Games, 1924–2006

Indicator	1924–1936	1948–1960	1964–1976	1980–1992	1994–2006
Venue Locations					
Europe	3	3	3	2	2
North America	1	1	0	2	1
Other Continents	0	0	1	0	1
Participating Countries					
Europe	18	22	24	30	45
North America	2	2	2	3	3
Other Continents	2	6	10	19	27
Sporting Events	15	24	35	47	73

In each case four Games per period (with Games suspended during World War II; offset since 1994 to take place midway between the Summer Games). For the participating countries (National Olympic Committees) and the sporting events: average of the four Games in each period. Source: data from the International Olympic Committee, provided by the IOC Research and Reference Service in Lausanne.

idea of its development and imbalances.[77] The beginnings of this industry can be dated to the mid-eighteenth century. At that time a new wanderlust was spreading among the elites of northern Europe, not only for the well-known cities and ancient monuments but also and increasingly for 'unspoiled, natural' landscapes – in particular, the mountains. The mountainous regions between central Switzerland and Chamonix became a classic early tourist destination. In this situation, and in many later ones, tourism also grew as a side effect of urbanisation. The more the population concentrated in the centres, the more a certain prosperity spread and the more efficient and affordable transportation became, so that leisure travel assumed a new importance. Tourism thus became a leading global industry over the course of the twentieth century. The cultural imaginings of 'other places', along with affiliated fashion trends, played an important role in this. As with the Winter Games, the development of tourism was extremely uneven in mountainous areas. It began in a few Alpine regions and gradually expanded into broader areas but hardly ever in a homogenous way. The dominance of Europe may be seen in the exported terms 'Switzerland' and 'Alps', which were turned into landscape designations and carried, especially during the nineteenth century, to many parts of the world. This also suggests

---

77. On the development of tourism, in general and in mountain regions, see, for example, Tissot 2000 and 2003; Price 1997; Busset 2004; Barton 2008.

that tourism – despite or even precisely because of its tendency toward stereotypes – was among the important factors in cultural transfer. Emanating from Europe, for example, it put into circulation new mountain images associated with romance and high-performance sports.[78]

In later phases, however, the dynamic could also extend from other regions and put the West into the more passive role. An example is the appropriation of the European and above all Swiss mountain world by 'Bollywood', as the commercial Hindi cinema in Bombay/Mumbai is also known. The first production of this type was the 1964 film *Sangam* ['The Union'], portraying a newlywed Indian couple on their honeymoon to Paris, Venice and the Bernese Alps. The film was an overwhelming success and started a trend that has led to a series of productions since the late 1980s. Post-colonial Indian society was their point of departure and target audience and, according to one film scholar, their customary composition differed from the iconography of tourism in the West: 'In Indian films, Swiss mountains are conveyed similarly in compositional terms to the mountains of Kashmir, which provide the traditional setting for romance in paintings, photographs, posters, and films.' The cultural background to this romantic use of mountain landscapes is often recognised in the tradition of the early modern Mughal Empire, in which Kashmir and its summer palaces played a significant role. Among other influential factors were the Hindu epics with their pertinent models and also in some cases imported British ideas from the nineteenth century. In any case, the Bollywood productions made the Alps into a stage for romantic musical and dance performances and thus into a landscape of love. Parallel to the success of these films came a sharp rise in Indian tourism to Swiss mountain destinations – an example of the power of imagination that has generally characterised the history of leisure travel.[79]

2002: The International Year of the Mountains

In this chapter, on the basis of selected examples, we have discussed several forms of large-scale, cross-cultural contacts that altered the perception of mountains. They may be characterised as follows:

1. Forced Assimilation – in the case of Spanish colonialism in Latin America during the sixteenth and seventeenth centuries, which regarded the indigenous mountain cults as 'idolatry' and meant to eradicate them.

---

78. See above, Chapter 1.3 (globalisation of the designation 'Alps') and Siedentop 1977 and 1984 (spread of the designation 'Switzerland').

79. Schneider 2002 (quote p. 138, original German) and 2006; Keller 2002.

2. Cultural Penetration – with the rise of tourism and Alpinism since the eighteenth and nineteenth centuries, initially extending from Europe, which brought romantic and performance-based athletic images of mountains into currency

3. Global Initiatives – as promoted by the Olympic movement, which showcased sports competitions 'on ice and snow' at regular intervals since the early twentieth century.

As seen in Part One of this book, a scientific tradition concerned with the world's mountains provided the impulse for yet another global initiative. The specialisation of research in many disciplines fostered a global orientation but led simultaneously to a segmented view. Then, with the politicisation of the environment in the late twentieth century, there emerged a current that was increasingly oriented toward public discourse and interdisciplinary approaches. One group involved in this movement succeeded in anchoring the topic on the diplomatic floor. At the UN Earth Summit of Rio de Janeiro in 1992, the mountains received a special chapter in the Agenda for the Twenty-First Century, a kind of global constitutional text. At the same time a unit was created within the Food and Agriculture Organization (FAO), where the Mountain Chapter was to be further elaborated within the framework of the UN system (see above, Chapters 1.1 and 1.5).

With this, there arose a process for transnational cultural contacts and a new problems- and policy-oriented mountain perception. The protagonists of the movement now had to assert themselves increasingly within the changing agendas of the world community. First and foremost it required the creation of an identity in this setting – in other words, winning over the broadest possible support for the ideas and providing them with the necessary coherence and consistency. An opportunity for this presented itself in the 'International Years', which the United Nations General Assembly proclaimed on a regular basis in order to sensitise the world public to certain themes. In 1998, for example, there was an 'International Year of the Ocean'. In response to the proposal from Kyrgyzstan, the assembly agreed in November of that same year to dedicate the year 2002 to the mountains. The resolution called on all governments, UN organisations and other actors to use the opportunity 'to increase awareness of the importance of sustainable mountain development'. The FAO, which took over the preparation and coordination, called the project an exciting challenge in the continuation of the Rio process. It summarised the message in the following words:

Mountains are fragile ecosystems and are globally important as water towers of the earth, repositories of rich biological diversity, target areas for recreation, and as a hub of cultural integrity and heritage. Occupying about one-fifth of the world's land surface area, mountains provide a direct life-support base for about one-tenth of humankind as well as goods and services to more than half the world's population.[80]

By the end of October 2002, the FAO unit was able to announce in an interim report that the Year of the Mountains was being celebrated around the globe with numerous national and international events and initiatives, organised and carried out by the most diverse institutions and individuals. The final report painted a similar picture: reaction to the Mountain Year had been enormous. In no less than 78 countries throughout Africa and Asia, the Pacific Rim, Europe, Latin and North America, national committees or similar bodies were reportedly active:

> Many of these national committees had a broad-based membership of stakeholders, including representatives of national government agencies, mountain people, grass-roots organizations, NGO's, civil society, academic and research institutions, the private sector, United Nations agencies, and decentralized authorities.

The list of reported events and items produced was colourful too: seminars, concerts, expeditions, school contests, media reports, commemorative postage stamps and telephone cards and more. At the global level, according to the FAO, ten major events were organised, among them a 'High Summit 2002' (telecommunications conferences linking high mountain locations on four continents); a new 'Mountain Initiative', launched at the UN World Summit on Sustainable Development in Johannesburg; and, in culmination, a 'Global Mountain Summit' in Bishkek, the capital of Kyrgyzstan where the idea for the International Year first originated.[81]

Among the major events there was also the meeting 'Celebrating Mountain Women', held in early October 2002, which drew around 250 participants from almost every continent to the small Buddhist country of Bhutan in the Himalayas (see Plate 16). The meeting is of special interest here because it accentuated social and cultural aspects. Under the theme of 'Culture and Indigenous Knowledge', the participating women identified globalisation as an essential driving force. In recent decades, they felt it had undermined

---

80. UNGA 1998, p. 3 and FAO 2000, p. 1.
81. FAO 2002, pp. 3–4; UNGA 2003, pp. 12–13.

indigenous knowledge. The rich traditions of storytelling, songs, myths and legends were being forgotten. The keynote speaker, who came from a position of international feminism, also emphasised diversity: 'The question of how to create unity while accommodating differences becomes a central problem for the future of the women's movement.' Following from this, 'An empowered woman honours diversity.' The discussion was accompanied by a 'Mountain Costume Show'. Most of the featured clothing and costumes were richly coloured and artistically handcrafted. They came from many parts of the world. Each costume told, according to the conference proceedings, 'a story about the mountain people's age-old traditions embedded in culture, customs, and a unique set of beliefs and values'. Among the enthusiastic visitors were two American women who came from Appalachia and represented their regional association, 'In Praise of Mountain Women'. A folklorist friend had helped design their clothing and they viewed their appearance in Bhutan as a success. 'They liked our energy when we went out on stage', they told one reporter. 'Everybody was cheering, and we were just dancing.'[82]

Many participants in such events must have been aware that they themselves were taking part in globalisation and that they could not vindicate their differences on these occasions without a certain artifice. Yet the effectiveness of the global agenda should not be overestimated, during the International Year of the Mountains or otherwise. In reality the coordinating powers were highly dependent on the participation of completely different organisations, which could place the global currency in service of their own objectives. In general, the 'Mountain Scene' of the year 2002 entered into that transnational political culture with its origins in the late twentieth century, whose colourful groups and networks had to constantly struggle for visibility and positioning. Together they developed a moral force not to be underrated. Many of them stood for particular ethnic or religious identities. A prominent and relatively successful example was the Tibetan movement, which, like others since the 1980s, underwent an ecological transformation.[83]

From historical perspective and experience, we can establish that the 'ancient' cultural elements thereby brought into play were seldom really old at all (the clothing from 2002 could just as easily have been made the previous year without being the less fascinating). The supposition that modernisation and globalisation lead to a general cultural homogeneity remains unconvincing.

---

82. IDIMOD 2003, pp. 6, 15, 52, 55 68, 81; the importance of diversity was also stressed in the concluding declaration; see also Anand/Josse 2002 and Zimmermann 2002.
83. Debarbieux/Rudaz 2010, pp. 245–75; Huber 1997b and 1997c.

The assessment also depended on that which was seen as 'unique' and on many other aspects that were commonly overlooked or left out of such definitions. Let us take, for example, the scientific investigation of the mountain world, which we can certainly designate as 'modern'. It developed a certain repertoire of shared standards but came to be divided precisely as a result of its growth into various directions and disciplinary cultures. As a further example, which likewise provides a fairly systematic overview, we may point to the naming of mountains. Before the nineteenth and twentieth centuries there were many unnamed peaks and yet, as they later received designations, these bore witness more to the contextual restraints and divisions inherent in modernity than to any levelling process. Everything indicates that, in many cases, development and cultural diversity presented no real antithesis but were in fact compatible.[84]

---

84. On the history of mountain research and naming see above, Chapters 1.2–1.4 and 4.2.

~ 5 ~

RESULTS AND OUTLOOK

A Three-Dimensional World

This study sets out to examine the three-dimensionality of the earth from a historical perspective. Other disciplines that treat this theme normally privilege spatial approaches. If we aim to enter the discussion as historians, then we should shift our focus to humans and their diachronic existence. This affords us the best hope of stimulating the research and making a meaningful contribution. The present study handles economic, social and cultural themes, namely: 1. Globalisation of Perception; 2. Population and Urbanisation; 3. Agriculture, Family, Mobility; and 4. Cultural Diversity and Modernity. It considers, each according to the subject of inquiry and the state of research, select mountain regions on different continents as well as in certain periods over the last five hundred years.

The recent research on intellectual and cultural representations emphasises the constructive aspect of universals and global concepts. In our case this becomes very clear. For the idea to conceive of the mountains as a universal whole does not result from mere visual inspection. No matter where one stands, only individual mountains can be seen. Even when the earth could be viewed from space, the widely scattered mountains did not readily impose themselves as a global object. Nevertheless, in the twentieth century they found their way as such into highly regarded documents, in particular the Agenda 21, which was achieved through great effort at the UN Earth Summit of 1992 in Rio de Janeiro. How and why did this historical construction come about?

European expansion and scientific departure provided important impulses in the early modern period. In the seventeenth century, there arose a major interest in altitude measurements (one speaks of the 'Birth of Altitude') and, in the eighteenth century, naturalists and philosophers began to conceive of the world's mountains as a system. The search for the highest mountain on earth now developed into an undertaking that drew many under its spell. It was the vertical pendant on the horizontal chain of historical discoveries and conquests.

Results and Outlook

The conceptual globalisation then accelerated from the nineteenth century by way of scientific specialisation. This made the investigated environmental units smaller, while often broadening the geographical field of observation. Finally, around 1970, there came a general politicisation of the environment. It formed the background for a variety of organisational efforts in mountain research and led to a certain anchoring of this theme on the institutional floor of the United Nations.

Globalisation movements can be a motive to emphasise in retrospect those aspects of history that are held in common, thereby underestimating cultural diversity. Such is the case with the idea of a general 'mountain sacredness', which took shape in the nineteenth century and caught on especially in the late twentieth century. Upon closer examination, this idea does not stand: in Asia, one finds structured and elaborated cultures of holy mountains throughout the entire modern period (and earlier), whereas in Europe and among the European settlers of North America no such parallels existed during the sixteenth and seventeenth centuries; only later did a certain sacralisation occur there, in conjunction with modernisation. From this Euro-American romanticisation of nature and the 'wilderness' concept there emerged the national park movement, which comprised by the year 2000 almost 4,000 parks worldwide, many of them in mountain regions.

The parks, essentially 'nature' reserves, are also an expression of the increasing disparities between highland and lowland that bear the mark of modern development. In a first phase, ecological differences appeared less often than other 'accidental' factors of population and settlement. At that time, areas with lower population densities could be found everywhere. In a second phase, however, clear regularities began to reveal themselves. In many places the differences between highland and lowland regions intensified, as can be seen especially in the process and varying tempo of urbanisation. This gave rise, above all in the nineteenth and twentieth centuries, to relatively systematic disadvantages for mountain regions. Even where enormous differences divided the regions in a country, or the countries of the North and South, on average there now prevailed in the mountains of the world relatively greater poverty and less prosperity than in the lowlands.

Major Ecosystems

On the theoretical level, two models have proven to be of special interest in this study: the idea of path-dependency and a particular concept of agrarian intensification. Path-dependency, as opposed to context-dependency, empha-

Results and Outlook

sises the temporal relationships between phenomena. A specific constellation of phenomena can have a decisive influence on development, in that it prejudices the direction forward, which will be abandoned later only under contextual pressure. This implies that synchronous relationships often assume a suboptimal quality: in the relationship between humans and environment, the 'adaptation' may have been in many cases more improvisation than a *fait accompli*. Path-dependency makes it easier to grasp certain spatial distributions and locations, such as those of the high-altitude metropolises of Latin America. In this view, such situations consequently came about not by 'coincidence' but through an otherwise defined, chronological 'necessity'.

The underlying model of preindustrial agrarian intensification stems from Ester Boserup and assumes that it was possible, under the pressure of a growing population, to substantially raise land productivity by employing simple technologies, though this might require greater expenditure and even the acceptance of a decline in labour productivity. The data suggest that agrarian growth presented an option in mountain regions too, but only up to a certain level of intensity – beyond this point, the mountain setting posed an obstacle. The handicap therefore developed greater strength in a second phase than in the first and this reinforcement of disadvantages for growth could take hold before an eventual industrialisation, thereby influencing its specific form. Thus a multi-phase model presents itself, with variable levels of intensity and correspondingly different relations to environmental conditions.

Lucien Febvre, a classic author of modern historiography, remarked in his 1922 treatment of geography and history (later reissued several times) that one could not speak of mountain society as a general type: 'In reality there exists no kind of mountain unity, which would appear regularly in any location, where one encounters a mountain relief on the globe.' Everywhere there were, in his view, only similar possibilities or offerings for humans to make use of, each in a particular way or not at all. If, however, in addition to monographs concerned with Europe, studies were to appear from mountain regions elsewhere in the world, he felt it would then perhaps be possible 'to ascertain a certain number of adaptational forms in human societies according to the possibilities of various mountain types.'[1] Today such non-European studies are available – what can we draw from them in response to Febvre's observation?

A central point for this discussion concerns the vertical organisation of land use and mobility, which can be observed in many mountain regions worldwide. Their forms differed to start with for climatic reasons. The mountains

---

1. Febvre 1922, p. 240 (original French).

of the tropics experienced pronounced temperature variations throughout the day but barely any seasonal fluctuations. Whereas vertical mobility in non-tropical mountains may be related to the seasonal rise and fall of temperature and snow cover, in tropical mountains it depends on other factors. Important for historical research is its dynamic modelling: much evidence suggests that vertical interwovenness often accompanied the intensification of land use. Where the mountain slopes were used in regular, short intervals of time, there was a greater likelihood that the individual altitude levels would find different uses for various forms of field cultivation and animal husbandry. This in turn may have been a prerequisite for the development of vertically organised economies.

The 'possibilism' of Lucien Febvre stood as an important alternative concept against the dominant environmental determinism of the early twentieth century, yet he shared the latter's basically static conception. From our view it seems necessary to bring diachronic and dynamic explanations into play, as represented by the aforementioned models of path-dependency and agrarian intensification. It would undoubtedly be interesting in this context to inquire about the long-term history of other major ecosystems as well. In 1922, Febvre laid out a wealth of material on the human uses of various vegetation belts, desert regions and oceanic islands. To this could be added cultural and political questions as to the historical perception of such forms and their institutional associations. The historical research of the twentieth century has often concerned itself with questions of this sort; most evident today may well be the achievements of 'maritime history'. Would it not be worth the effort to bring these things together and evaluate them anew?

Towards Kamchatka

The UN Conference on Environment and Development of 1992 in Rio de Janeiro, which I used in this book as the starting point for a journey through the history of mountains, was a forward-looking event. In the mountain sphere, as in other areas, it sought to provide a breakthrough in sustainable development. Adopted on this occasion, the Agenda for the Twenty-First Century was a remarkable document, the preparation of which required an estimated 24 million pages and the synthesis another 500 pages. Even more astonishing is the fact that such a document remained a topic of discussion for many years afterwards, attaining through its high rate of citation a constitutional character, though it held no legal obligation for individual governments. Clearly, this moment in history was driven by the '*Zeitgeist*', the staying power of which one can seldom predict. In the future, will the Mountain Chapter continue

Results and Outlook

to motivate people to action all around the world, as it did during the 2002 International Year of the Mountains?

Many mountain regions serve as water towers for wide areas of the surrounding lowlands, and one can safely assume that future water resources will take on even greater importance in the future. Still, it is difficult to say if and to what extent this fact will find application in an argument to empower mountain people. In view of the existing disadvantages, this would certainly be justified in many cases. Also hard to predict is the future of a socio-political argument that played a by no means inconsequential role in 1992. At that time the wealthy countries of the North demanded 'environmental protection' from the less developed South, whereas the South called for a 'technology transfer' and financial compensation from the North. The mountains were among the few themes that brought these two opposing blocs together.

This North–South problematic continues to deserve our attention, in historical work as elsewhere. Methodologically, its cultural aspects deserve particular attention, because this issue requires a detailed understanding of the completely different contexts within which claims to power and attributions of meaning are negotiated and expressed by individual groups, each according to its own agenda. 'These are not necessarily agendas of power and domination as such; often they are not', writes Sherry B. Ortner in her important investigation of the Sherpas on Mount Everest, 'But the de facto differentials of power and resources shape even the most well-meaning encounters, and produce the ongoing friction – sometimes pleasurable, often tragic, always generative – of history.'[2]

In the present study we have observed the North–South conflict community in mountain regions on the basis of selected stopovers and distinguished between several forms of contact (forced assimilation, cultural penetration, global initiatives). One should perhaps go a step further and also include, for example, such a remote and impressive history as is encountered on Kamchatka. This large peninsula in East Asian Russia found itself far from the centres of development, yet it was repeatedly exposed to their influences. Three quarters of Kamchatka's surface consists of mountains and volcanoes, a few of them extremely active: the Pacific Plate is subducted here beneath the Eurasian Plate at a rate of almost ten centimetres annually. At the end of the seventeenth century the peninsula was spotted by Russian Cossacks who soon occupied it, engaging in bloody clashes with the tribal population. Some decades later, travelling researchers came to Kamchatka and generated extensive descriptions. The next

---

2.   Ortner 1999, p. 17.

Results and Outlook

chapter began in the twentieth century, when the peninsula assumed a world political role as an outpost and military blockade zone in the struggle between the Soviet Union and the United States. What is provisionally the final chapter came about after the cold war, as ecotourism gained currency and UNESCO declared the volcanic region a Natural World Heritage site.[3]

In his 2003 novel *Kamchatka*, the Argentinian author Marcelo Figueras uses the distant Russian peninsula as an imaginary bastion against the terror of the generals, and he reflects on the temporal course of events as follows: 'Time is weird. Sometimes I think it is like a book. Everything is inside, between the front and back covers, the whole story, from beginning to end.' For the narrator, all these occurrences and memories are gathered here in one place and they run together as if they happened in the same moment. Presented by several people, a polyphonic choir could emerge.[4] The author does not pretend any attempt to portray the real nature and culture of the volcanic world of Kamchatka. Yet his efforts to understand the chronological sequences, along with the insight that this requires many voices and various tonalities, could offer us one way forward.

---

3. Posselt 1990 (reader-friendly collection of texts; German-Russian research has now published many documents from the Kamchatka expeditions); Zoelen 2002.
4. Figueras 2010 (2003), p. 308; the 'simultaneous' unfolding of history is a *leitmotiv* of the novel.

BIBLIOGRAPHY

Acosta, Joseph de: *Historia natural y moral de las Indias*, Mexico 2006 (first edition 1590).

Aitmatow, Tschingis: *Kindheit in Kirgisien*, Zurich 1998.

Albera, Dionigi: 'Oltre la norma e la strategia: per una comparazione ragionata dell'organizzazione domestica alpina', in *Histoire des Alpes* 6 (2001), pp. 117–132.

Albert, Jean-Pierre: 'Les montagnes sont-elles bonnes à penser en termes religieux?' in Serge Brunet *et al.* (eds.) *Montagnes sacrées d'Europe*, Paris 2005, pp. 65–71.

Anand, Anita / Ojaswi Josse: 'Celebrating Mountain Women: Moving Mountains, Moving Women', in *Mountain Research and Development* 22/3 (2002), pp. 233–235.

Andrian, Ferdinand von: *Der Höhencultus asiatischer und europäischer Völker. Eine ethnologische Studie*, Vienna 1891.

Arnaud, Pierre / Thierry Terret: *Le rêve blanc. Olympisme et Sport d'hiver en France, Chamonix 1924, Grenoble 1968*, Bordeaux 1993.

Asbury, Francis: *The Journal and Letters*, ed. by Elmer T. Clark, 3 vols. London 1958.

Assadourian, Carlos Sempat: 'Agriculture and Land Tenure', in *The Cambridge Economic History of Latin America*, vol. 1: *The Colonial Era and the Short Nineteenth Century*, Cambridge 2006, pp. 275–314.

Badenkov, Yuri P.: 'Sustainable Development of the Mountain Regions of the USSR. The Realities, the Role of Science, and Research Orientations', in *Mountain Research and Development* 10/2 (1990), pp. 129–139.

Bairoch, Paul *et al.*: *La population des villes européennes de 800 à 1850 / The Population of European Cities from 800 to 1850*, Geneva 1988.

— 'Agriculture and the Industrial Revolution 1700–1914', in Carlo M. Cipolla (ed.) *The Fontana Economic History of Europe*, vol. 3, Glasgow 1973, pp. 452–506.

— *De Jéricho à Mexico. Villes et économie dans l'histoire*, Paris 1996 (second corrected edition).

— *Taille des villes, conditions de vie et développement économique*, Paris 1977.

Baker, Dwight Condo: *T'ai Shan. An Account of the Sacred Eastern Peak of China*, Shanghai 1925.

Bandyopadhyay, Jayanta / Shama Perveen: 'Emergence of and Future Steps for Sustainable Mountain Development in the Global Environmental Agenda', in Tullio Treves *et al.* (eds.) *Sustainable Development of Mountain Areas. Legal Perspectives Beyond Rio and Johannesburg*, Milan 2004, pp. 9–25.

Barbero, Amilcare / Stefano Piano (eds.): *Religioni e Sacri Monti. Atti del Convegno Internazionale Torino, Moncalvo, Casale Monferrato, 12–16 ottobre 2004*, Ponzano Monferrato 2006.

Barfield, Thomas J.: *The Nomadic Alternative*, New Jersey 1993.

Bibliography

Barrett, Thomas M.: *At the Edge of Empire. The Terek Cossacks and the North Caucasus Frontier 1700–1860*, Boulder 1999.

Barton. Susan: *Healthy Living in the Alps. The Origins of Winter Tourism in Switzerland, 1860–1914*, Manchester 2008.

Bätzing, Werner: 'Die Alpen im Spannungsfeld der europäischen Raumordnungspolitik', in *Raumforschung und Raumordnung* 57 (1999), pp. 3–13.

Bätzing, Werner *et al.*: *Der sozio-ökonomische Strukturwandel des Alpenraumes im 20. Jahrhundert. Eine Analyse von 'Entwicklungstypen' auf Gemeinde-Ebene im Kontext der europäischen Tertiarisierung*, Berne 1993.

Beck, Hanno: *Alexander von Humboldt*, vol. 1: *Von der Bildungsreise zur Forschungsreise 1769–1804*; vol. 2: *Vom Reisewerk zum 'Kosmos' 1804–1859*, Wiesbaden 1959/1961.

— *Grosse Geographen. Pioniere – Aussenseiter – Gelehrte*, Berlin 1982.

— 'Landschaften, Profile und Karten aus Alexander von Humboldts Atlanten zum amerikanischen Reisewerk', in *Mitteilungen der Alexander von Humboldt-Stiftung* 10/40 (1982), pp. 31–38. Quoted as 1982b.

Becker, Alfred / Harald Bugmann (eds.): *Global Change and Mountain Regions. The Mountain Research Initiative (IGBP Report 49)*, Stockholm 2001.

Beltrán y Rózpide, Ricardo: *Colección de las memorias o relaciones que escribieron los virreyes del Perú acerca del estado en que dejaban las cosas generales del reino*, vol. 1, Madrid 1921.

Bendik-Keymer, Jeremy: 'Sacred Places', in *Encyclopedia of World Environmental History*, ed. by Shepard Krech *et al.*, New York 2003, vol. 3, pp. 1081–1084.

Berghaus, Heinrich: *Physikalischer Atlas zu Alexander von Humboldt, Kosmos. Entwurf einer physischen Weltbeschreibung*, ed. by Ottmar Ette and Oliver Lubrich, Frankfurt a.M. 2004 (first edition 1845–1848).

Bergier, Jean-François: *Pour une histoire des Alpes, Moyen Âge et Temps modernes*, Aldershot 1997.

Bergier, Jean-François / Gauro Coppola (eds.): *Vie di terra e d'acqua. Infrastrutture viarie e sistemi di relazioni in area alpina (secoli XIII–XVI)*, Bologna 2007.

Bernand, Carmen / Serge Gruzinski: 'Les enfants de l'Apocalypse: la famille en Méso-Amérique et dans les Andes', in André Burguière *et al.* (eds.) *Histoire de la famille*, Paris 1986, vol. 2, pp. 157–209.

Bernbaum, Edwin: *Sacred Mountains of the World*, Berkeley 1997 (first edition 1990).

— 'Sacred Mountains: Themes and Teachings', in *Mountain Research and Development* 26/4 (2006), pp. 304–309.

— 'The Spiritual and Cultural Significance of Mountains', in Bruno Messerli / Jack D. Ives (eds.) *Mountains of the World. A Global Priority*, New York 1997, pp. 39–60. Quoted as 1997b.

Bert, Paul: *La pression barométrique. Recherches de physiologie expérimentale*, Paris 1878.

Bertrand, Elie: *Essai sur les usages des montagnes, avec une lettre sur le Nil*, Zurich 1754.

Biermann, Frank: 'Weltumweltpolitik auf den sieben Meeren. Von der Meeresnutzungs- zur Meeresschutzordnung', in Udo E. Simonis (ed.) *Weltumweltpolitik. Grundriss und Bausteine eines neuen Politikfeldes*, Berlin 1996, pp. 197–216.

Bibliography

Biermann, Kurt-R. et al.: *Alexander von Humboldt. Chronologische Übersicht über wichtige Daten seines Lebens* (second revised edition), Berlin 1983.

Biraben, Jean-Noël: 'Essai sur l'évolution du nombre des hommes', in *Population* 34 (1979), pp. 13–25.

Biswas, Asit K.: *History of Hydrology*, Amsterdam 1970.

Bitterli, Urs: *Alte Welt – neue Welt. Formen des europäisch-überseeischen Kulturkontakts vom 15. bis zum 18. Jahrhundert*, Munich 1986.

— *Die Entdeckung Amerikas. Von Kolumbus bis Alexander von Humboldt*, Munich 1999.

Blache, Jules: *Le Grand Refus. Pamphlet pour notre rééducation civique*, Paris 1945.

— *L'Homme et la Montagne* (Géographie Humaine 3), Paris 1934.

Blanckaert, Claude: 'La discipline en perspective. Le système des sciences à l'heure du spécialisme (XIXᵉ–XXᵉ siècle)', in Jean Boutier et al. (eds.) *Qu'est-ce qu'une discipline?* Paris 2006, pp. 117–148.

Blatter, Michael: 'The Transformation of the Alpine Economy, 14th–18th Centuries', in *Nomadic Peoples* 13/2 (2010), pp. 146–159.

Blondeau, Anne-Marie / Ernst Steinkellner (eds.): *Reflections of the Mountain. Essays on the History and Social Meaning of the Mountain Cult in Tibet and the Himalaya*, Vienna 1996.

Blunden, Caroline / Mark Elvin: *Cultural Atlas of China*, Oxford 1983.

Boerma, Pauline: 'Assessing Forest Cover Change in Eritrea – A Historical Perspective', in *Mountain Research and Development* 26/1 (2006), pp. 41–47.

Böhm, Hans: 'Annäherungen an Carl Troll (1899–1975) – Wissenschaftler in der NS-Zeit', in Mathias Winiger (ed.) *Zeitumstände und Forschungsperspektiven. Kolloquium im Gedenken an den 100. Geburtstag von Carl Troll*, St. Augustin 2003, pp. 1–99.

Bonilla, Heraclio: *El futuro del pasado. Las coordenadas de la configuración de los Andes*, 2 vols. Lima 2005.

— 'Religious Practices in the Andes and their Relevance to Political Struggle and Development: the Case of El Tío and Miners in Bolivia', in *Mountain Research and Development* 26/4 (2006), pp. 336–342.

Bonilla, Heraclio et al.: *Los Andes y la Amazonía: la metamorfosis y los particularismos de una región* (Maestría internacional de estudios andinos y amazónicos), unpublished paper, Bogotá 2004.

Boscani Leoni, Simona (ed.): *Wissenschaft – Berge – Ideologien. Johann Jakob Scheuchzer (1672–1733) und die frühneuzeitliche Naturforschung*, Basel 2010.

— 'Tra Zurigo e le Alpi: le "Lettres des Grisons" di Johann Jakob Scheuchzer (1672–1733). Dinamiche della comunicazione erudita all'inizio del Settecento', in Jon Mathieu / Simona Boscani Leoni (eds.) *Die Alpen! Zur europäischen Wahrnehmungsgeschichte seit der Renaissance*, Berne 2005, pp. 157–171.

Boserup, Ester: *Economic and Demographic Relationships in Development*. Essays Selected and Introduced by T. Paul Schulz, Baltimore 1990.

— *Population and Technology*, Oxford 1981.

— *The Conditions of Agricultural Growth. The Economics of Agrarian Change Under Population Pressure*, London 1993 (first edition 1965).

Bibliography

Bossus, Pierre: *Les cinquante premières années de l'Union Internationale des Associations d'Alpinisme / The First Fifty Years of the International Union of Mountaineering Associations*, Geneva 1982.

Bouguer, Pierre: *La Figure de la Terre, déterminée par les Observations des Messieurs Bouguer, & De La Condamine, de l'Académie Royale des Sciences, envoyés par l'ordre du Roy au Perou, pour observer aux environs de l'Equateur*, Paris 1749.

Bourdieu, Pierrre: 'Le champ scientifique', in *Actes de la recherche en sciences sociales* 1976/2–3, pp. 88–104.

Braudel, Fernand: *The Mediterranean and the Mediterranean World in the Age of Philip II*, 2. vols. Berkeley 1995 (first French edition 1949/66).

— *Civilisation and Capitalism, 15th-18th Century*, 3 vols. Berkeley 1992 (first French edition 1967/1979).

Braun, Georg / Franz Hogenberg: *Beschreibung und Contrafactur der vornembster Stät der Welt*, 2 vols. Cologne 1576–1618.

Brendecke, Arndt: 'Informing the Council. Central Institutions and Local Knowledge in the Spanish Empire', in Wim Blockmans / André Holenstein / Jon Mathieu (eds.) *Empowering Interactions. Political Cultures and the Emergence of the State in Europe 1300–1900*, Farnham 2009, pp. 235–252.

Brereton, Joel P.: 'Sacred Space', in *The Encyclopedia of Religion*, ed. by Mircea Eliade, New York 1987, vol. 12, pp. 526–535.

Bronger, Dirk: *Lhasa. Vom Zentrum des Tibetischen Buddhismus zu einem Chinesischen Regionalzentrum. Historische, strukturelle und funktionale Entwicklung 633–1998 n. Chr.*, Bochum 2001.

Browman, David L.: 'High Altitude Camelid Pastoralism of the Andes', in John G. Galati / Douglas L. Johnson (ed.) *The World of Pastoralism. Herding Systems in Comparative Perspective*, London 1990, pp. 323–352.

Bruce-Chwatt, Leonard Jan / Julian de Zulueta: *The Rise and Fall of Malaria in Europe*, Oxford 1980.

Brunet, Serge / Dominique Julia / Nicole Lemaitre (eds.): *Montagnes sacrées d'Europe*, Paris 2005.

Brunnbauer, Ulf: 'Environment, Markets, and the State: Human Adaptation in the Balkan Mountains, 19th–early 20th Centuries', in *Ethnologia Balkanica* 8 (2004), pp. 129–154.

Brunschwig, Murielle: 'La montagne des encyclopédistes du XIIIe siècle: entre brouillard et air pur', in Jon Mathieu / Simona Boscani Leoni (eds.) *Die Alpen! Zur europäischen Wahrnehmungsgeschichte seit der Renaissance*, Berne 2005, pp. 99–114.

Bruun, Ole / Arne Kalland: 'Images of Nature. An Introduction to the Study of Man–Environment Relations in Asia', in Brun and Kalland (eds.) *Asian Perceptions of Nature: A Critical Approach*, Richmond 1995, pp. 1–24.

Buache, Philippe: 'Essai de Géographie Physique, où l'on propose des vûes générales sur l'espèce de Charpente du Globe, composée des chaînes de montagnes qui traversent les mers comme les terres; avec quelques considérations particulières sur les différens bassins de la mer, et sur sa configuration intérieure', in *Mémoires de l'Académie Royales des Sciences* 1752, pp. 399–416.

Bibliography

— 'Parallèle des Fleuves des Quatre Parties du Monde, pour servir à déterminer les haueurs des montagnes du Globe physique de la Terre, qui s'exécute en relief au dôme du Luxembourg', in *Mémoires de l'Académie Royales des Sciences* 1753, pp. 586–588.

Buffetrille, Katia: *Pèlerins, lamas et visionnaires. Sources orales et écrites sur les pèlerinages tibétains*, Vienna 2000.

— 'Reflections on Pilgrimages to Sacred Mountains, Lakes and Caves', in Alex McKay: *Pilgrimage in Tibet*, Richmond 1998, pp. 18–34.

Burga, Conradin A. *et al.* (eds.): *Gebirge der Erde. Landschaft, Klima, Pflanzenwelt*, Stuttgart 2004.

Bürgi, Andreas (ed.): *Europa Miniature. Die kulturelle Bedeutung des Reliefs, 16.–21. Jahrhundert*, Zurich 2007.

Burke, Peter: *History and Social Theory*, Cambridge 1992.

— *A Social History of Knowledge: from Gutenberg to Diderot*, Cambridge 2000.

Burri, Katrin: *Umweltschutz in der Kailashregion. Präfektur Ngari, Westtibet. Eine Situationsanalyse*, s.l. [Zurich/Kriens] 2005.

Busset, Thomas / Luigi Lorenzetti / Jon Mathieu (eds.): *Anden – Himalaja – Alpen* (Geschichte der Alpen 8), Zurich 2003.

— *Tourisme et changements culturels / Tourismus und kultureller Wandel* (Geschichte der Alpen 9), Zurich 2004.

Busset, Thomas / Marco Marcacci (eds.): *Pour une histoire des sport d'hiver / Zur Geschichte des Wintersports*, Neuchâtel 2006.

Butzer, Karl W.: 'Practicing Geography in a Totalitarian State: (Re)Casting Carl Troll as a Nazi Collaborator?' in *Erde* 135/2 (2004), pp. 223–231.

— 'The Indian Legacy in the American Landscape', in Michael P. Conzen (ed.) *The Making of the American Landscape*, Boston, 1990, pp. 27–50.

Cajori, Florian: 'History of Determinations of the Heights of Mountains', in *Isis. An International Review Devoted to the History of Science* 13 (1929), pp. 482–514.

Cannon, Susan Faye: *Science in Culture: The Early Victorian Period*, New York 1978.

Cardwell, Donald S. L.: *From Watt to Clausius. The Rise of Thermodynamics in the Early Industrial Age*, London 1971.

— *The Organisation of Science in England*, London 1972.

Carey, Mark: 'Mountaineering', in *Encyclopedia of World Environmental History*, ed. by Shepard Krech *et al.*, New York, 2003 vol. 2, pp. 859–861.

CERSO Centre d'études et de recherches sur le sport et l'olympisme: *La participation aux Jeux Olympiques d'hiver: une ouverture timide*, unpublished paper, Besançon 2002 (by order of the CIO, accessible on www.olympic.org).

Chandler, Tertius: *Four Thousand Years of Urban Growth. An Historical Census*, Lewiston NY 1987.

Chang, Sen-Dou: 'The Historical Trend of Chinese Urbanization', in *Annals of the Association of American Geographers* 53/2 (1963), pp. 109–143.

Chape, Stuart *et al.*: *United Nations List of Protected Areas*, Gland 2003.

Bibliography

Chavannes, Edouard: *Le T'ai Chan. Essai de monographie d'un culte chinois*, Paris 1910.

Ciancio, Luca: *Teatro del mutamento. Immagini del 'Tempio di Serapide' a Pozzuoli (1750–1900)*, Trento 2005.

Clark, Peter (ed.): *Small Towns in Early Modern Europe*, Cambridge 1995.

Clark, William: *Academic Charisma and the Origins of the Research University*, Chicago 2006.

Claval, Paul: *Histoire de la géographie française de 1870 à nos jours*, Paris 1998.

Cole, John W. / Eric R. Wolf: *The Hidden Frontier. Ecology and Ethnicity in an Alpine Valley*, New York 1974.

Collantes, Fernando: 'Élevage extensif, industrialisation et économies montagnardes en Europe occidentale: un schéma comparatif', in Pierre-Yves Laffont (ed.) *Transhumance et estivage en Occident des origines aux enjeux actuels*, Toulouse 2006, pp. 355–366.

— 'Farewell to the Peasant Republic: Marginal Rural Communities and European Industrialisation, 1815–1990', in *The Agricultural History Review* 54/2 (2006), pp. 257–273. Quoted as 2006b.

— 'Rural Europe Reshaped: the Economic Transformation of Upland Regions, 1850–2000', in *Economic History Review* 62/2 (2009), pp. 306–323.

— 'The Demise of European Mountain Pastoralism: Spain 1500–2000', in *Nomadic Peoples* 13/2 (2010), pp. 124–145.

Colpe, Carsten: 'The Sacred and the Profane', in *The Encyclopedia of Religion*, ed. by Mircea Eliade, New York, 1987, vol. 12, pp. 511–526.

Comaroff, John / Jean Comaroff: *Ethnography and the Historical Imagination*, Boulder 1992.

Conrad, Christoph: 'Die Dynamik der Wenden. Von der neuen Sozialgeschichte zum cultural turn', in Jürgen Osterhammel *et al.* (eds.) *Wege der Gesellschaftsgeschichte* (Geschichte und Gesellschaft, Sonderheft 22), Göttingen 2006, pp. 133–160.

'Convergences and Differences in Mountain Economies and Societies. A Comparison of the Andes and Himalaya', ed. by Benjamin S. Orlove and David W. Guillet, special issue of *Mountain Research and Development* 5/1, 1985.

Cook, Noble David: *Demographic Collapse. Indian Peru, 1520–1620*, Cambridge 1981.

Coubertin, Pierre de: *Mémoires Olympiques*, Lausanne 1931.

Cronon, William: 'The Trouble with Wilderness; or, Getting Back to the Wrong Nature', in Cronon (ed.) *Uncommon Ground. Towards Reinventing Nature*, New York 1995, pp. 69–90.

Crosby, Alfred W.: *Ecological Imperialism. The Biological Expansion of Europe*, Cambridge 2004 (first edition 1986).

— *The Columbian Exchange. Biological and Cultural Consequences of 1492*, Westport 1972.

Cuaz, Marco: *Le Alpi*, Bologna 2005.

Dakang, Zuo / Zhang Peiyuan: 'The Huang-Huai-Hai Plain', in by B. L. Turner *et al.* (eds.) *The Earth As Transformed by Human Action. Global and Regional Changes in the Biosphere over the Past 300 Years*, Cambridge 1990, pp. 473–477.

Dalence, José María: *Bosquejo estadístico de Bolivia*, La Paz 1975 (first edition 1851).

Bibliography

Dangwal, Dhirendra Datt: *Himalayan Degradation. Colonial Forestry and Environmental Change in India*, New Delhi 2009.

Darbellay, Charly: 'L'agriculture de montagne en mutation', in Ernst A. Brugger *et al.* (eds.) *Umbruch im Berggebiet. Die Entwicklung des schweizerischen Berggebietes zwischen Eigenständigkeit und Abhängigkeit aus ökonomischer und ökologischer Sicht*, Berne 1984, pp. 407–437.

Davis, Donald Edward: *Where There Are Mountains. An Environmental History of the Southern Appalachians*, Athens Georgia, 2000.

De Beer, Gavin: *Travellers in Switzerland*, London 1949.

Debarbieux, Bernard: 'La nomination au service de la territorialisation. Réflexions sur l'usage des termes "alpe" et "montagne"', in *Le Monde alpin et rhodanien* 25 (1997), pp. 227–241.

— 'The Mountains Between Corporal Experience and Pure Rationality: the Contradictory Theories of Philippe Buache and Alexander von Humboldt', in Denis Cosgrove / Veronica della Dora (eds.) *High Places. Cultural Geographies of Mountains, Ice and Science*, London 2009, pp. 87–104.

Debarbieux, Bernard / François Gillet (eds.): *Mountain Regions: a Research Subject?* International Mountain Research Workshop, Autrans 2000.

Debarbieux, Bernard / Gilles Rudaz: *Les faiseurs de montagne. Imaginaires politiques et territorialités: XVIIIe-XXIe siècle*, Paris 2010.

Debarbieux, Bernard / Martin F. Price: 'Representing Mountains: From Local and National to Global Common Good', in *Geopolitics* 13/1 (2008), pp. 148–168.

Dech, Stefan *et al.*: *Berge aus dem All*, ed. by Deutsches Zentrum für Luft- und Raumfahrt, Munich 2005.

Demiéville, Paul: 'La montagne dans l'art chinois', in Demiéville: *Choix d'études sinologiques (1921–1970)*, Leiden 1973, pp. 364–389.

Denevan, William M. (ed.): *The Native Population of the Americas in 1492*, Madison 1992 (first edition 1976).

— 'The Native Population of Amazonia in 1492 Reconsidered', in *Revista de Indias* 63/227 (2003), pp. 175–188.

Derouet, Bernard / Luigi Lorenzetti / Jon Mathieu (eds.): *Pratiques familiales et sociétés de montagne, XVIe–XXe siècles*, Basel 2010.

Desideri, Ippolito: *An Account of Tibet. The Travels of Ippolito Desideri of Pistoia, S.J., 1712–1727*, ed. by Filippo de Filippi, London 1937.

Díaz del Castillo, Bernal: *Historia Verdadera de la Conquista de la Nueva España*, ed. by Carmelo Sáenz de Santa Maria, Madrid 1989.

Dixit, Kanak Mani: 'Mountaineering's Himalayan Face', in *Himal* Nov/Dec 1992, pp. 11–18.

Dollfus, Olivier: *Territorios andinos. Retos y memoria*, Lima 1991.

Durand, John D.: 'Historical Estimates of World Population: An Evaluation', in *Population and Development Review* 3 (1977), pp. 253–296.

Dürr, Renate *et al.* (eds.): *Expansionen in der Frühen Neuzeit* (Beiheft 34 Zeitschrift für Historische Forschung), Berlin 2005.

Bibliography

Duviols, Pierre: *La lutte contre les religions autochtones dans le Pérou colonial. "L'extirpation de l'idolâtrie" entre 1532 et 1660*, Lima 1972.

Ebel, Johann Gottfried: *Anleitung auf die nützlichste und genussvollste Art in der Schweitz zu reisen*, 2 parts, Zurich 1793.

Eckholm, Erik P.: 'The Deterioration of Mountain Environments. Ecological stress in the highlands of Asia, Latin America, and Africa takes a mounting social toll', in *Science* 189 (1975), pp. 764–770.

Ehlers, Eckart: *Bevölkerungswachstum – Nahrungsspielraum – Siedlungsgrenzen der Erde*, Frankfurt a.M., 1984.

— 'Die Organisation von Raum und Zeit – Bevölkerungswachstum, Ressourcenmanagement und angepasste Landnutzung im Bagrot/Karakorum', in *Petermanns Geographische Mitteilungen* 139/2 (1995), pp. 105–120.

Ehlers, Eckart / Hermann Kreutzmann (eds.): *High Mountain Pastoralism in Northern Pakistan*, Stuttgart 2000.

Elvin, Mark: 'Chinese Cities since the Sung Dynasty', in Philip Abrams and E. A. Wrigley (eds.) *Towns in Societies. Essays in Economic History and Historical Sociology*, Cambridge 1978, pp. 79–89.

— *The Retreat of the Elephants. An Environmental History of China*, New Haven 2004.

Elvin, Mark / Liu Ts'ui-jung (eds.): *Sediments of Time. Environment and Society in Chinese History*, Cambridge 1998.

Emeljanenko, Tatjana: 'Nomadic Year Cycles and Cultural Life of Central Asian Livestock-Breeders Before the 20th Century', in Carel van Leeuwen *et al. Nomads in Central Asia. Animal Husbandry and Culture in Transition (19th – 20th Century)*, Amsterdam 1994, pp. 37–68.

Engelhardt, Wolfgang / Hubert Weinzierl (eds.): *Der Erdgipfel. Perspektiven für die Zeit nach Rio*, Bonn 1993.

Eriksen, Wolfgang: 'Eco-Climatological Aspects of the Bolivian Puna – with Special Reference to Frost Frequency and Moisture Conditions', in Wilhelm Lauer (ed.) *Natural Environment and Man in Tropical Mountain Ecosystems*, Stuttgart 1984, pp. 197–210.

Escobar, Gabriel / Cynthia M. Beall: 'Contemporary Patterns of Migration in the Central Andes', in *Mountain Research and Development* 2/1 (1982), pp. 63–80.

Ezcurra, Exequiel: 'The Basin of Mexico', in B.L. Turner *et al.* (eds.) *The Earth As Transformed by Human Action. Global and Regional Changes in the Biosphere over the Past 300 Years*, Cambridge 1990, pp. 577–588.

FAO Food and Agriculture Organization of the United Nations: *International Year of the Mountains 2002. Concept Paper*, Rome 2000.

— *Progress Report on the International Year of the Mountains 2002. Hundred and Twenty-Third Session of the FAO Council, Rome 28 October – 2 November 2002* (internet publication, www.fao.org/DOCREP/MEETING/005/Y7382e.HTM Accessed 2 June 2009).

Farrington, Brian: 'Words as New as the Hills. Concept Formation in the Field of High Altitude Topography (1750–1850)', in *French Language Studies* 10 (2000), pp. 45–72.

Bibliography

Farrington, John D.: 'De-development in Eastern Kyrgystan and Persistence of Semi-Nomadic Livestock Herding', in *Nomadic Peoples* NS 9 (2005), pp. 171–197.

Favier, René: *Les villes du Dauphiné aux XVIIe et XVIIIe siècles*, Grenoble 1993.

— 'Raoul Blanchard et la découverte des Alpes', in Jon Mathieu / Simona Boscani Leoni (eds.) *Die Alpen! Zur europäischen Wahrnehmungsgeschichte seit der Renaissance*, Berne 2005, pp. 53–72.

Febvre, Lucien: *La terre et l'évolution humaine. Introduction géographique à l'histoire*, Paris 1970 (first edition 1922).

Felmy, Sabine: 'Division of Labour and Women's Work in a Mountain Society. Hunza Valley in Pakistan', in Saraswati Raju / Deipica Bagchi (eds.) *Women and Work in South Asia. Regional Patterns and Perspectives*, London 1993, 196–208.

Felsch, Philipp: *Laborlandschaften. Physiologische Alpenreisen im 19. Jahrhundert*, Göttingen 2007.

Feuchtwang, Stephan: 'School-Temple and City God', in G. William Skinner (ed.) *The City in Late Imperial China*, Stanford 1977, pp. 581–608.

Fiedler, Horst / Ulrike Leitner: *Alexander von Humboldts Schriften. Bibliographie der selbständig erschienenen Werke*, Berlin 2000.

Figueras, Marcelo: *Kamchatka*. Translated from the Spanish by Frank Wynne, London 2010 (original Spanish edition of the novel, Madrid 2003).

Finke, Peter: *Nomaden im Transformationsprozess. Kasachen in der post-sozialistischen Mongolei*, Münster 2004.

Fontaine, Laurence: 'Les résaux de colportage des alpes françaises entre 16e et 19e siècles', in *Col bastone e la bisaccia per le strade d'Europa. Migrazioni stagionali di mestiere dall'arco alpino nei secoli XVI–XVIII*, Bellinzona 1991, pp. 105-129.

— 'Montagnes et migrations de travail (XVe–XXe siècles). Un essai de comparaison globale', in *Revue d'histoire moderne et contemporaine* 52/2 (2005), pp. 26–48.

— *Pouvoir, identités et migrations dans les hautes vallées des Alpes occidentales (XVIIe–XVIIIe siècle)*, Grenoble 2003.

Ford, Robert E.: 'The Dynamics of Human-Environment Interactions in the Tropical Montane Agrosystems of Rwanda: Implications for Economic Development and Environmental Stability', in *Mountain Research and Development* 10/1 (1990), pp. 43–63.

Fourny, Marie-Christine / Anne Sgard (eds.): *Ces géographes qui écrivent les Alpes. Une relecture de la Revue de Géographie Alpine à travers le siècle*, Grenoble 2007.

Francke, August Hermann: *Tibetische Geschichtsforschung und was man dabei erleben kann*, Herrnhut 1911.

Frödin, John: *Zentraleuropas Alpwirtschaft*, 2 vols. Oslo 1940/1941.

Furter, Reto: 'Traffico di transito nell'area alpina tra XIV e XIX secolo', in Jean-François Bergier / Gauro Coppola (eds.) *Vie di terra e d'acqua. Infrastrutture viarie e sistemi di relazioni in area alpina (secoli XIII–XVI)*, Bologna 2007, pp. 83–122.

Furter, Reto: *Urbanisierung – Transitverkehr – Bädertourismus – Alpinismus. Indikatoren zum Hintergrund des Alpendiskurses, 15. bis 19. Jahrhundert*, dissertation at the University of Berne 2005.

Bibliography

Galaty, John G. / Douglas L. Johnson: 'Introduction: Pastoral Systems in Global Perspective', in Galaty and Douglas (eds.) *The World of Pastoralism. Herding Systems in Comparative Perspective*, London 1990, pp. 1–31.

Gerbi, Antonello: *La naturaleza de las Indias nuevas. De Cristóbal Colón a Gonzalo Fernández de Oviedo*, Mexico 1978.

Gerlach, Larry (ed.): *The Winter Olympics. From Chamonix to Salt Lake City*, Salt Lake City 2004.

Gestrich, Andreas / Jen-Uwe Krause / Michel Mitterauer: *Geschichte der Familie*, Stuttgart 2003.

Gidl, Anneliese: *Alpenverein: Die Städter entdecken die Alpen. Der Deutsche und Österreichische Alpenverein von der Gründung bis zum Ende des Ersten Weltkrieges*, Vienna 2007.

Gieryn, Thomas F.: 'Boundary-Work and the Demarcation of Science from Non-Science: Strains and Interests in Professional Ideologies of Scientists', in *American Sociological Review* 48 (1983), pp. 781–795.

Gil Montero, Raquel: *Caravaneros y trashumantes en los Andes meridionales. Población y familia indígena en la puna de Jujuy, 1770–1870*, Lima 2004.

— *La construcción de Argentina y Bolivia en los Andes Meridionales. Población, tierras y ambiente en el siglo XIX*, Buenos Aires 2008.

Gil Montero, Raquel / Jon Mathieu / Chetan Singh: 'Mountain Pastoralism 1500–2000: An Introduction', in *Nomadic Peoples* 13/2 (2010), pp. 1–16.

Gilbert, Daniel L.: 'The First Documented Report of Mountain Sickness: the Andean or Pariacaca Story', in *Respiration Physiology* 52 (1983), pp. 327–347.

Goethe, Johann Wolfgang von: 'Höhen der alten und neuen Welt bildlich verglichen. Ein Tableau von Hrn. Geh. Rath v. Göthe mit einem Schreiben an den Herausg. der A. G. E.', in *Allgemeine Geographische Ephemeriden* 41 (1813), pp. 3–8.

Gratzl, Karl (ed.): *Die heiligsten Berge der Welt*, Graz 1990.

Gratzl, Karl: *Mythos Berg. Lexikon der bedeutenden Berge aus Mythologie, Kulturgeschichte und Religion*, Purkersdorf 2000.

Greyerz, Kaspar von: *Religion und Kultur. Europa 1500–1800*, Göttingen 2000.

Grötzbach, Erwin: 'Bagrot – Beharrung und Wandel einer peripheren Talschaft im Karakorum', in *Die Erde* 115 (1984), pp. 305–321.

— 'Heilige Berge und Bergheiligtümer im Hochgebirge – ein Vergleich zwischen verschiedenen Religionen', in *Alpenwelt – Gebirgswelten. Inseln, Bücken, Grenzen*, Heidelberg 2004, pp. 457–463.

— 'High Mountains as Human Habitat', in Nigel J. R. Allan et al. (eds.) *Human Impact on Mountains*, New Jersey 1988, pp. 24–35.

— 'Mobility of Labour in High Mountains and the Socio-Economic Integration of Peripheral Areas', in *Mountain Research and Development* 4/3 (1984), pp. 229–235. Quoted as 1984b.

Grove, Richard H.: *Green Imperialism. Colonial Expansion, Tropical Island Edens and the Origins of Environmentalism, 1600–1860*, Cambridge 1995.

Grubb, Michael et al.: *The Earth Summit Agreements. A Guide and Assessment*, London 1993.

Bibliography

Guicciardini, Francesco: 'Storia d'Italia, libri I–X', in *Opere di Francesco Guicciardini*, ed. by Emanuella Scarano, vol. 2, Turin 1981.

Guillet, David W.: 'Toward a Cultural Ecology of Mountains: The Central Andes and the Himalaya Compared', in *Current Anthropology* 24/5 (1983), pp. 561–574.

Hambis, Louis (ed.): *Marco Polo. La description du monde. Texte intégral en français moderne avec introduction et notes*, Paris 1955.

Hambloch, Hermann: *Der Höhengrenzsaum der Ökumene. Anthropogeographische Grenzen in dreidimensionaler Sicht* (Westfälische Geographische Studien 19), Münster 1966.

Hansen, Peter H.: 'Albert Smith, the Alpine Club and the Invention of Mountaineering in Mid-Victorian Britain', in *Journal of British Studies* 34 (1995), pp. 300–324.

— 'Confetti of Empire: The Conquest of Everest in Nepal, India, Britain and New Zealand', in *Comparative Studies in Society and History* 42 (2000), pp. 307–332.

— 'Debate – Tenzing's Two Wrist-Watches: The Conquest of Everest and Late Imperial Culture in Britain 1921–1953', in *Past and Present* 157 (1997), pp. 159–177.

— 'Partners: Guides and Sherpas in the Alps and Himalayas, 1850s–1950s', in Jaś Elsner / Joan-Pau Rubiés (eds.) *Voyages and Visions: Towards a Cultural History of Travel*, London 1999, pp. 210–231.

— 'The Dancing Lamas of Everest: Cinema, Orientalism, and Anglo-Tibetan Relations in the 1920s', in *The American Historical Review* 101/3 (1996), pp. 712–747.

— 'Vertical Boundaries, National Identities: British Mountaineering on the Frontiers of Europe and the Empire, 1868–1914', in *Journal of Imperial and Commonwealth History* 24 (1996), pp. 48–71. Quoted as 1996b.

Harten, Hans-Christian / Elke Harten: *Die Versöhnung mit der Natur. Gärten, Freiheitsbäume, republikanische Wälder, heilige Berge und Tugendparks in der Französischen Revolution*, Hamburg 1989.

Heim, Albert: *Handbuch der Gletscherkunde*, Stuttgart 1885.

Helbling, Jürg: *Verwandtschaft, Macht und Produktion. Die Alangan-Mangyan im Nordosten von Mindoro, Philippinen*, Berlin 1996.

Henze, Dietmar: *Enzyklopädie der Entdecker und Erforscher der Erde*, 5 vols. Graz 1978–2004.

Herbers, Hiltrud: 'Ernährungssicherung in Nord-Pakistan: Der Beitrag der Frauen', in *Geographische Rundschau* 47/4 (1995), pp. 234–239.

Herder, Johann Gottfried: 'Ideen zur Philosophie der Geschichte der Menschheit (4 Teile 1784–1791)', in *Johann Gottfried Herder – Werke*, vol. 3 in two parts, ed. by Wolfgang Pross, Munich 2002.

Herrmann, Klaus: *Pflügen, Säen, Ernten. Landarbeit und Landtechnik in der Geschichte*, Hamburg 1985.

Hewitt, Farida: 'Woman's Work, Woman's Place: the Gendered Life-World of a High Mountain Community in Northern Pakistan', in *Mountain Research and Development* 9/4 (1989), pp. 335–352.

Hewitt, Kenneth: 'The Study of Mountain Lands and Peoples: A Critical Overview', in Nigel J. R. Allan *et al.* (eds.) *Human Impact on Mountains*, New Jersey 1988, pp. 6–23.

Bibliography

Hewsen, Robert H.: 'Russian Conquest of Caucasus', in *The Modern Encyclopedia of Russian and Soviet History*, Gulf Breeze 1978, vol. 6, pp. 145–151.

Ho, Ping-ti: *Studies on the Population of China, 1368–1953*, Cambridge MA 1959.

Hoheisel, Karl: 'Berge, heilige', in *Religion in Geschichte und Gegenwart*, fourth edition, ed. by Hans-Dieter Betz *et al.* Tübingen, 1998, vol. 1, cols. 1307–1308.

Hoibian, Olivier (ed.): *L'invention de l'alpinisme. La montagne et l'affirmation de la bourgeoisie cultivée (1786–1914)*, Paris 2008.

Horn, Peter: 'Die Namen der Berge im Südlichen Afrika', in INST (ed.) *Die Namen der Berge*, (internet publication 2002, www.inst.at/berge Accessed 16 Nov. 2008).

Hostetler, Laura: *Qing Colonial Enterprise. Ethnography and Cartography in Early Modern China*, Chicago 2001.

Huber, Toni: 'A Guide to the La-Phyi Mandala. History, Landscape and Ritual in South-Western Tibet', in Alexander W. Macdonald (ed.) *Mandala and Landscape*, New Delhi 1997, pp. 233–286.

— 'Green Tibetans. A Brief Social History', in Frank J. Korom (ed.) *Tibetan Culture in the Diaspora*, Wien 1997, pp. 103–119. Quoted as 1997b.

— 'Shangri-La im Exil: Darstellungen tibetischer Identität und transnationale Kultur', in Thierry Dodin / Heinz Räther (eds.) *Mythos Tibet. Wahrnehmungen, Projektionen, Phantasien*, Köln 1997, pp. 300–312. Quoted as 1997c.

— 'Territorial Control by "Sealing" (rgya sdom-pa): A Religio-Political Practice in Tibet', in *Zentralasiatische Studien* 33 (2004), pp. 127–152.

— *The Cult of Pure Crystal Mountain. Popular Pilgrimage and Visionary Landscape in Southeast Tibet*, Oxford 1999.

— 'Traditional Environmental Protectionism in Tibet Reconsidered', in *The Tibet Journal* 16/3 (1991), pp. 67–77.

— 'Where Exactly are Caritra, Devikota and Himavat? A Sacred Geography Controversy and the Development of Tantric Buddhist Pilgrimage Sites in Tibet', in Alex McKay (ed.) *The History of Tibet*, vol. 2, London 2003, pp. 392–424.

Huddleston, Barbara *et al.*: *Towards a GIS-Based Analysis of Mountain Environments and Populations* (Environmental and Natural Resources Working Paper No. 10, UNO/FAO), Rome 2003.

Humboldt, Alexander von: *Ansichten der Natur*, ed. by Adolf Meyer-Abich, Stuttgart 1969 (first edition 1807, ed. according to the 1849 edition).

— *Asie centrale. Recherches sur les chaînes de montagnes et la climatologie comparée*, 3 vols. Paris 1843.

— *Examen critique de l'histoire de la géographie du nouveau continent et des progrès de l'astronomie nautique aux quinzième et seizièmes siècles*, 5 vols. Paris 1836–1839.

— *Kosmos. Entwurf einer physischen Weltbeschreibung*, ed. by Ottmar Ette and Oliver Lubrich, Frankfurt a.M. 2004 (first edition 1845–1862).

— *Schriften zur Geographie der Pflanzen*, ed. and commented by Hanno Beck (Alexander von Humboldt Studienausgabe vol. 1), Darmstadt 1989.

Bibliography

Hunter, Michael: *Establishing the New Science. The Experience of the Early Royal Society*, Woodbridge 1989.

Hunter, Michael / Edward B. Davis (eds.): *The Works of Robert Boyle*, 14 vols. London 1999–2000.

Hyde, Anne Farrar: *An American Vision. Far Western Landscape and National Culture, 1820–1920*, New York 1990.

ICIMOD International Centre for Integrated Mountain Development: *Advancing the Mountain Women's Agenda: a Report on a Global Gathering 'Celebrating Mountain Women' in Bhutan, October 2002*, Kathmandu 2003 (internet publication, http://css.mtnforum.org/en/node/8622 Accessed 4 June 2009).

Imhof, Viola: 'Minya-Konka-Expedition von Eduard Imhof 1930', in *Die Alpen* 71(1995), pp. 145–159.

Inamura, Tetsuya: 'The Pastoralism in the Andes and the Himalayas', in *Global Environmental Research* 6/1 (2002), pp. 85–102.

INST (ed.): *Die Namen der Berge* (internet publication 2002, www.inst.at/berge Accessed 16 Nov 2008).

Isserman, Maurice / Stewart Weaver: *Fallen Giants. A History of Himalayan Mountaineering from the Age of Empire to the Age of Extremes*, New Haven 2008.

Ives, Jack D.: 'Carl Troll 1899–1999 Centennial Dedication / Editorial', in *Mountain Research and Development* 19/4 (1999), unnumbered frontispiece.

Jacob, Ernst Gerhard (ed.): *Christoph Columbus. Bordbuch, Briefe, Berichte, Dokumente*, Bremen 1956.

Jahn, Ilse / Fritz G. Lange (eds.): *Die Jugendbriefe Alexander von Humboldts 1787–1799*, Berlin 1973.

Johnson, Stanley P.: *The Earth Summit: The United Nations Conference on Environment and Development (UNCED)*, London 1993.

Jourdanet, Denis: *Influence de la pression de l'air sur la vie de l'homme. Climats d'altitude et climats de montagne*, 2 vols. Paris 1875.

Jouty, Sylvain: 'Naissance de l'altitude', in *Compar(a)ison. An International Journal of Comparative Literature* 1 (1998), pp. 17–32.

Kahlaoui, Tarek: 'On a Western Islamic School of Mediterranean Navigational Knowledge and Mapmaking in the Late Medieval Period (12th–16th centuries)', in Markus Oehrli (ed.) *Paper and Poster Abstracts of the 22nd International Conference on the History of Cartography*, Berne 2007, pp. 150–151.

Kamper, Erich: *Lexikon der Olympischen Winterspiele*, Stuttgart 1964.

Kandell, Jonathan: *La Capital. The Biography of Mexico City*, New York 1988.

Kanwar, Pamela: *Imperial Simla. The Political Culture of the Ray*, Delhi 2003 (first edition 1990).

Kapos, V. et al.: 'Developing a Map of the World's Mountain Forests', in M. F. Price / N. Butt (eds.) *Forests in Sustainable Mountain Development: a State of Knowledge Report*, Wallingford 2000, pp. 1–9.

Bibliography

Kastrop, Rainer: *Ideen über die Geographie und Ansatzpunkte für die moderne Geographie bei Varenius unter Berücksichtigung der Abhängigkeit des Varenius von den Vorstellungen seiner Zeit*, Saarbrücken 1972.

Kates, Robert W. / Viola Haarmann: 'Where the Poor Live. Are the Assumptions Correct?' in *Environment* 34/4 (1992), pp. 4–11, 25–28.

Kaufmann, Jeffrey C.: 'The Long Walk – an Interview with Anatoly M. Khazanov', in *Nomadic Peoples* NS 4/1 (2000), pp. 5–22.

Keller, Urs: *Der indische Tourismus in der Schweiz. Eine empirische Untersuchung unter besonderer Berücksichtigung der Beziehung von Tourismus und Film*, diploma thesis at the University of Zurich 2002.

Kempe, Michael: *Wissenschaft, Theologie, Aufklärung. Johann Jakob Scheuchzer (1672–1733) und die Sintfluttheorie*, Epfendorf 2003.

Kertz, Walter: *Geschichte der Geophysik*, ed. by Ruth Kertz and Karl-Heinz Glaßmeier, Hildesheim 1999.

Khazanov, Anatoly M.: *Nomads and the Outside World*, Madison 1994 (first edition 1984).

King, Anthoni: *Colonial Urban Development. Culture, Social Power and Environment*, London 1976.

Kish, George: 'Early Thematic Mapping: The Work of Philippe Buache', in *Imago Mundi. The Journal of the International Society for the History of Cartography* 28 (1976), pp. 129–136.

Klemp, Egon (ed.): *America in Maps, Dating from 1500 to 1856*, New York 1976.

Kohler, Alfred: *Columbus und seine Zeit*, Munich 2006.

Kollmar-Paulenz, Karénina: *Kleine Geschichte Tibets*, Munich 2006.

Körner, Martin: '"Berg", "Gebirg" und "Pass" bei Andreas Ryff und Heinrich Schickhart um 1600', in Martin Körner / François Walter (eds.) *Quand la Montagne aussi a une Histoire. Mélanges offerts à Jean-François Bergier*, Berne 1996, pp. 265–278.

Korol, Juan Carlos / Enrique Tandeter: *Historia económica de América Latina: problemas y procesos*, Mexico 2000.

Korom, Frank J.: 'Tibet und die New-Age-Bewegung', in Thierry Dodin / Heinz Räther (eds.) *Mythos Tibet. Wahrnehmungen, Projektionen, Phantasien*, Cologne 1997, pp. 178–192.

Krader, Laurence: *Peoples of Central Asia*, Bloomington 1966.

Krätz, Otto: *Alexander von Humboldt. Wissenschaftler – Weltbürger – Revolutionär*, München 2000.

Kreutzmann, Hermann (ed.): *Karakoram in Transition. Culture, Development, and Ecology in the Hunza Valley*, Oxford 2006.

— 'Challenge and Response in the Karakoram: Socioeconomic Transformation in Hunza, Northern Areas, Pakistan', in *Mountain Research and Development* 13/1 (1993), pp. 19–39.

— *Hunza – Ländliche Entwicklung im Karakorum*, Berlin 1989.

— 'Livestock Economy in Hunza: Societal Transformation and Pastoral Practices', in Eckart Ehlers / Hermann Kreutzmann (eds.) *High Mountain Pastoralism in Northern Pakistan*, Stuttgart 2000, pp. 121–150.

Bibliography

— 'Mobile Viehwirtschaft der Kirgisen am Kara Köl: Wandlungsprozesse an der Höhengrenze der Ökumene im Ostpamir und im westlichen Kun Lun Shan', in *Petermanns Geographische Mitteilungen* 139/3 (1995), pp. 159–178.

Krüger, Arnd: 'The History of the Olympic Winter Games, the Invention of Tradition', in Matti Goksoyr et al. (eds.) *Winter Games, Warm Traditions. Selected papers from the 2. International ISHPES Seminar*, Lillehammer 1994, pp. 101–122.

Kühnel, Josef: *Thaddaeus Haenke. Leben und Wirken eines Forschers*, Prague 1960.

Kupper, Patrick: 'Science and the National Parks: A Transatlantic Perspective on the Interwar Years', in *Environmental History* 14 (2009), pp. 58–81.

Laffont, Pierre-Yves (ed.): *Transhumance et estivage en Occident des origines aux enjeux actuels*, Toulouse 2006.

Lains, Pedro / Vicente Pinilla (eds.): *Agriculture and Economic Development in Europe since 1870*, London 2009.

Larsen, Knud / Amund Sinding-Larsen: *The Lhasa Atlas. Traditional Tibetan Architecture and Townscape*, Boston 2001.

Lauer, Wilhelm (ed.): *Argumenta geographica. Festschrift Carl Troll zum 70. Geburtstag*, Bonn 1970.

Lenoir, Timothy: *Instituting Science. The Cultural Production of Scientific Disciplines*, Stanford 1997.

Livi Bacci, Massimo: *Storia minima della popolazione del mondo*, Bologna 2005 (new edition).

Lombard-Salmon, Claudine: *Un exemple d'acculturation chinoise. La province du Gui Zhou au XVIIIe siècle*, Paris 1972.

Lorenzetti, Luigi / Raul Merzario: *Il fuoco acceso. Famiglie e migrazioni alpine nell'Italia d'età moderna*, Rome 2005.

MacCormack, Sabine: *Religion in the Andes. Vision and Imagination in Early Colonial Peru*, Princeton 1991.

Mackintosh, A. J.: 'Mountaineering Clubs', in *Alpine Journal* 23 (1907), pp. 542–570.

Mägdefrau, Karl: *Geschichte der Botanik. Leben und Leistung grosser Forscher*, Stuttgart 1992.

Malthus, Thomas Robert: 'An Essay on the Principle of Population. The sixth editon (1826) with variant readings from the second edition (1803)', in *The Works of Thomas Robert Malthus*, ed. by E. A. Wrigley and David Souden, vol. 2 (Part I) and vol. 3 (Part II), London 1986.

Marchal, Guy P.: 'La naissance du mythe du St-Gothard ou la longue découverte de l'"homo alpinus helveticus" et de l'"Helvetia mater fluviorum" (XVe siècle – 1940)', in *La découverte des Alpes*, ed. by Jean-Francois Bergier and Sandro Guzzi, Basel 1992, pp. 35–53.

Marcil, Yasmine: 'Découvrir, comprendre, ressentir la montagne dans la presse périodique des années 1780', in Gilles Bertrand / Alain Guyot (eds.) *Discours sur la montagne (XVIIIe–XIXe siècles): rhétorique, science, esthétique*, Berne 2003, pp. 145–170.

Mathieu, Jon: 'Alpenwahrnehmung: Probleme der historischen Periodisierung', in Jon Mathieu / Simona Boscani Leoni (eds.) *Die Alpen! Zur europäischen Wahrnehmungsgeschichte seit der Renaissance*, Berne 2005, pp. 53–72.

Bibliography

— *Eine Agrargeschichte der inneren Alpen. Graubünden, Tessin, Wallis 1500–1800*, Zurich 1992.

— 'From Ecotypes to Sociotypes. Peasant Household and State-Building in the Alps, Sixteenth-Nineteenth Centuries', in *The History of the Family. An International Quarterly* 5/1 (2000), pp. 55–74.

— Gibt es eine Geschichte der Berge? L'Homme et la Montagne von Jules Blache neu gelesen, in *Historische Anthropologie* 14/2 (2006), pp. 305–316.

— *History of the Alps 1500–1900. Environment, Development, and Society*, Morgantown WV 2009 (first German edition 1998).

— 'The Mountains in Urban Development: Lessons from a Comparative View', in *Geschichte der Alpen* 8 (2003), pp. 15–33.

— 'The Sacralization of Mountains in Europe during the Modern Age', in *Mountain Research and Development* 26/4 (2006), pp. 343–349. Quoted as 2006b.

— 'Von den Alpen zu den Anden: Alexander von Humboldt und die Gebirgsforschung', in Simona Boscani Leoni (ed.) *Wissenschaft – Berge – Ideologien. Johann Jakob Scheuchzer (1672–1733) und die frühneuzeitliche Naturforschung*, Basel 2010, pp. 293–308.

Mathieu, Jon / Chetan Singh (guest editors): 'Religion and Sacredness in Mountains: A Historical Perspective', Special Issue of *Mountain Research and Development*, 26/4 (2006).

Mathieu, Jon / Reto Furter: 'Urban Development in Early Modern Europe: the Significance of Altitude', in *Città e Storia* 5/1 (2010), pp. 71-83.

Mathieu, Jon / Simona Boscani Leoni (eds.): *Die Alpen! Zur europäischen Wahrnehmungsgeschichte seit der Renaissance / Les Alpes! Pour une histoire de la perception européenne depuis la Renaissance*, Berne 2005.

Mathis, Franz: 'Wie die Europäer satt und süchtig wurden', in Karl Kohut *et al.* (eds.) *Deutsche in Lateinamerika – Lateinamerika in Deutschland*, Frankfurt a.M. 1996, pp. 234–254.

— *Zur Bevölkerungsstruktur österreichischer Städte im 17. Jahrhundert*, Munich 1977.

Matthies, Volker: *Äthiopien, Eirtrea, Somalia, Djibouti. Das Horn von Afrika*, Munich 1997.

Maurer, Eva: 'Cold War, "Thaw" and "Everlasting Friendship": Soviet Mountaineers and Mount Everest, 1953-1960', in *The International Journal of the History of Sport* 26/4 (2009), pp. 484–500.

— *Wege zum Pik Stalin. Sowjetische Alpinisten, 1928–1953*, Zurich 2010.

McCann, James C.: *Green Land, Brown Land, Black Land. An Evironmental History of Africa, 1800–1990*, Oxford 1999.

— *People of the Plow. An Agricultural History of Ethiopia, 1800–1990*, Madison 1995.

McCormick, John: *The Global Environmental Movement: Reclaiming Paradise*, London 1989.

McEvedy, Colin / Jones, Richard: *Atlas of World Population History*, Harmondsworth 1978.

McKay, Alex (ed.): *Pilgrimage in Tibet*, Richmond 1998.

— *The History of Tibet*, 3 vols. London 2003.

Bibliography

— 'Kailas-Manasarovar in "Classical" (Hindu) and Colonial Sources. Asceticism, Power, and Pilgrimage', in McKay (ed.): *Pilgrimage in Tibet*, Richmond 1998, pp. 165–183. Quoted as 1998b.

McNeill, John R.: *The Mountains of the Mediterranean World. An Environmental History*, Cambridge 1992.

— 'Observations on the Nature and Culture of Environmental History', in *History and Theory* 42 (2003), pp. 5–43

Meckelein, Wolfgang: *Nordkaukasien. Eine landeskundliche Untersuchung*, Stuttgart 1998 (written in 1951).

Medicus, Ludwig Wallrath: *Bemerkungen über die Alpen-Wirthschaft auf einer Reise durch die Schweiz gesammlet*, Leipzig 1795.

Menzies, Nicholas K.: *Forest and Land Management in Imperial China*, New York 1994.

Messerli, Bruno: 'Introduction', in Tullio Treves et al. (eds.) *Sustainable Development of Mountain Areas. Legal Perspectives Beyond Rio and Johannesburg*, Milan 2004, pp. 3–7.

— 'United Nations University (UNU) and the Mountains of the World', unpublished paper 2002.

— 'Work and History of the Commission on Mountain Geoecology of the International Geographical Union (IGU)', in Wilhelm Lauer (ed.) *Natural Environment and Man in Tropical Mountain Ecosystems*, Stuttgart 1984, pp. 9–11.

Messerli, Bruno / Jack D. Ives (eds.): *Mountains of the World. A Global Priority*, New York 1997.

Meybeck, Michel et al.: 'A New Typology for Mountains and Other Relief Classes. An Application to Global Continental Water Resources and Population Distribution', in *Mountain Research and Development* 21/1 (2001), pp. 34–45.

Meyer, Kurt / Pamela Deuel Meyer: *In the Shadow of the Himalayas. Tibet, Bhutan, Nepal, Sikkim. A Photographic Record by John Claude White 1883–1908*, Ahmedabad 2005.

Mills, Kenneth: *Idolatry and its Enemies. Colonial Andean Religion and Extirpation, 1640–1750*, Princeton 1997.

Miquel, André: *La géographie humaine du monde musulman jusqu'au milieu du XIe siècle*, 4 vols. Paris 1967–1988.

Mitterauer, Michael: *Historisch-anthropologische Familienforschung. Fragestellungen und Zugangsweisen*, Vienna 1990.

Morales, Yves: 'La genèse des jeux olympiques d'hiver et l'idéologie universaliste: Chamonix 1924', in Paul Dietschy et al. (eds.) *Sport et idéologie. VIIe Congrès International du Comité Européen de l'Histoire du Sport*, Besançon 2002, pp. 69–82.

Mountain Agenda (ed.): *An Appeal for the Mountains*, Berne 1992.

— *Mountains of the World. Sustainable Development in Mountain Areas. The Need for Adequate Policies and Instruments*, Berne 2002.

Mousson, Albert: *Die Gletscher der Jetztzeit. Eine Zusammenstellung und Prüfung ihrer Erscheinungen und Gesetze*, Zurich 1854.

Müller, Bertrand: *Lucien Febvre, lecteur et critique*, Paris 2003.

Bibliography

Mullikin, Mary Augusta / Anna M. Hotchkis: *The Nine Sacred Mountains of China. An Illustrated Record of Pilgrimages Made in the Years 1935–1936*, Hong Kong 1973.

Murra, John V.: *El mundo andino. Población, medio ambiente y economía*, Lima 2002.

Nash, Roderick Frazier: *The Rights of Nature. A History of Environmental Ethics*, Madison 1989.

— *Wilderness and the American Mind*, New Haven 2001 (first edition 1967).

Needham, John et al.: 'Agriculture', in *The Cambridge Encyclopedia of China*, Cambridge 1991, pp. 434–435.

Netting, Robert McC: *Balancing on an Alp. Ecological Change and Continuity in a Swiss Mountain Community*, Cambridge 1981.

— *Smallholders, Householders. Farm Families and the Ecology of Intensive, Sustainable Agriculture*, Stanford 1993.

Newson, Linda: 'The Demographic Impact of Colonization', in *The Cambridge Economic History of Latin America*, vol. 1: *The Colonial Era and the Short Nineteenth Century*, Cambridge 2006, pp. 143–184.

— 'Pattern of Indian Depopulation in Early Colonial Ecuador', in *Revista de Indias* 63/227 (2003), pp. 135–156.

Nicolson, Marjorie Hope: *Mountain Gloom and Mountain Glory. The Development of the Aesthetics of the Infinite*, Seattle 1997 (first edition 1959).

Olcott, Martha Brill: *The Kazakhs*, Stanford 1987.

Oppitz, Ulrich-Dieter: 'Der Name der Brüder Humboldt in aller Welt', in *Alexander von Humboldt. Werk und Weltgeltung*, ed. by Heinrich Pfeiffer, Munich 1969, pp. 277–482.

Orlove, Benjamin S. / David W. Guillet: 'Theoretical and Methodological Considerations on the Study of Mountain Peoples: Reflections on the Idea of Subsistence Type and the Role of History in Human Ecology', in *Mountain Research and Development* 5 (1985), pp. 3–18.

Ortner, Sherry B.: *High Religion. A Cultural and Political History of Sherpa Buddhism*, Delhi 1992.

— *Life and Death on Mt. Everest. Sherpas and Himalayan Mountaineering*, Princeton 1999.

— 'Thick Resistance: Death and the Cultural Construction of Agency in Himalayan Mountaineering', in *Representations* 59 (1997), pp. 135–162.

Osterhammel, Jürgen / Niels P. Petersson: *Geschichte der Globalisierung. Dimensionen, Prozesse, Epochen*, Munich 2003.

Outram, Dorinda: *The Enlightenment*, Cambridge 1995.

Pallière, Johannes: *Les premiers Jeux d'hiver de 1924. La grande bataille de Chamonix*, Chambéry 1991.

Parnreiter, Christof: 'Mexico City. Die Produktion einer "Megastadt" 1930–1980', in Wolfgang Schwentker (ed.) *Megastädte im 20. Jahrhundert*, Göttingen 2006, pp. 165–184.

Parvez, Safdar / Stephen F. Rasmussen: 'Sustaining Mountain Economies: Poverty Reduction and Livelihood Opportunities', in Martin F. Price et al. (eds.) *Key Issues for Mountain Areas*, Tokyo 2004, pp. 86–110.

Bibliography

Peattie, Roderick: *Mountain Geography. A Critique and Field Study*, Cambridge MA 1936.

Penck, Albrecht: 'Das Hauptproblem der physischen Anthropogeographie', in *Sitzungsberichte der Preussischen Akademie der Wissenschaften. Physikalisch-mathematische Klasse*, 1924, pp. 242–257.

— 'Die Tragfähigkeit der Erde', in Karl H. Dietzel *et al.* (eds.) *Lebensraumfragen europäischer Völker*, vol. 1: *Europa*, Leipzig no year (1940/41).

— *Morphologie der Erdoberfläche*, 2 parts, Stuttgart 1894.

'Perspectives on Global History: Concepts and Methodology', in *Proceedings, 19th International Congress of Historical Sciences*, Oslo 2000, pp. 2–52.

Platt, Tristan / Therese Bouysse-Cassagne / Olivia Harris: *Qaraqara-Charka. Mallku, Inka y Rey en la provincia de Charcas (siglos XV–XVII). Historia antropológica de una confederación aymara*, La Paz 2006.

Pommaret, Françoise (ed.): *Lhasa in the Seventeenth Century. The Capital of the Dalai Lamas*, Leiden 2003.

Posselt, Doris (ed.): *Die Grosse Nordische Expedition von 1733 bis 1743. Aus Berichten der Forschungsreisenden Johann Georg Gmelin und Georg Wilhelm Steller*, Munich 1990.

Prete, Ivano Dal: 'Valerio Faenzi e l'origine dei monti nel Cinquecento veneto', in Simona Boscani Leoni (ed.) *Wissenschaft – Berge – Ideologien. Johann Jakob Scheuchzer (1672–1733) und die frühneuzeitliche Naturforschung*, Basel 2010, pp. 197–214.

Price, Martin F. (ed.): *Global Change in Mountain Regions*, Duncow 2006.

— 'Introduction: Sustainable Mountain Development from Rio to Bishkek and Beyond', in Martin F. Price *et al.* (eds.) *Key Issues for Mountain Areas*, Tokyo 2004, pp. 1–17.

— *Mountain Research in Europe. An Overview of MAB Research from the Pyrenees to Siberia*, Paris 1995.

Price, Martin F. *et al.*: 'Tourism and Amenity Migration', in Bruno Messerli / Jack D. Ives (eds.) *Mountains of the World. A Global Priority*, New York 1997, pp. 249–280.

Pryor, Frederic L.: 'The Adoption of Agriculture: Some Theoretical and Empirical Evidence', in *American Anthropologist* 88 (1986), pp. 879–897.

Radkau, Joachim: *Natur und Macht. Eine Weltgeschichte der Umwelt*, Munich 2002.

Radvanyi, Jean: 'Tradition et modernisation au Caucase. La politique soviétique de developpment de la montagne', in Erwin Grötzbach / Gisbert Rinschede (eds.) *Beiträge zur vergleichenden Kulturgeographie der Hochgebirge*, Regensburg 1984, pp. 213–234.

Ramírez, Susan Elizabeth: *To Feed and Be Fed. The Cosmological Bases of Authority and Identity in the Andes*, Stanford 2005.

Raphael, Lutz: *Geschichtswissenschaft im Zeitalter der Extreme. Theorien, Methoden, Tendenzen von 1900 bis zur Gegenwart*, Munich 2003.

Rassem, Mohammed / Jusin Stagl (eds.): *Geschichte der Staatsbeschreibung. Ausgewählte Quellentexte 1456–1813*, Berlin 1994.

Raveri, Massimo: 'Paradisi e labirinti: la montagna sacra in Giappone', in Amilcare Barbero / Stefano Piano (eds.) *Religioni e Sacri Monti. Atti del Convegno Internazionale Torino, Moncalvo, Casale Monferrato, 12–16 ottobre 2004*, Ponzano Monferrato 2006, pp. 287–299.

Bibliography

Reardon-Anderson, James: 'Land Use and Society in Manchuria and Inner Mongolia during the Qing Dynasty', in *Environmental History* 5 (2000), pp. 503–530.

Reinhard, Johan: 'Sacred Mountains: An Ethno-Archaeological Study of High Andean Ruins', in *Mountain Research and Development* 5/4 (1985), pp. 299–317.

Rhoades, Robert E. / Stephen I. Thompson: 'Adaptive Strategies in Alpine Environments: Beyond Ecological Particularism', in *American Ethnologist* 2/3 (1975), pp. 535–551.

Richards, John F.: *The Unending Frontier. An Environmental History of the Early Modern World*, Berkeley 2005.

Richter, Sabine / Hans Böhm: 'Erschliessungsprojekt Nachlass Carl Troll', in Mathias Winiger (ed.) *Zeitumstände und Forschungsperspektiven. Kolloquium im Gedenken an den 100. Geburtstag von Carl Troll*, St. Augustin 2003, pp. 100–103.

Rinschede, Gisbert: 'Wanderviehwirtschaft im Vergleich Alpen/Pyrenäen – Hochgebirge der westlichen USA', in Erwin Grötzbach / Gisbert Rinschede (eds.) *Beiträge zur vergleichenden Kulturgeographie der Hochgebirge*, Regensburg 1984, pp. 285–304.

Roder, W.: 'Slash-and-Burn Rice Systems in Transition: Challenges for Agricultural Development in the Hills of Northern Laos', in *Mountain Research and Development* 17/1 (1997), pp. 1–10.

Romero, Emilio Pérez: 'L'historiographie sur la transhumance en Espagne 1983–2003', in Pierre-Yves Laffont (ed.) *Transhumance et estivage en Occident des origines aux enjeux actuels*, Toulouse 2006, pp. 97–108.

Rudaz, Gilles: 'Swiss Mountain Communities in a Global Network: Local/Global Consequences of the International Rise of Mountain Issues', in Martin F. Price (ed.) *Global Change in Mountain Regions*, Duncow 2006, pp. 328–329.

Ruthenberg, Hans: *Farming Systems in the Tropics*, Oxford 1983 (first edition 1971).

Salaman, Redcliffe N.: *The History and Social Influence of the Potato*, Cambridge 1985 (first edition 1949).

Salati, Eneas *et al.*: 'Amazonia', in B.L. Turner *et al.* (eds.) *The Earth as Transformed by Human Action. Global and Regional Changes in the Biosphere over the Past 300 Years*, Cambridge 1990, pp. 479–493.

Salisbury, Richard / Elizabeth Hawley: *The Himalaya by the Numbers. A Statistical Analysis of Mountaineering in the Nepal Himalaya*, 2007 (internet publication; www.himalayandatabase.com).

Sánchez-Albornoz, Nicolás: 'El debate inagotable', in *Revista de Indias* 63/227 (2003), pp. 9–18.

Sanz, Ángel García: 'El final de la Mesta (1808–1836)', in Gonzalo Anes / Ángel García Sanz (eds.) *Mesta, trashumancia y vida pastoril*, Madrid 1994, pp. 191–203. Quoted as 1994b.

— 'El siglo XVIII: entre la prosperidad de la trashumancia y la crítica antimesteña de la Ilustración (1700–1808)', in Gonzalo Anes / Ángel García Sanz (eds.) *Mesta, trashumancia y vida pastoril*, Madrid 1994, pp. 137–158.

Sarmiento, Fausto O.: 'Mount Chimborazo: In the Steps of Alexander von Humboldt', in *Mountain Research and Development* 19 (1999), pp. 77–78.

Bibliography

Sauer, Carl O.: *Agricultural Origins and Dispersals. The Domestication of Animals and Foodstuffs*, Cambridge MA 1969 (first edition 1952).

Saussure, Horace-Bénedict de: *Voyages dans les Alpes, précédés d'un essai sur l'histoire naturelle des environs de Genève*, 4 vols. Neuchâtel 1779–1796.

Scharfe, Martin: *Berg-Sucht. Eine Kulturgeschichte des frühen Alpinismus*, Vienna 2007.

— 'Erste Skizze zu einer Geschichte der Berg- und Gipfelzeichen', in *Hessische Blätter für Volks- und Kulturforschung* 35 (1999), pp. 97–124.

— 'Kruzifix mit Blitzableiter', in *Österreichische Zeitschrift für Volkskunde* 53/102 (1999), pp. 289–336. Quoted as 1999b.

Schlee, Günter: 'Forms of Pastoralism', in Stefan Leder / Bernhard Streck (eds.) *Shifts and Drifts in Nomad-Sedentary Relations*, Wiesbaden 2005, pp. 17–53.

Schlee, Susan: *A History of Oceanography. The Edge of an Unfamiliar World*, London 1973.

Schneider, Alexandra (ed.): *Bollywood. Das indische Kino und die Schweiz*, Zurich 2002.

— '"The Best of Both Worlds": Film und Tourismus als Industrien des Begehrens am Beispiel von Indien und Deutschland', in Ralf Adelmann et al. (eds.) *Ökonomien des Medialen. Tausch, Wert und Zirkulation in den Medien- und Kulturwissenschaften*, Bielefeld 2006, pp. 265–282.

Scholz, Fred, 'Nomads/Nomadism in History', in *International Encyclopedia of the Social and Behavioral Sciences*, Amsterdam 2001, vol. 16, pp. 10650–10655.

— *Nomadismus. Theorie und Wandel einer sozio-ökonomischern Kulturweise*, Stuttgart 1995.

Schönwiese, Christian-Dietrich: *Klimatologie*, Stuttgart 1994.

Schwentker, Wolfgang: 'Die Megastadt als Problem der Geschichte', in Schwentker (ed.) *Megastädte im 20. Jahrhundert*, Göttingen 2006, pp. 7–26.

Scott, James C.: *The Art of Not Being Governed. An Anarchist History of Upland Southeast Asia*, New Haven 2009.

Sezgin, Fuat: *Mathematische Geographie und Kartographie im Islam und ihr Fortleben im Abendland, Historische Darstellung Teil 1 und 2; Kartenband* (Geschichte des arabischen Schrifttums vols. X–XII), Frankfurt a.M. 2000.

Sgard, Anne: 'Un moment de la construction du savoir sur la montagne: Jules Blache dans l'Homme et la Montagne (1934)', in Bernard Debarbieux / Maire-Christine Fourny (eds.) *L'effet géographique. Construction sociale, appréhension cognitive et configuration matérielle des objets géographiques*, Grenoble 2004, pp. 37–53.

— 'Voyage dans les montagnes du monde. Sur les traces de Jules Blache en 1934', in *Revue de Géographie Alpine* 89 (2001), pp. 107–120.

Shayakhmetov, Mukhamet: *The Silent Steppe. The Story of a Kazakh Nomad under Stalin*, London 2006.

Siedentop, Irmfried: 'Die geographische Verbreitung der Schweizen', in *Geographica Helvetica* 1 (1977), pp. 33–43.

— 'Die Schweizen – eine fremdenverkehrsgeographische Dokumentation', in *Zeitschrift für Wirtschaftsgeographie* 28 (1984), pp. 126–130.

Siegrist, Dominik: *Sehnsucht Himalaya. Alltagsgeographie und Naturdiskurs in deutschsprachigen Bergsteigerreiseberichten*, Zurich 1996.

Bibliography

Simo, David: 'Die Eroberung der Landschaften. Alte und neue Namen der Berge in Afrika', in INST (ed.) *Die Namen der Berge* (internet publication 2002, www.inst.at/berge Accessed 16 Nov. 2008).

Simons, Elisabeth / Oswald Oelz: *Kopfwehberge. Eine Geschicht der Höhenmedizin*, Zurich 2001.

Singh, Chetan: 'Polyandry and Customary Rights in the Western Himalaya', in Chetan Singh (ed.) *Recognizing Diversity: Society and Culture in the Himalaya*, Delhi 2011, pp. 98-120.

— 'Du fond des vallées aux sommets. Les villes précoloniales de l'Himachal et l'impact de la domination britannique sur la croissance urbaine', in *Histoire des Alpes* 8 (2003), pp. 125–144.

— 'Forests, Pastoralists and Agrarian Society in Mughal India', in David Arnold / Ramachandra Guha (eds.) *Nature, Culture, Imperialism. Essays on the Environmental History of South Asia*, Delhi 1995, pp. 21–48.

— 'Humans and Forests: The Himalaya and the Terai during the Medieval Period', in Ajay S. Rawat (ed.) *History of Forestry in India*, New Delhi 1991, pp. 163–178.

— *Natural Premises. Ecology and Peasant Life in the Western Himalaya 1800–1950*, Delhi 1998.

Skeldon, Ronald: 'Population Pressure, Mobility, and Socio-Economic Change in Mountainous Environments: Regions of Refuge in Comparative Perspective', in *Mountain Research and Development* 5/3 (1985), pp. 233–250.

Snellgrove, David / Hugh Richardson: *A Cultural History of Tibet*, Boulder 1980.

Snelling, John: *The Sacred Mountain. Travellers and Pilgrims at Mount Kailas in Western Tibet and the great Universal Symbol of the Sacred Mountain*, Delhi 2006 (first edition 1983).

Solano, Francisco de (ed.): *Cuestionarios para la formación de las relaciones geograficas de Indias, siglos XVI/XIX*, Madrid 1988.

Spencer, J. E. / G. A. Hale: 'The Origin, Nature and Distribution of Agricultural Terracing', in *Pacific Viewpoint* 2/1 (1961), pp. 1–40.

Staszewski, Józef: *Vertical Distribution of World Population* (Geographical Studies No. 14, Polish Academy of Sciences, Institute of Geography), Warsaw 1957.

Steinke, Hubert: 'Die Einführung der Kartoffel in der Waadt 1740–1790. Agrarmodernisierung aus bäuerlicher Sicht', in *Zeitschrift für Agrargeschichte und Agrarsoziologie* 45 (1997), pp. 19–44.

Stewart, Gordon T.: 'Tenzing's Two Wrist-Watches: The Conquest of Everest and Late Imperial Culture in Britain 1921–1953', in *Past and Present* 149 (1995), pp. 170–197.

Stichweh, Rudolf: *Wissenschaft – Universität – Profession. Soziologische Analysen*, Frankfurt a.M. 1994.

— *Zur Entstehung des modernen Systems wissenschaftlicher Disziplinen. Physik in Deutschland 1740–1890*, Frankfurt a.M. 1984.

Stückelberger, Alfred / Gerd Graßhoff (eds.): *Klaudios Ptolemaios. Handbuch der Geographie*, 2 vols. Basel 2006.

Stutfield, H. E. M.: 'Mountaineering as a Religion', in *The Alpine Journal* 32 (1918–1919), pp. 241–247.

Bibliography

Tableau comparatif des principales montagnes, des principaux fleuves et cataractes de la terre. D'apres les observations des plus Savants Voyageurs (single sheet, 40/55 cm), Paris chez Bulla et Pictet no year [1820–1829].

Thargyal, Rinzin: *Nomads of Eastern Tibet. Social Organization and Economy of a Pastoral Estate in the Kingdom of Dege*, ed. by Toni Huber, Leiden 2007.

The Cambridge Economic History of India, ed. by Tapan Raychaudhuri and Irfan Habib, vol. 1, Cambridge 1982.

The Cambridge World History of Human Disease, ed. by Kenneth F. Kiple, Cambridge 1993.

The Humboldt Library. A Catalogue of the Library of Alexander von Humboldt with a Bibliographical and Biographical Memoir by Henry Stevens, London 1863 (Reprint Leipzig 1967).

Thomas, Keith: *Man and the Natural World. Changing Attitudes in England 1500–1800*, London 1983.

Tichy, Herbert: *Zum heiligsten Berg der Welt. Auf Landstrassen und Pilgerfahrten in Afghanistan, Indien und Tibet. Geleitwort von Sven Hedin*, Vienna 1937.

Tiffen, Mary et al.: *More People, Less Erosion. Environmental Recovery in Kenya*, Chichester 1994.

Tilly, Charles: *Coercion, Capital and European States, AD 990-1992*, Cambridge MA 1992.

Tissot, Laurent (ed.): *Construction d'une industrie touristique aux 19e et 20e siècles: perspectives internationales / Development of a tourist industry in the 19th and 20th centuries: international perspectives*, Neuchâtel 2003.

— *Naissance d'une industrie touristique: les Anglais et la Suisse au XIXe siècle*, Lausanne 2000.

Tissot, Laurent / Béatrice Veyrassat (eds.): *Technological Trajectories, Markets, Institutions. Industrialized Countries, 19th–20th Centuries; from Context Dependency to Path Dependency*, Berne 2002.

Troll, Carl: *Ausgewählte Beiträge. Zusammengestellt und gewidmet Carl Troll zum 65. Geburtstag von seinen Kollegen und Mitarbeitern*, 3 vols. Wiesbaden 1966.

— 'Die dreidimensionale Gliederung der Erde', in Harald Uhlig / Willibald N. Haffner (eds.) *Zur Entwicklung der vergleichenden Geographie der Hochgebirge*, Darmstadt 1984, pp. 218–250 (first published in 1962 and quoted as such).

— 'Studien zur vergleichenden Geographie der Hochgebirge der Erde', in Harald Uhlig / Willibald N. Haffner (eds.) *Zur Entwicklung der vergleichenden Geographie der Hochgebirge*, Darmstadt 1984, pp. 128–169 (first published in 1941 and quoted as such).

— *Tagebücher der Reisen in Bolivien 1926/1927*, ed. by Felix and Ingeborg Monheim, Wiesbaden 1985.

— 'The Cordilleras of the Tropical Americas. Aspects of Climatic, Phytogeographical and Agrarian Ecology', in Carl Troll (ed.) *Geo-Ecology of the Mountainous Regions of the Tropical Americas*, Bonn 1968, pp. 15–56.

— 'Über das Wesen der Hochgebirgsnatur', in Harald Uhlig / Willibald N. Haffner (eds.) *Zur Entwicklung der vergleichenden Geographie der Hochgebirge*, Darmstadt 1984, pp. 170–195 (first published in 1955 and quoted as such).

Turner, B. L. / Stephen B. Brush (eds.): *Comparative Farming Systems*, New York 1987.

Bibliography

Turner, Frederick: *John Muir. From Scotland to the Sierra*, Edinburgh 1997 (first edition 1985).

Uhlig, Harald: 'Bergbauern und Hirten im Himalaya. Höhenschichtung und Staffelsysteme – ein Beitrag zur vergleichenden Kulturgeographie der Hochgebirge', in Harald Uhlig / Willibald N. Haffner (eds.) *Zur Entwicklung der vergleichenden Geographie der Hochgebirge*, Darmstadt 1984, pp. 427–479.

— 'Die Profildarstellungen von Geo-Ökosystemen in Profilen und Diagrammen als Mittel der Vergleichenden Geographie der Hochgebirge', in Erwin Grötzbach / Gisbert Rinschede (eds.) *Beiträge zur vergleichenden Kulturgeographie der Hochgebirge*, Regensburg 1984, pp. 93–152. Quoted as 1984b.

UNGA United Nations General Assembly: *Fifty-eighth Session, Sustainable Mountain Development, International Year of Mountains, 2002*, 11 July 2003.

— *Press Release, 10 November 1998, Assembly Proclaims Year 2002 International Year of Mountains, Debates Establishing 2001-2010 Decade for Culture of Peace*.

United Nations (ed.): *Agenda 21: Programme of Action for Sustainable Development. Rio Declaration on Environment and Development. Statement of Forest Principles*, New York 1993.

— *The Global Partnership for Environment and Development. A Guide to Agenda 21, Post Rio Edition*, New York 1993.

— *Urban Agglomerations 2001*, New York 2003.

Vaj, Daniela: 'La montagne qui guérit: altitude, médecins et voyages au XIXe siècle', in Sophie Linon-Chipon / Daniela Vaj (eds.) *Relations savantes. Voyages et discours scientifiques*, Paris 2006, pp. 205–229.

— 'Tra ricerca scientifica e approccio empirico. Il contributo dei medici allo sviluppo delle stazioni climatiche montane nel corso del XIX secolo', in Jon Mathieu / Simona Boscani Leoni (eds.) *Die Alpen! Zur europäischen Wahrnehmungsgeschichte seit der Renaissance*, Berne 2005, pp. 315–336.

Varela, Consuelo / Juan Gil (eds.): *Cristóbal Colón. Textos y documentos completos*, Madrid 1992.

Varenius, Bernhard: *Geographia Generalis, in qua affectiones generales Telluris explicantur*, Amsterdam 1664 (first edition 1650).

Velthuizen, Harrij van et al.: *Mapping biophysical facors that influence agricultural production and rural vulnerability* (FAO Environment and natural resources series 11), Rome 2007.

Veyret, Paul: 'Jules Blache (1893–1970)', in *Revue de Géographie Alpine* 58 (1970), pp. 589–592.

Viazzo, Pier Paolo: 'Migrazione e mobilità in area alpina: scenari demografici e fattori sociostrutturali', in *Storia delle Alpi* 3 (1998), pp. 37–48.

— *Upland Communities. Environment, Population and Social Structure in the Alps since the Sixteenth Century*, Cambridge 1989.

Villamarín, Juan / Judith Villamarín: 'Native Colombia: Contact, Conquest and Colonial Populations', in *Revista de Indias* 63/227 (2003), pp. 105–134.

Vries, Jan de: 'The Industrial Revolution and the Industrious Revolution', in *The Journal of Economic History* 54/2 (1994), pp. 249–270.

Bibliography

Wachtel, Nathan: *La vision des vaincus. Les Indiens du Pérou devant la Conquête espagnole 1530–1570*, Paris 1992 (first edition 1971).

Walter, François: *Les figures paysagères de la nation. Territoire et paysage en Europe (16ᵉ–20ᵉ siècle)*, Paris 2004.

Weber, Wolfgang E. J.: *Geschichte der europäischen Universität*, Stuttgart 2002.

White, John Claude: 'The World's Strangest Capital', in *National Geographic Magazine* 29 (1916), pp. 273–295.

White, Lynn: 'The Historical Roots of Our Ecologic Crisis', in *Science* 155/3767 (1967), pp. 1203–1207.

Whiteman, Peter T. S.: 'Mountain Agronomy in Ethiopia, Nepal and Pakistan', in Nigel J. R. Allan et al. (eds.) *Human Impact on Mountains*, New Jersey 1988, pp. 57–82.

Williams, John Alexander: *Appalachia. A History*, Chapel Hill 2002.

Wilson, Joseph: *A History of Mountains, Geographical and Mineralogical. Accompanied by a Picturesque View of the Principal Mountains of the World in their Respective Proportions of Height above the Level of the Sea, by R. A. Riddell*, 3 vols., London, 1807–1810.

Wyckoff, William / Lary M. Dilsaver (eds.): *The Mountainous West. Explorations in Historical Geography*, Lincoln 1995.

Wyder, Margrit: 'Vom Brocken zum Himalaja. Goethes "Höhen der alten und neuen Welt" und ihre Wirkungen', in *Goethe-Jahrbuch* 121 (2004), pp. 141–164.

Xiao-Gan, Yu: 'Untersuchung zur Obergrenze des Nassreisanbaus in China', in Wilhelm Lauer (ed.) *Natural Environment and Man in Tropical Mountain Ecosystems*, Stuttgart 1984, pp. 43–54.

Yushu, Zhang: 'Die Benennung der Berge in China', in INST (ed.) *Die Namen der Berge*, internet publication 2002 (consulted on 16. 11. 2008: www.inst.at/berge).

Zedler, Johann Heinrich (ed.): *Grosses vollständiges Universal-Lexicon aller Wissenschaften und Künste*, 64 vols. and supplements, Halle/Leipzig 1732–1752.

Ziak, Karl: *Der Mensch und die Berge. Eine Weltgeschichte des Alpinismus*, Salzburg 1956.

Zimmermann, Anne: 'Celebrating Mountain Women: A Move to Empower Women in Mountain Regions', in *Mountain Research and Development* 22/4 (2002), pp. 400–401.

Zoelen, Aaltje van: 'A World of Mountains, Yet to Conquer: The Kamtschatka Peninsula', in *Mountain Research and Development* 22/2 (2002), pp. 191–193.

INDEX

A

Adam's Peak (Ceylon, Sri Lanka) 27
adaptation, environmental 86, 88, 157–8
Addis Ababa 54, 97
Africa; *see also* East Africa, South Africa, West Africa 7, 29, 43, 53–4, 57, 83, 92, 95, 101, 103, 139, 152
Agenda 21 6–10, 42, 45–6, 118, 155, 158
agrarian intensification 62–3, 66–7, 83, 86–7, 95–100, 107–9, 111–13, 127, 156–7
agrarian reform 107
agricultural revolution 88, 98–101
agriculture; *see also* agrarian intensification, animal husbandry, fallow, field cultivation, fodder production, hoeing, irrigation, multicropping, pastoralism, ploughing 39–40, 61–2, 83–4, 88–108
Aitmatow, Tschingis 104
Alaska 21
Alfraganus (astronomer) 14
Algiers 67
alpacas 101
alpiculture (*Alpwirtschaft, économie alpestre*) 38, 89–91
Alpine Association, German and Austrian 43, 136
Alpine Club (London) 43, 124, 143
Alpinism; *see* mountaineering
Alps 20, 27–31, 36, 38, *Plate* 12, 58, 62, 67, 76, 84, 92, 106, 107, 115, 116, 121–22, 124–25, 138, 143, 148–50
    economy 57–8, 62, 76, 83–4, 106–7, 116–17
    research 20, 25, 36–7
Alpujarras (Spain) 61
Altai Mountains ix
altitude
    levels 88–92, 110

measurements; *see* mountains (altimetry)
sickness 28
Amazon 68–9, 81
America; *see also* Latin America, North America, South America, United States of America ix, 16–7, 29, 56
Andalusia 68
Andes 2, 7, 23, 27–8, *Plate* 10, 56–60, 76, 81, 140–43
animal husbandry 17, 62, 65, 88, 90, 92–5, 101–8, 158
anthropology (discipline) 89–90, 96, 108
Apennine Mountains 61
Appalachia *Plate* 7, 64–7, 118, 153
Aragon 12
Argentina 16, 94, 160
arid regions; *see* climate (dry), desert
Asia; *see also* Central Asia 28, 29, 30, 32, 38, 39, 43, 44, 53–4, 56–7, 68, 77, 83, 92, 95, 101–2, 114, 121, 128–39, 152, 156
Assadourian, Carlos Sempat 60
asynchrony 58–69, 81–2, 116
Atlas Mountains 26
Australia 30
Austria 123
Azores 27
Aztec *Plate* 9, 78–9

B

Bagrot Valley (Pakistan) 109–10
Bairoch, Paul 74
Bandyopadhyay, Jayanta 8
barometer 18, 27–8
Beardmore, Nathaniel 35
Beijing 63
Berghaus, Heinrich 32, 35
Berlin 24, 31
Bernbaum, Edwin 128
Bert, Paul 35–6

Index

Bhutan 9, *Plate* 16, 152–3
Bierstadt, Albert *Plate* 13
biology (discipline) 41
Bishkek 104, 152
Blache, Jules 34–5, 37–40, 84–6
Blanchard, Raoul 37, 48
Bloch, Marc 1
Bogotá 54
Bolivia 9, 25, *Plate* 10, 54, 73, 82, 91
Bollywood 150
Bombay; *see* Mumbai
Bön (religion) 136
Bonn 40
Boserup, Ester 86, 95, 157
botany, plant geography 1, 7, 25, 35, 40–1, *Plate* 3, 92
boundaries, national 117
Boyle, Robert 19, 29
Braudel, Fernand 61, 67–8, 115
Brazil 21
Bromme, Traugott 32
Brundtland, Gro Harlem 44
Buache, Philippe 21–2
Buddhism 77, *Plate* 15, 131–35, 144–47
Buenos Aires 2–3, 94
buffalo 94, 101

C

California 16
camels 101, 103
Canada 30
Caribbean 12–15, 92
cartography 20–2, 35
Castile 12, 89, 104–6
cattle 15, 92, 94, 97, 101–3, 106–7
Caucasus ix, 27, 117–18
Central Asia 16, 30, 72, 101–3, 105–7
Chaco 94
Chamonix 147–48
Chave, Olivier 8
Cherokee, Native Americans *Plate* 7, 65
Chile 16
Chimborazo (volcano) 23–4, 27, 29–30, 32, *Plate* 3, *Plate* 4
China 2, 9, *Plate* 6, *Plate* 8, *Plate* 14, 16, 30, 38, 59, 62–4, 67–8, 75–8, 81, 87, 93, 116, 130–2, 135–37, 139, 140, 145
Christianity 15, 123–28, 141–43
cities
  concept of 70–1
  growth of; *see also* urbanisation 53–5, 77–82, 117, 147
  size 71, 74–80
civilisation 70, 125, 132, 147
climate history 87
climate; *see also* mountain climate
  daily (tropical) 41, 90, 100, 158
  dry; *see also* desert 103–4, 110
  seasonal (non-tropical) 41, 90, 100, 158
climatology (discipline) 1, 35
Collantes, Fernando 81
Colombia 60
colonialism; *see also* decolonisation 11–2, 16–19, 30, 38, 56, 69, 72–3, 83, 136–43
Columbian Exchange 92–3
Columbus, Christopher 12–16, 92
communication; *see also* traffic 39, 44, 46, 84, 113, 127
Confucius 130
Cortés, Hernán *Plate* 9
Cortina d'Ampezzo 148
Cossacks 117, 160
Coubertin, Pierre de 148
cows; *see* cattle
Cronon, William 126
cropping systems; *see* agrarian intensification, fallow, field cultivation, multi-cropping, shifting cultivation
crosses, Christian 123, 143, 146
Cusco 56–9

D

Dagestan 118
Dalai Lama 5, *Plate* 8, 77, 135, 145
Daulaghiri 30
decolonisation 118, 139, 146
deforestation; *see also* environmental degradation, forests, shifting cultivation 9, 44, 62, 96–7
Demiéville, Paul 132

Index

desert; *see also* climate (dry) 2, 7, 9, 16, 44, 48, 59, 122, 125, 158
Desideri, Ippolito 77
disciplines, scientific; see also individual disciplines 23, 33–7, 151, 155
disparity, between uplands and lowlands 58, 74–6, 81–2, 118–19, 156
donkeys 101

E

Earth Summit; *see* United Nations Conference on Environment and Development (UNCED)
East Africa 40, 91, 96–8, 102–3
Ebro River 67
ecology; *see also* ecosystem, environmental movement 23, 40–2
ecosystem, major 2, 6, 8–9, 42, 48, 152, 156–8
Ecuador 27, 54, 60, 90
Egypt 26
Elvin, Mark 87
England; *see also* Great Britain 12, 19–20, 29, 37, 100, 121
Enlightenment 15, 121–22, 127
environmental
 degradation; *see also* deforestation, erosion, overgrazing 6, 87, 94
 determinism; *see also* adaptation (environmental) 84–5, 157–58
 factors 86, 98–9, 101, 109, 113, 119
 movement 43–4, 69, 85, 128, 151, 153
 protection 6, 42, 66, 158–59
epidemics 83
erosion 6, 44, 97–8
Estonia 2
Ethiopia 40, *Plate* 5, *Plate* 11, 54, 96–7
Europe 1, 2, 13, 14, 16, 23, 24, 25, 29, 30, 38–9 51–4, 56–62, 74–6, 80, 81, 89, 92, 106, 115, 121, 122–5, 137–8, 140, 143, 148–52, 156–7
European expansion 11–21, 30, 42, 56, 120, 140–43, 155
explorers 12–16, 23–32, 160

F

fallow; *see also* high-altitude fallow 95–8, 101–2
family 104, 108–14, 115–16
farming, farming systems; *see* agriculture, animal husbandry, field cultivation, pastoralism
Febvre, Lucien 84–5, 157–8
Felsch, Philipp 36
field cultivation 39, 62, 93–4, 106, 158
Figueras, Marcelo 160
flooding 44, 68
fodder production 62, 84, 89, 102, 106–7
Fontaine, Laurence 3, 115
Food and Agriculture Organization (FAO) 46, 98, 151–52
forest science 49
forests; *see also* deforestation 6–7, 44, 48, 63, 65, 68, 125
France 35, 37, 46, 115–16, 121, 123
Frödin, John 89

G

Gallimard (publishing house) 38
Ganges River 68
Garmisch-Partenkirchen 148
gender; *see also* women 112–13, 152–53
Geneva 8, 25
geography (discipline) 1, 14, 20–2, 27, 35, 58, 85
geology (discipline) 35
geomorphology (discipline) 35
geophysics (discipline) 35
Gerbi, Antonello 16
Germany 24, 35, 41, 59, 76, 100, 136
Gilgit (Pakistan) 99
glaciology (discipline) 35–6
global history 10–11, 13
globalisation 11, 14, 34, 36, 43, 120, 127, 151–53, 155–6
goats 101, 103, 111–12
Goethe, Johann Wolfgang von 31–2, *Plate* 4
grain 92, 93, 96, 99–100, 105–6, 110
Great Britain; *see also* England 24, 72, 110, 143–47
Greece 61, 67

Index

Greenland 36
Grenoble 37–8, 76, 148
Gressler, F.G.L. 32
Grisebach, A. 41
growing season 62, 91, 93, 100, 114
Grueber, Johannes *Plate* 8
Guamán Poma de Ayala, Felipe *Plate* 10
Guicciardini, Francesco 61
Guizhou (China) *Plate* 6, 64

H

Haenke, Thaddaeus 25
Haiti 13–15
Haller, Albrecht von 20
Hambloch, Hermann 51–2, 55, 66
Hann, Julius 35
hay; *see* fodder production, wild hay
health; *see also* high altitude medicine, mountain climate 69, 83
Heim, Albert 36
Hekla (volcano) 27
Herder, Johann Gottfried 22
high altitude medicine (discipline) 35–6, *Plate* 5
high-altitude climate; *see* mountain climate
high-altitude fallow 97
Hill Stations (Asia) 72–3
Hillary, Edmund 146
Himachal Pradesh 71–3
Himalayanism; *see* mountaineering
Himalayas 30, 39–40, 57–8, 71–3, 76, 102, 114, 133, 143–47
Hinduism 136, 150
history (discipline) 1, 10–11, 49–50
hoeing 95, 97–8
holiness; *see* mountains (sacred), sacralisation
horses 92, 94, 100, 101–3, 105
Huaca 142
Huber, Toni 134, 137
human geography; *see* geography
Humboldt, Alexander von 13, 22–7, 29–32, 34–5, 40–1, 48, *Plate* 3, *Plate* 4, 59, 89, 123
hydrology (discipline); *see also* irrigation, water towers 7, 35

I

Iceland *Plate* 5
Inca 56, 59–60, 69, 90, 141
India 9, 12, 57–8, 68, 72–3, 76, 133
Indian Council [*Consejo de Indias*] 16–17
Indian Removal Act 65
Indians, American; *see* indigenous people, Native Americans
indigenous people 60, 89
Indonesia 93
industrialisation 33, 87, 98–101, 108, 116–17, 157
Innsbruck 148
intensification; *see* agrarian intensification
interdisciplinarity 37, 40–1, 43
International Mountaineering and Climbing Federation 43
International Year of the Mountains (2002) 1–2, 10, 23, 45–6, 49, *Plate* 2, *Plate* 16, 140, 150–54, 159
irrigation 63, 67, 99, 109–10
Islam 14, 20, 83, 111–12
islands 14, 58
Italy 24, 61, 76, 82, 107, 115, 121
Ives, Jack D. 8, 47

J

Jainism 136
Japan 30, 102, 132, 148
Jehol (China) 63
Jesuits 28, *Plate* 8, 77, 141
Johannesburg 49, *Plate* 2, 152
Jourdanet, Denis 36

K

Kamchatka 158–60
Karakoram 2, 36, 99–100, 109–14, 144
Karakoram Highway 110
Kashmir 150
Kazakhstan 103
Kenya 98
Kreutzmann, Hermann 112
Kunlun Mountains 130
Kyrgyzstan 103–5, 107–8, 151

Index

L

La Paz 54, 73, 86
labour productivity 86, 93, 102, 157
labour, division of; *see also* markets 33–4, 70–1, 111–14
Ladakh 135
Lake Tahoe 125
land improvement 67–8
land use; *see* agrarian intensification, agriculture, fallow, mountains (vertical land use), multicropping
Lander's Peak *Plate* 13
Lapchi (Tibet) 134
Lapland *Plate* 3, 31–2
Latin America; *see also* South America 16–17, 36, 44–5, 53–4, 56–7, 76, 86, 101, 140, 150, 152, 157
Leo XIII, Pope 143
Lhasa *Plate* 8, 77–8, 133, 135, 145
Lima 25, 58, 141–42
Lisbon 14
livestock; *see* animal husbandry
llamas 101, 142
London 19, 31–2, 43, 124, 143
lowlands 67–9, 76
Lyell, Charles 35

M

Madrid 27, 76
maize 91–3, 96, 99–100, 110, 142
malaria 68, 83
Malthus, Thomas Robert 83–4, 87
Mangyans 96
Mao Zedong 132
markets 70–1, 77, 100–1, 105–8, 114–17
Mauss, Marcel 111
Mecca 14
mechanisation; *see* technology
Mechel, Christian von 31
medicine; *see* high altitude medicine
Mediterranean 2, 14, 59, 61–2, 66–7, 81, 102, 115
Messerli, Bruno 8–9, 47
Mesta, Honoured Council of the (Spain) 105–6
metropolis 54, 73, 86, 118

Mexico 16, *Plate* 5, 53–4, 102
Mexico City *Plate* 9, 54, 77–80, 86
Miao *Plate* 6, 64
migration 38, 39, 63–4, 73, 80, 103–4, 106, 108–10, 114–17
Milan 107
Mindoro 95
mineralogy (discipline) 18
Ming Dynasty 129
mining 30, 60, 66, 76
mobility 90–1, 103–7, 111–14, 116, 157–8
modernity 11, 16, 18, 50, 81, 118–20, 137, 146–7, 153–4
monastery; *see* monasticism
monasticism 78, 133, 145–47
Mongolia 75, 103, 106
Mont Blanc 25, 32, *Plate* 3, *Plate* 4, 148
montology (discipline) 23, 47
Morocco 61
Mount Ararat *Plate* 4
Mount Cameroon 139
Mount Etna 13, 27
Mount Everest (Chomolungma, Sagarmatha) 30, 136, 144–47, 159
Mount Kailash *Plate* 15, 134–37, 147
Mount Kilimanjaro 139
Mount Stanley 139
Mount Taishan 129–31
Mountain Agenda 8–9, 42, 46–7, 49, *Plate* 2
mountain
  climate 16, 73, 83
  names 131, 139, 154
  regions examined 2, 49
mountaineering 43, 143–47
mountains
  altimetry 18, 27–30, 34, 42, 155
  definition 48–9, *Plate* 2, 52, 80
  highest 23, 27–30, 42
  perception 12–50, 83–6, 120–54
  relief 40, 84, 100–1, 109
  sacred *Plate* 14, *Plate* 15, 123–24, 127–38, 156
  vertical land use 88–91, 111–14, 157
Mousson, Albert 35–6
Mughal 68, 150
Muir, John 125–26

Index

mules 101, 142
Müller, Johann 35
multicropping 62–3, 93, 95, 99–100, 101–2, 110
Mumbai 150
Murra, John V. 89–90

N

Napoleon, Napoleonic period 26
National Parks 66, 124, 126, 156
nationalism 117, 124–27, 146
Native Americans; *see also* indigenous people *Plate* 7, 64–5, 124
Nature, perception of; *see also* mountains (perception), Romanticism 12–16, 25–6, 121–22, 124, 129, 143, 149
Nepal 7, 9, 44, 134, 144, 146
Netherlands 148
New World; *see* America
New York 9
New Zealand 30, 43, 102
Newton, Isaac 27
nomadism 89, 91, 102–6
Non-Governmental Organisations (NGOs) 5, 7, 47, 152
Norgay, Tenzing 146
North America 24, *Plate* 13, 53–4, 56–7, 64–6, 81, 116, 148–49, 152
Norway *Plate* 5, 84

O

Oceania 29, 53–4, 57, 102, 152
oceanography (discipline) 48
oceans, seas; *see also* oceanography, seafaring 2, 7, 48, 158
old-settled lands 58–62, 81
Olympic Winter Games 147–49
oronymy; *see* mountains (names)
Ortner, Sherry B. 159
overgrazing; *see also* environmental degradation 94, 107
oxen *Plate* 11, 96–7

P

Pakistan 99, 109, 111

Pamir Mountains 103
Paris 24, 26, 32, 36–8, 123, 150
Pascal, Blaise 11
pastoralism; *see also* alpiculture, nomadism, transhumance 39, 83–4, 89–91, 95, 101–7
Patagonia 94
path-dependency 60, 73, 86, 117, 156–8
Penck, Albrecht 35, 69
Peru 9, 59–60, 67, 89, 94, 141
Philip II, Spanish King 16–17
Philippines 73, 95–6, 98
physio-theology 127–28
Pico del Teide 27–8
pigs 92, 94, 101, 135
pilgrimage 14, 78, 123, 130–31, 133–37
Pindus Mountains 61
Pius XI, Pope 143
plant geography; *see* botany
ploughing *Plate* 11, 94–7
Po Valley 68
Polo, Marco 14, 16, 27
polyandry 114
Pope 141, 143
population
  crisis 56, 60, 87
  density 52–3, 66, 83–4, 95, 114
  growth 55–9, 74–5, 80–2, 93, 96–8, 106, 108, 110–12
Portugal 14, 25, 97
possibilism 84–5, 158
Potala Palace *Plate* 8, 77
potato; *see also* sweet potato, tubers *Plate* 10, 91–3, 110
Potosí 60, 76
poultry 101, 135
poverty 6, 117–19
Prussia 23, 30
Pryor, Frederic 85
Ptolemy 14
Puebla 54
Pure Crystal Mountain (Tsari) 134–35
Puritans 124
Pyrenees 11, 31, *Plate* 3, *Plate* 5, 57–8

Index

Q

Qing Dynasty 64, 68
Qualla Reservation, Appalachia *Plate* 7
questionnaire 16–20
Quito 29, 54, 90

R

racism 39
rainforest; *see* deforestation, forests
Reclus, Élisée 128
revolution 22, 117, 123, 131–32
rice 39, 63, 92–3, 96, 98
Rif Mountains 61
Rio de Janeiro; *see* United Nations Conference on Environment and Development
Rocky Mountains *Plate* 13, 66, 126
Romanticism 15, 18, 89, 121–26, 128, 132, 150–51, 156
Rongbuk Monastery 145
Rousseau, Jean-Jacques 121–22
Royal Academy of Sciences (France) 21, 29
Royal Society of London 19
Ruskin, John 128
Russia; *see also* Soviet Union 24, 26, 38, 104, 117–18, 159–60
Rwanda 98

S

sacralisation; *see also* mountains (sacred) 120–21, 123, 127–28, 134–39
Salonica 67
San Francisco 125
Sana'a (Yemen) 54
Sapporo 148
Saussure, Horace-Bénédict de 20, 25, 29, 32, *Plate* 4
Scandinavia *Plate* 5
scarcity 98, 113–14
Scheuchzer, Johann Jakob 20
science; *see also* disciplines (scientific), individual disciplines 19–20, 23–4, 33–7, 41–2
Scotland 82, 84
seas; *see* oceans
seafaring 12
secularisation 120, 127
sheep 92, 94, 101, 103, 104–6, 111–12
sherpas 146, 159
shifting cultivation 64, 91, 96
Shimla 72–3, 86
Siberia 2, 21
Sichuan 30
Sierra Nevada (California) 125–26
Sierra Nevada (Spain) 61–2
Singh, Chetan 71
South Africa 40, 139
South America; *see also* Latin America 24–5, 53, 56–60, 76, 81, 116
Soviet Union; *see also* Russia 101, 104, 108, 117, 160
Spain 12–19, 24, 27, 59–60, 78–9, 82, 89–90, 96, 104, 140–43
specialisation; *see* labour (division of), disciplines (scientific)
Spitsbergen (Norway) *Plate* 5
St. Gotthard 28
St. Moritz 138, 148
St.Veit 138
Stalin, Joseph 101, 104
stall-feeding *Plate* 12, 89, 95, 102–3, 106–8
Staszewski, Józef 51–2, 55
Stockholm 7, 44
subsistence economy 60, 89–90, 95, 101–2, 106–7
Sulitjelma Mountain *Plate* 3
summit crosses; *see* crosses (Christian)
surplus 71
sustainability 6, 44, 47, 87, 152, 158
sweet potato 92–3, 96
Switzerland 8–9, 20, 35, 43, 46, 84, 121, 149–50

T

Table Mountain 139
taboo 112, 130, 135, 137, 144
Tantrism 133
Taoism *Plate* 14, 130
Taurus Mountains 27, 61
technology, agricultural 88, 95–101, 108, 112

Index

technology transfer 6, 159
Tenerife 13, 15, 27, 29
Tengboche Monastery 147
Tenochtitlán *Plate* 9, 79
Terai (India, Nepal) 68
terraces 97–8
thermometer 18
Thomas, Keith 123
Tianmushan (mountain) 139
Tianshan (mountain) 139
Tianszhushan (mountain) 139
Tiantaishan (mountain) 139
Tibet 26, *Plate* 8, *Plate* 15, 76–8, 106, 114, 129, 132–37, 139, 144–47, 153
Tibet Initiative Germany 136
Tichy, Herbert *Plate* 15, 136
Ticlla, María Poma 142
Toluca (Mexico) 54
tourism 43, 66, 129, 131, 136–37, 147–50
traffic; *see also* transport 17, 59–61, 76, 84–6, 131
transcendentalism 125
transhumance 89–91, 102–7
transport; *see also* traffic 60–1, 71–3, 100, 101, 105, 110–12, 127
Transylvania 30
Troll, Carl 40–2, 48
Tropics 38, 40–1, 54–5, 69, 83, 85, 90–1, 158
Tsari (Pure Crystal Mountain) 134–35
tubers 91, 96
Turkey 61, 84, 102
Tyrol 92

U

UNESCO World Heritage 98, 131, 160
United Nations (UN) 5, 8–10, 43–5, 51, 151–53
United Nations Conference on Environment and Development (UNCED), Rio de Janeiro 1992 1, 5–10, 23, 45–7, 118, 151, 155, 158
United States of America 6, 9, 43, 65–6, 100, 118, 124–27, 147, 160
urban supply 60, 70–1, 74–5, 77–8, 97

urbanisation; *see also* city (growth) 54–8, 70–80, 86, 108, 115–16, 156

V

Varenius, Bernhard 27
vegetation belts; *see also* growing season, mountains (vertical land use) 31–2, *Plate* 3
Venice 107, 150
Veracruz 79
vertical control; *see* mountains (vertical land use)
Vesuvius 13
volcanoes 13, 17–18, 23, 160

W

Wanli, Chinese Emperor 129–31
Washington D.C. 66
water towers, mountains as; *see also* irrigation 6, 152, 159
West Africa 12, 14, 21
wild hay *Plate* 12, 106–7
wilderness 59, 62, 65–6, 124–26, 156
Winter Games *see* Olympic Winter Games
women; *see also* gender *Plate* 16, 111–14, 147, 152–54
World Heritage; *see* UNESCO World Heritage
World War II 39, 43, 67, 85, 126

Y

yaks 101, 106, 111–12
Yangtze River 130
Yellow River 68
Yellowstone National Park 126
Yemen 54, 82
Yosemite Valley 125–26
Younghusband, Francis 145
Yunnan (China) 93

Z

Zugspitze (mountain) 136

www.ingramcontent.com/pod-product-compliance
Lightning Source LLC
Chambersburg PA
CBHW061444300426
44114CB00014B/1826